The Death of Homo Economicus

The Death of Homo Economicus

Work, Debt and the Myth of Endless Accumulation

Peter Fleming

PLUTO  PRESS

First published 2017 by Pluto Press
345 Archway Road, London N6 5AA

www.plutobooks.com

British Library Cataloguing in Publication Data
A catalogue record for this book is available from the British Library

ISBN	978 0 7453 9942 3	Hardback
ISBN	978 0 7453 9940 9	Paperback
ISBN	978 1 7868 0129 6	PDF eBook
ISBN	978 1 7868 0131 9	Kindle eBook
ISBN	978 1 7868 0130 2	EPUB eBook

This book is printed on paper suitable for recycling and made from fully managed
and sustained forest sources. Logging, pulping and manufacturing processes are
expected to conform to the environmental standards of the country of origin.

Typeset by Stanford DTP Services, Northampton, England

Simultaneously printed in the United Kingdom and United States of America

Contents

Introduction:
Welcome to the New Dark Ages

Joy breaking like a dawn! But only for an instant. It is not merely that clouds begin to cross this new, radiant sky. It is as if at the moment when the sun comes forth in its glory, another sun appears too, a shadow sun, an anti-sun sliding across its face. The dawning sun is there not for itself but to undergo eclipse; joy shines out only to reveal what the annihilation of joy will be like. (J.M Coetzee, *The Master of Petersburg*)

It's popular to compare the 2007–08 financial crisis and the global recession that followed to a massive tsunami, violently washing away the socio-economic certainties of the past and bringing capitalism to the brink of oblivion. The metaphor was probably attractive because for the first time we gained explicit insight (with the aid of mobile phone cameras) into what a real one looked like close up after the 2004 Boxing Day wave, which killed around 250,000 people. The awful 2011 Tōhoku tsunami in Japan only reinforced its aptness concerning the economic and cultural demolition job that we've witnessed over the last ten years, especially during the age of austerity and the unexpected comeback of the obscenely rich.

The trouble with the metaphor, in my mind at least, when it comes to understanding the nature of global capitalism over the last ten years is that it's applied only partially. Just two aspects of the killer wave are mentioned: the triggering event (the earthquake or subprime meltdown after years of risky debt) and then the wall of water hitting land (collapsing banks, the recession, etc.). However, seismologists point out that there are at least four phases involved. The earthquake in which a large piece of ocean floor is displaced, the drawback where the ocean recedes from the shoreline

1

sometimes by many metres (people often wander out to look at the strange scene and are first to be wiped away), the enormous impact of the wave as it destroys society and then the final stage, which is seldom cited. The great backwash. This is where all the water, ruins and sludge *return to the sea* ... creating an undercurrent of dark mayhem as it does, sucking everything back out with it, both dead and alive.

This book seeks to complete the metaphor by concentrating on that fourth phase, which I suggest is where Western capitalism presently stands at the moment. The initial wave was certainly catastrophic, egged on by greedy bankers, easy credit, lax and corrupt governments and a near religious faith in the dubious assumptions of neoclassical economics, particularly the 'alchemy' of monetary policy practised by central banks.[1] Our mistake, however, similar to those who survive a real tsunami, was to think that the devastation would cease after the initial impact, with calls to rebuild the economy, reform the banks and so forth. But now the wave is rapidly coming back, returning to sea and redoubling the carnage as it does. It's no longer 'newsworthy' like the first big wave. Nevertheless, the damage is even worse because the already weakened survivors are now being overrun by the deluge again. No wonder the present state of the world feels even worse than it did immediately after the Great Recession nearly ten years ago. Neoliberalism – the reduction of *all* social life to the logic of profit-seeking behaviour – ought to have disappeared in 2008, and a form of it certainly did. Only now its worst excesses are rolling back through town, more potent than ever, stripping whole communities of the meagre pickings that were left as it attempts to take us out with the mangled debris.

We can see this widening corporate hellscape everywhere. The uber-rich are wealthier now than ever. The wave appeared to serve them well and they're cashing in bigtime as it rages back towards the abyss. Tax laws remain outlandishly unfair, stacked in favour of a corporate elite who are laughing all the way to the bank (the same ones that the average taxpayer bailed out only a few years ago) … now ordinary working people and consumers carry a dispro-portionate burden of funding society.[2] The financial services sector today acts as if 2008 never happened. It remains largely unreformed, shameless in its support of tax evasion and money laundering as the leaked Panama Papers revealed, abetted by governments that still believe banks can regulate themselves.[3] If globalisation still does exist, it's mainly of the 'deviant' kind fuelled by transnational crime organisations so powerful they constitute ghost states in their own right.[4] They've thrived under neoliberal capitalism, generally at our expense.[5] In public life, arrogant demigods, vapid technocrats, Rupert Murdoch and Goldman Sachs have commandeered the state and effectively de-democratised it. Indeed, it's no surprise that Murdoch's senior executives met with the British prime minister and chancellor ten times in one year during 2015–16 or that Goldman Sachs alumni hold key positions in the Trump administration.[6] But they're just the elite we can see. There's also the ominous reign of 'dark money' behind the scenes, with ethereal billionaires like Michael Hintze and the Koch brothers who are dictating the rules that you and I have to live by. In short, in just a few short years we have witnessed the rise of what could only be termed 'vulture capitalism', the worst variety of a bad lot.

Languishing at the other end of the income spectrum is the expansive majority, where holding down an average job has become intolerable and levels of exploitation not seen since the Victorian era are commonplace. Here salary growth has come to an abrupt halt, of course. But that's just the tip of the iceberg. Thirty-seven per cent of British workers find their occupations completely devoid of any meaning, disconnected from anything remotely beneficial to society.[7] According to another study, the typical US worker spends only 39 per cent of their time performing the task they were hired to do.[8] The rest is clogged up with emails, useless meetings and sorting the mess created by inexplicable management hierarchies. To make matters worse (not to mention unhealthy), this is all experienced in a highly private and personal way: the concept of the public is withering on the vine and dying. There are few social spaces left to shelter us from the reversing economic wave. In January 2017, for example, the National Health Service (NHS) in the UK was found to be so short of cash that the British Red Cross declared a 'humanitarian crisis' and intervened to help. Young people in Western economies have been abandoned by their forebears, with a retiree earning more than the average millennial, a generational disparity that has pronounced race and class dimensions to boot. It's obvious that commerce hates kids. And let's not even mention the eco-system, which has nearly given up the ghost and teeters on the brink of collapse. The Pacific Ocean, for example, is now one giant rubbish tip.[9] The promise of 'green capitalism' was a confidence trick and it's not surprising that our civilisation is on the verge of committing ecocide. Unsustainability is not only inherent to how business is done, however, but also a *way of life* for the average person, which gives the economic lunacy of late capitalism strong existential reverberations.

It is in this context that the central character of this book is examined: the over-promoted, overrated and totally mythical figure of homo economicus – rational economic man. The financial human being. Similar to the Soviets in the 1920s (but towards very different ends, of course), the early zealots of free market economics believed that the human self could be remade.

Character. Personality. Emotional infrastructure. Neoclassical economics of the 1960s and 1970s had a definite character in mind. They drew on the ideas of Adam Smith among others showing how everyday people act like capitalist enterprises in most facets of their lives. In order for their increasingly abstract models and mathematical formulae to make sense, a tremendously impractical conception of being human had to be presumed. Governments swallowed the idea almost too readily in the 1980s and 1990s, rebuilding society to faithfully reflect its image, particularly in relation to work and employment. From the beginning, homo economicus was defined by an extreme form of individualism, driven largely by monetary gain and profoundly suspicious of anyone but themselves, particularly 'the public'. The project was a complete failure, of course, because it could only exist in the realm of fantasy. But even as the dirty wave retreats to sea, we're still being lectured on how homo economicus is the only way to be. What a joke. It's a little like telling a gambler who's lost everything that one last wager might save the day.

In order to fully comprehend the painful vagaries of being enclosed in an over-economized world today, we have no choice but to stand outside the narrative of mainstream academic economics. That's not just because much of the discipline today has been taken over by mathematical theorems only a select few can understand.[10] Nor because it's largely useless at predicting events that really matter, like the subprime meltdown. No, the main reason comes down to the fact that it's so stubbornly wedded to a completely inoperative vision of society. You immediately lose touch with reality as soon as its assumptions are adopted. Let's be frank. It's no secret that most theoretical and applied economics today intrinsically functions in a parallel universe, a kind of nerd's dreamtime, selling a narrative that defies the daily experiences of the 99%-ers as the backwash of debt, stress and insecurity threatens to drag us under. The models look neat on paper. When applied to reality, however, the prescriptions (and even descriptions) forwarded by neoconservative economists like Milton Friedman, James M. Buchanan and more recently Stephen Moore (advisor to Donald Trump whose books include *It's*

Getting Better All the Time and *Privatization: A Strategy for Taming the Deficit*) cause chaos on the ground and frequently defy basic common sense. That's why it is strange that this post-real orthodoxy has only intensified since the 2007/08 crash.[11] The reasons why will be carefully investigated in this book. But languishing at the heart of the disaster is homo economicus, who in the UK and USA, for example, is now struggling against the tide of unprecedented economic trends and is about to be pulled under.[12]

Most economics textbooks don't tell us the real reason why homo economicus was probably invented. Capitalism creates a good deal of socio-economic 'crap' as a rule (e.g., pollution, stress, insecurity, in work poverty, waste, etc.), the inevitable collateral damage of profit-seeking behaviour. When the business system offloads this crap, it gets passed down a vast chain until it can't be passed any further. Nobody wants to be at the end of the shit chain, usually reserved for the global poor, women, the natural environment and so forth. Homo economicus was meant to be an effective relay mechanism, shifting capitalism's excrement to the next least powerful party in the sequence. This is what *rationality* and *efficiency* really means in the context of free market capitalism. But now the shit's starting to stick, an outcome of both the rising flood of economic disrepair (debt, etc.) and years of governmental policy that has sought to propagate 'economic man' throughout the entire social body. In short, homo economicus find him or herself at the end of the shit chain and is now practically drowning in the stuff.

It is no surprise that in these bleak times the defenders of the 'reversing wave' (i.e., neoliberal capitalism, warts and all) tell the critics to lighten up. Things aren't that bad, no matter how much life is being squeezed out of the present like the hue from an oil painting. According to pop psychologist Steven Pinker, for example, modern civilisation has never had it so good. He looks back to the Dark Ages, the capricious injustice, perverse levels of poverty, illiteracy and disease.[13] In light of that, we shouldn't be complaining too much – especially in relation to global inequality, which might seem bad today but is nothing like it was: 'As one becomes aware of the decline of violence, the world begins to look different. The past seems less innocent; the present less sinister.'[14] Right-wing hacks have latched onto this misplaced optimism too. When it was reported in early 2017 that just eight billionaires are as rich as the world's poorest half, a spokesperson for the Adam Smith Institute, a free enterprise think-tank in London, gave this bizarre reading of the situation: 'It is not the wealth of the world's rich that matters, but the welfare of the world's poor, and this is improving every year ... Inequality is a side-effect of stability, peace, and growth; clamping down on it through foolish wealth taxes risks everybody's living standards.'[15]

The comment is too vacuous to warrant too much reflection; as if radical inequality has little connection to the ongoing problem of poverty; as if trickledown economics – the expectation that everyone will benefit if we encourage the rich to get even wealthier – hadn't been completely discredited years ago. In any case, the quote does inadvertently tell us how bad things have got for the Western middle classes and working poor. Apologists seeking to justify a broken economic paradigm in the UK and USA, for example, are now so desperate for material given the horrible facts before us they must evoke the most destitute denizens of the Global South or even medieval rituals of torture as a point of comparison. These are the standards we're now measured against, absolute rather than relative immiseration, which would have been unimaginable a few years ago. Perhaps a sign of things to come?

There is very good reason to feel terminally deflated at the present juncture. As the cultural critic Mark Fisher insightfully demonstrated, contemporary capitalism wages a psychological war as much as a pecuniary one, where melancholy is systematically induced on a mass scale to tame the revolutionary rage that marked the 1960s and 1970s apart.[16] For sure, in this climate it would be *irrational* not to feel gravely out of sync with the world. As I will argue in the coming pages, the growing evidence points to a major breakdown in the norms that once governed the distribution of wealth, regulated employment and provided spaces for democratic voice. The events of 2007–08 were just the beginning. Thriving amidst this neo-feudalist flood is a detached, largely secretive and unaccountable elite that holds massive amounts of power in the public and private sectors. For the first time in some years their avowed interests stand directly, openly and stubbornly against those of 99 per cent of the population, locked in a zero-sum game. What they gain we lose. And they've gained a lot.[17] The tacit agreement between capital and labour forged after World War II (WWII) concerning wages and conditions has effectively been dissolved, and the income/power differentials between us and the rich are now so stark that even the highest earners among the 99 per cent have more in common with the lowest (on minimum wage) than they do with the 1 per cent.[18] The plutocrats and their state lackeys truly live far away, on dry land.

But this book is no nostalgic pining for a bygone age, since the deal workers got in the past was never brilliant, even during the post-WWII boom.[19] Instead, this book seeks to provide a set of conceptual tools for navigating a path away from the torrential socio-economic grime that is surging around us as it heads back out to the unrelenting deep.

Chapter 1 introduces the argument by focusing on how the crisis of work and the economy has become normalised, inducing a latent psychosis in everyday exchanges and the terminal decline of homo economicus. The approach is extended in Chapter 2. The term 'wreckage economics' is proposed to designate the theoretical and practical paradigm of choice when dominant powers seek to preserve the spirit of capitalism, even if it is on fire all around us. This part of the book also questions whether the liberating effects of information technology is enough to save us, as some have rather optimistically proposed. Chapter 3 concentrates on the sad and lonely figure of homo economicus: the economic human being. He or she now embodies an inbuilt tendency for disaster, frequently lived as a personal nightmare of debt and insecurity. If homo economicus today is obsessed with money, then it's purely in the negative sense, of being kept up at night worrying about the kid's school fees and so forth. In Chapter 4 the question of work is examined more closely. Employment has entered into an almost paradoxical phase. Useless and symbolic on the one hand, universally necessary on the other, rendering it into a sort of theatre of cruelty. The rise of depressing new work forms associated with the 'gig economy' and 'zero-hour' contracts is the topic of Chapter 5, which I trace back to the seemingly harmless notion of 'human capital theory' in neoclassic economics. This approach to economic activity truly represents the apogee of neoliberal economic (un) reason in its catastrophic glory. Chapter 6 then explores the problem of resistance and conflict in an era of total economics, where the poison of a cash-centricity has seeped into every social crevasse. If mainstream economic thought and practice is effectively dead, as the emblematic figure of homo economicus readily implies, then the conclusion attempts to envisage what might come to replace it.

1

Cash Psychosis

The last time 85-year-old pensioner Isabella Purves was seen alive was back in 2004. The Canonmills resident – a district in the city of Edinburgh – was a woman of few words and only seen picking up a newspaper from the local shop.[1] A neighbour nevertheless remembered Isabella fondly:

> She was always cleaning her brasses and keeping the stair clean and would go out hiking. She was very fit and only became frail in later years. She was an old-fashioned lady, quite a Miss Marple, Morningside-type, but not glam – no pearls or twin sets, but she would wear thick tights and long skirts and was always very well turned out.[2]

And then, in the words of another Canonmills resident, Isabella disappeared off the face of the earth. Some thought she'd moved away or into a retirement home. Others simply forgot about her. However, in 2009 water started to drip from her council flat into the property below. The local authorities were called to investigate. After pushing through all the unopened mail piled up behind Isabelle's door, they discovered her remains. She had been dead for five years and nobody had noticed.

The case of Isabella Purves caught the headlines because it exemplified everything that was wrong with elderly care in the UK, and particularly the decline of society more generally. Loneliness has become an epidemic in neoliberal Britain and elsewhere, especially among the elderly who are deemed to be no longer useful to society.[3] It doesn't help matters that governmental social care services have been chronically underfunded. For example, in 2017 it was reported that 900 people are leaving the social care sector every day in England.[4] Who can blame them? The pay is terrible. The government treats these jobs as an unnecessary drain on resources and its employees as second-class citizens. In the vacuum, family networks have tried to step in to do the work, mainly other senior citizens, unpaid of course. A spate of similar examples to Isabella have occurred across the UK.[5] In societies that have embraced the ethos of market individualism it appears that the very fabric of the community has evaporated. One Canonmills resident said that things turned bad when a large supermarket chain arrived a few years back, typifying what might be called the truculent *anonymisation* of Britain: 'Tesco changed things. There used to be a butcher's, baker's, we had everything, and you would just meet people. Having a supermarket makes things less personal.'[6]

When I first read about Isabella Purves I was shocked. But not that surprised in the context of austerity and a decimated welfare state. It was an extreme case compared to the norm and certainly had little to do with the topic of this book, homo economicus, the super-rational, money-chasing individual whom neoclassical economics believes we all resemble at heart, like wanna-be bankers, ruthless real estate agents or ambitious entrepreneurs. I made a brief note about Isabella and moved on. But the story kept niggling me. It was something about her isolation and abandonment, how she was partially placed outside the loop of monetary value but still inescapably defined by it. Ossified by a bad ideology and trapped in a symbolic no-man's land. Making matters more complex, news reports implied that Isabella might have desired her seclusion. A neighbour said, 'People will say, no-one looked out for her, but I don't think she wanted to be reached out to. But the area has changed. Not just this area, but other areas have as well.' Could it be that Isabella intentionally sought the solitude that would eventually nullify not only her memory but the farewell rites (i.e., mourning, commemoration, etc.) customary to the newly dead? As a fitting end to the story, it was later reported that a cousin happily swooped in to inherit Isabella's £100,000 estate, including cash and an apartment.[7]

Then it dawned upon me. What happened to Isabella Purves was not just an extreme case. Her fate was somehow symptomatic of a broader underlying logic concerning what economy and society has become more generally, especially the so-called hero of neoliberal policy, homo economicus. Economic man was designed to be a standalone creature, militantly selfish and the natural adversary of anything remotely social, even though he is reliant on other people as much as anyone else, perhaps more so. As this code was disseminated among the populations of Western economies (the rich, by the way, wanted nothing to do with homo economicus), he was inevitably mangled into an unworkable monstrosity, especially following the largest economic crisis in generations. Today, ten years later, the blind adherence to free market capitalism has not waned. It's perhaps even deepened, sucking the life out of an already crippled social body and mummifying its inhabitants one by one: anonymised, secretive and alone.

On the one hand Isabella was just another elderly person who had slipped through the net. A tragic story to be sure. But nothing compared to the awful wars we have recently seen, economic inequality that's spiralling out of control and the vast environmental destruction unleashed by the unrelenting corporatisation of the living ... and dead. By the same token, Isabella seemed to me a small but not insignificant emblem of an unfolding reality that has gripped *everyone* like a bad dream since 2007. Symptomatic not only of a malfunctioning economic ideology or failing neoliberal discourse but of a broken reality, a twisted and desperate world that feels devoid of any future. Angry and nihilistic in its outlook. Obsessed with anything remotely smelling of cash, the most private of all exchangeable commodities. If economic man is dead, then it isn't signified by the suicidal banker or cocaine-addled real estate agent, as I've suggest in an earlier book.[8] No, we see the fatality most evidently among those at the bottom of the heap and in the norms that the majority are pressured to follow as if nothing wrong has happened.

Like homo economicus, who has now been thoroughly ravaged by a noxious economic dogma and anonymising commercial milieu, Isabella represents what happens when society is stripped of *the public*. From about the mid-1980s successive regimes in the West have pursued a tireless battle against the public. This is not just about the sale of basic state-owned assets and the incessant commercialisation of everyday life. The war is against the very concept of the public sphere itself. For example, at no other time since its inception has the welfare state been so hated by the governing elite. Social care. Unemployment assistance. Health. Local councils and libraries. Municipal parks. Anything relating to what used to be called 'the public good' is attacked at the roots. Austerity redefines it as a fiscal liability or deficit rather than a shared investment in common decency. The ruling credo is now clear. For better or worse (usually worse), the private, moneyed individual reigns and anyone who claims otherwise must be some old, crusty collectivist – a dinosaur from another bygone age. It's not that all social connections have been evacuated in this economic wasteland. There are still plenty of those. It's just that we only now get the bad kind, the type that makes people like Isabella Purves want to disappear rather than face another ankle-biting bureaucrat or Tesco's carpark attendant. Indeed, when the public disappears like this, it could be argued, a veritable avalanche of social forces descend on the individual, separating him or her from the protective pack and exposing them to the worst excesses of economic collectivism otherwise known as post-2007 capitalism.

The tragic figure of Isabella Purves therefore opens a window onto a broader social landscape, revealing the shared devastation that this miscarriage of individualism has inflicted on an increasingly ill and emaciated social body. When corporations rule the world and a myopic state apparatus transforms our lives into one enormous, badly managed K-Mart, a special type of backwardness emerges. Innovation stalls. Skills that took generations to accumulate waste away. Democracy becomes farcical … nay, a bad joke. Personal debt hangs around one's neck like some medieval torture device. And people like Isabella, who were once young and full of life, are cast to the wayside and forgotten.

Privatised to death

The public. What does the idea mean? And perhaps more importantly, why does it grate so badly with the dominant norms of capitalist culture today? The word has Latin origins from *publicus* and *populus*, meaning the people. But this understanding of 'the people' is not simply the sum of different individuals since *populus* implies a shared and common interest: survival, wellbeing, freedom, the good life and so forth. It binds us to the fate of others, a sort of distributive responsibility in which we are all answerable to each other. We can extrapolate from the concept to include the people's voice (e.g., democracy) and a shared stake in our future or mutual self-determination: *res publica*. The state and civil society were once seen as the champion of this public claim over self-governance. Unfortunately, both have now become its professed enemy. After society was reconfigured into a brutalist paradise of self-serving individualism, using neoclassic economics as the blueprint, any sense of the 'public good' has been squashed with distain. Look at what has happened to local councils in the UK. In an excellent essay on the topic, Tom Crewe argues that

14

the real seat of public democratic expression isn't the centralised state but local authorities.[9] Since 2010 their funding has been slashed by 37 per cent. The forecast is 60 per cent by 2020. The result? Disappearing public toilets. School budgets slashed. Parks crumbling into disrepair. Street lights turned off at midnight to save money. Hundreds of public libraries closed and a 25 per cent reduction in staff since 2010. Indeed, only after a few years of vilification it's remarkable how hard it is to now remember what the word 'public' was like before the rise of neoliberal capitalism. It is like trying to recall how things got done before email.

When I was a child in 1970s (semi-socialist) New Zealand, a school teacher tried to astonish us by holding up a glass of water. The lesson was on money and the latent dangers of an exchange society. 'One day children,' he intoned, 'even water might someday be something you can only buy with money.' We laughed, totally unconvinced. There's no way water, which falls freely from the sky and flows off the mountains, could be privately owned or sold as such. It intrinsically belongs to everyone.

My, how times have changed. Today my London water bill – issued by a distant, foreign-owned monopoly who most likely doesn't give a shit about the residents of Stoke Newington – is astronomical. The same goes for energy, transport, sport, education, music, culture. The list goes on and on. Even air is now considered a private good: purified 'bottled air' can be purchased in heavily polluted sectors of the global economy.[10] It is obvious that this concerted offensive against common ownership is reaching new heights, despite the conclusive evidence that neoliberal economics and its devotion to private property simply doesn't work ... even by its own standards. It is important to note, however, that the public sphere has not been entirely eradicated from society. A part of it still remains, but as a gross caricature, designed to manipulate and control rather than express the spirit of the people. I am speaking here, of course, of the state, which is as much in need of total reform as the financial industries. Most people woke up following the bank bailouts and recognised in the state a perverted type of public domain, one that we ironically fund ourselves through taxation, bankrolling our own non-access to a dignified life. That recognition ought to have triggered the widespread rejection of capitalism, something even the Governor of the Bank of England said he expected during the financial crisis.[11] But it didn't quite turn out that way. The connection between economic trends and political attitude is never so simple.

It's true that the Western liberal state has always represented an objectification that stands over its creators like an alien force. But never has it been so removed and hostile to the common interest as it is today. It legitimises shameful levels of inequality. Paves the way for the corporate colonisation of almost everything. Engages in expensive and unjust oil wars. This is what unfortunately makes the modern state so dangerous to the spirit of democracy. In its wake we inevitably witness the rise of populism (e.g., Brexit in the UK and corporate fascism in the USA) as well as wanton riots like those that spread across London in 2011 as thousands of young people finally snapped. When governments become this type of tax-funded, anti-social *publicus*, it serves to displace the negative externalities of 'extreme economics' onto the individual him or herself, immigrants and the poor.

One such externality is typified by our manic attachment to money, a human artefact that has mysteriously taken over much of life as we know it. It becomes the only way of relating to each other under extreme capitalism. The only available means to do anything. Everything has a price and that fact is revealed with persistent and piercing clarity. While money sometimes seems like an instrument of empowerment, allowing us to do this or that, it is also fundamentally defined by its *absence*. This is why money inherently makes the world and us in it so inadequate. As the philosopher Walter Benjamin put it, money ultimately 'brings nearly every human relationship up short'.[12] Moreover, the source of cash and our ability to obtain it becomes a continuous, perpetual anxiety. What might be termed a sort of money madness infiltrates our social imagination, which has been convincingly linked to the epidemic of mental illness in many Western societies.[13] Although some might retaliate and direct their bile towards the state, it is typically rechannelled towards easier and more accessible targets, including ethnic or religious groups. This too is why nationalism and neoliberalisation are often so closely aligned, despite what some say about the alt-right being against market fundamentalism. On the contrary. It's what happens when cash-centricity meets nouveau fascism that is really worrying, something I dub *cashism* later in this book.

Commando capitalism

Why has neoliberalism entered into this authoritarian phase? I believe things really shifted up a gear in 2003, when war become the Western state's key motif for tackling problems of governmentality. As US and UK officials deceived the public, ignored their protests and went to war in Iraq and Afghanistan, the thousands of innocent men, women and children who died as a result were not the only causalities. Something also radically died in the civic capacities of people governed in pan-capitalist societies, most notably in England, America, France, Australasia and South East Asia. State policy became openly militarised, as did daily life. With the arrival of Tony Blair and George. W. Bush we see most of the gains of the 1960s counter-cultural movement swiftly retracted, heralding a new type of bullish mentality towards statecraft. Blend that trend with the rise of 'extreme inequality' in terms of wealth distribution, then punitive hierarchies in the public and private sector are probably inevitable, as does the growth of technocrats who now must police the gulf between the 99%-ers and the elite.[14]

Like an occupying military, unpopular policy is pushed through now regardless of whether we like it or not. Power exudes such confidence in its own influence that it seldom bothers to convince or persuade people of this or that policy's rightfulness. It just does what it wants and then says, 'What are you going to do about it? Nothing? That's what we thought.' Think here of government's militant stance towards junior doctors in the UK at the end of 2016 who were protesting about the implementation of potentially dangerous employment contracts. Or the passenger (physician,

David Dao) who was viciously removed from a United Airlines aircraft in April 2017 when it was discovered the flight was overbooked.[15] Economic power transitions from persuasion to brute, almost military-style force very easily today. In this respect, it is telling that when the architect of economic austerity in England, George Osborne, stepped down in 2016 and went on summer vacation, he was spotted in Vietnam. However, he wasn't sunning himself by a swimming pool or exploring the local cuisine, as other tourists might. Osborne was instead seen firing what looked to be an M60 light machine gun in an old Vietcong base.[16] It seems that he'd finally got to live out his Rambo-complex after all, an attitude clearly evident in his approach to the British public too.

This type of 'commando capitalism' certainly militarises economic life. But it also encourages a certain attitude towards dissent and disobedience among the powerful. For example, in 2013 the New Zealand Minister of Finance, Bill English, simply couldn't accept that the country's love affair with neoclassical economics had created extraordinary levels of inequality. But recent figures show that the number of children living under the poverty line has doubled since 1984, coming in at 300,000. By chance, Bill English met Professor Robert Wade from the London School of Economics in a television studio. The academic was in New Zealand to help promote a book revealing how bad inequality was in a country that was once proud of its egalitarianism. In his interview Wade stated, 'Over the past two decades or so, economic policy in the US, the UK and New Zealand has increasingly been set by the top 1 per cent or so for the top 1 per cent.' In the lobby, the academic was allegedly accosted by English, who angrily pointed at him warning 'Don't you say that again.' According to Professor Wade, the Finance Minister:

> Just sort of exploded like a volcano out in the anteroom ... I was surprised by the sort of menace in his voice. He was like a schoolmaster and he sort of jabbed his finger in the direction of my chest like a school master wagging the finger ... just asserting, in a rather bullying way I thought, his point of view ... he wasn't

in any mood to actually discuss … I just thanked him for his kind advice and proceeded on out.[17]

Bill English later became Prime Minister of New Zealand. A couple of disconcerting things are occurring here, other than the pugilistic thuggishness displayed. There is a fear of knowledge, facts that might disconfirm the rhetoric and surface the dirty reality of life under free markets. But it is the hatred of democratic dialogue and exchange that stands out, debate about the figures and open policy discussion. This *hatred of democracy*, as the French philosopher Jacques Rancière terms it, coupled with the vast distance between the state technocracy and ordinary people, has resulted in some bizarre developments.[18] Since facts no longer matter and official liars aren't held accountable in any meaningful manner (i.e., Tony Blair), the democratic process becomes worse than a spectacle, where leaders pretend to tell the truth. Instead, unabashed deception is now informally condoned and even expected by a public that sadly sees itself reflected in this post-factum theatre of the absurd.

Such post-truth politics was on full view during the 2016 Brexit campaign, of course, with ludicrous claims being made and openly revealed as such (sometimes by the claimants themselves!) after the vote took place. The 2016 US presidential election campaign and the rise of Donald Trump ('we will build a wall') also demonstrated how bad democracy has become. Not only bad entertainment (since we can always switch the TV off or walk out of a movie), but very unsafe entertainment in which the audience – 'us' – are not just distant observers but profoundly implicated in the terrifying spectacle. In January 2017 White House officials even used the term 'alternative facts' to justify Donald Trump's false boast that his inaugural attracted record-breaking crowds. Here the relationship between lying and truthfulness takes on new complexities. In the old days we used to believe the government until certain statements were proven false. To a certain extent, that's still the case, according to Harvard psychologist Daniel Gilbert. The problem is that the constant barrage of lies is relentless. It means that people give up on the second step that is meant to follow 'comprehension'; namely, critically disconfirming the split second belief in a patent mistruth: 'When faced with shortages of time, energy, or conclusive evidence, many fail to unaccept the ideas that they involuntarily accept during comprehension.'[19] This is why widely accepted information sources – like Wikipedia – are so picky about the evidence used to backup so-called factual statements. It's a sad testament to how bad the news is in the UK when the amateur editors of Wikipedia feel the need to ban the country's bestselling newspaper, the *Daily Mail*, deeming it an unreliable source *tout court*.[20]

But perhaps matters are even worse than this. If weary acceptance was simply the problem then critical truth telling would still have a fighting chance. However, running alongside this blind belief in falsehoods is a paradoxical cynicism concerning all statements, the stubborn feeling there is no correct information. That stance is just as corrosive to democracy. Now we act on the premise that even Noam Chomsky and Jeremy Paxman might also be somehow fudging the truth. Importantly, this is something that politicians implicitly *draw upon* to make even bolder falsehoods because by doing so they are merely satisfying a public expectation. When a senior official or CEO lies to us it oddly represents a sort of perverse fidelity. And herein lies the real danger of 'alternative fact' telling Trump style. We know it's a lie. They know it's a lie. But the point is to subtly change the tone of the debate through repetition, which can successfully occur regardless of the statement's veracity.

A selfish ghost ...

There is no doubt that the modern state has become a bastardised version of democracy. But something similar too has happened to the business world, the supposed lovechild of neoliberal economic theory. Exploiting the dogma of free markets, competition and privatisation, large and exceedingly powerful multinational enterprises have certainly evolved to dominate society. But they bear little resemblance to the original ideas of Milton Friedman, Murray Rothbard, Friedrich Hayek or even the theories of present-day academic acolytes working in the neoclassical tradition. Corporations today are more about monopolistically *capturing* societal wealth, much of which is produced *despite* of capitalism rather than because of it. That is to say, produced by you and me when we have to work around the unrealistic rules of economic formalism. Exploitation today relies upon a great deal of goodwill to function. This is why the critical commentator Paul Mason argues that we're potentially entering a post-capitalist period following the 2007–08 crisis and the rise of new forms of exchange based around the gift, digital sharing and cooperation.[21] But his analysis is far too optimistic. We may certainly be entering a post-capitalist world, but not in any hopeful and emancipatory way. With current trends unfolding as they are, a new dark age appears imminent, in which corporate fiefdoms and global plutocrats preside over an increasingly disenfranchised transnational population and dying natural environment. And there's the point. Neoliberal capitalism *is dead*, which is why we must use the term with much circumspection. To reiterate, the system is no longer 'non dead', a 'zombie' or staggering 'monster' as some have suggested.[22] No, it's verifiably deceased. The body economic has basically flat-lined, its vital organs, including the brain, are shutting down and the first signs of rigor mortis have set in.

Ever since the Great Recession of 2008 we have notably seen how big business and its twin-sun, big government, follow few of the ideas prescribed by neoliberal economic orthodoxy in practice. The state was happy to act as a generous 'safety net' for reckless financiers following the subprime crisis, and now that has become an expected norm that all mega-firms can rely upon. For sure, large corporates require hefty, intrusive governments of the nastiest kind to prop up their unproductive activities and ensure the next dividend payment is made to shareholders. So-called open markets have been captured by overarching cartels. Economic waste burgeons under inefficient subcontracting arrangements, with the UK government alone spending £80 billion a year on firms like Serco, G4S and others to provide scandal-ridden services (e.g., the London Olympics debacle, etc.).[23] The sad irony is that privatisation in the UK has patently failed to bring improved infrastructure, choice, cheaper prices or customer satisfaction. Just look at the railways, where multinational investors have 'sweated' assets to the point of decrepitude, extorted commuters and syphoned off millions from the public purse to offshore bank accounts.[24]

If neoliberalism is probably dead, then what do we have in its place? Its unhappy and maladroit *ghost* no doubt. But a very selfish one. The business model that predominates today shelters itself from the inclement forces of crisis capitalism, which are largely left to the general public to deal with. Moreover, corporations are marked by an aggressive opportunism, which is characterised by the logic of *extraction* rather than production, as mentioned earlier. Extraction of natural resources. Extraction of funds from the state coffers. Indeed, extraction of life itself by way of the so-called 'sharing economy' – what else could you call Uber apart from a tax scam? This is perhaps why growth and productivity figures have plummeted so dramatically in many Western economies. Not much is being produced. Value is being drained away (or up) instead.

Executive pay functions precisely in this way. It has increased by 80 per cent over the last ten years and has been found to have little or no relationship to business performance or returns on invested capital.[25] CEO remuneration operates more as a type of 'rent', which in 2017 ballooned to an incredible 386 times more than the average living wage in the UK.[26] When executives are paid in stock options, which began to occur from the 1980s onwards, they become purely motivated by short-term share price gains, and to hell with all other parties (workers, consumers, etc.) or even the sustainability of the firm itself.[27] Income growth for everyone else, of course, has stagnated for years.[28] The corporate class as a whole has applied this extractive formula to the languishing post-crash economy, leveraging the state in particular. In Britain, for example, it's been estimated that 'corporate welfare' – the money flow from the state (via taxes) to the business sector in the form of subsidies, grants and exemptions – is in the region of £93 billion per year.[29] Think here also of the cash *that isn't* collected. Not only do corporations have ingenious ways to avoid tax, but the employment systems they employ (zero-hours contracts, etc.) has indirectly resulted in an estimated loss of £4 billion a year.[30] That's a lot of money being diverted from much needed public investment.

Another instance of how this 'drainage economics' works was recently reported in relation to the ongoing attempt to privatise the National Health Service in England concerning an especially controversial scheme called Private-Finance-Initiative.[31] It was introduced in the Tony Blair years. Private investors help fund the establishment and management of a hospital, receiving payments in return over a long-term period. However, the immediate profits are so good (since they ultimate derive from the state ... or more accurately, the taxpayer), some private investors simply sell on the contracts and double their original investment. This is called 'flipping' in which a private investor breaks the deal with the government (e.g., long-term management) and seeks to make a quick profit.

The programme has been an expensive (or very lucrative if you are a private investor) mess, with one observer stating, 'Let's face it, they are not doing this because they love the NHS. We need a full, open investigation into what has happened here.'[32] In 2016 the Northumbria Healthcare NHS Foundation Trust highlighted what was at stake. They decided to borrow £114 million from the local council and buy out the investor who helped fund a new hospital. Now free from the private investor's lopsided conditions, the trust will save £3.5 million a year over the next 19 years the original contract was meant to run.

Perhaps the worst case of big business relentlessly jabbing its 'blood funnel into anything that smells like money' (as Matt Taibbi memorably described Goldman Sachs a few years back) concerns those firms that benefited from the Iraq war. The economic and human costs of this modern catastrophe are still being calculated. But we now know that several multinational firms literally made a killing out of the contracts funded by the US government. According to one study, the ten-year conflict saw private firms receive $138 billion in US taxpayers' money, with ten companies receiving over 50 per cent of that sum.[33] The top earner was Halliburton. It soaked up $39.5 billion in contracts, which is unsurprising given that one of the war's chief architects – Dick Cheney – was the company's CEO between 1995 and 2000. What I call 'wreckage economics' in the next chapter really comes into its own with this example because the forces of irresponsible destruction and unscrupulous profiteering are so closely aligned. This is a useful metaphor for much of the economy today, controlled by faceless shareholders and multinational goliaths who have only one thing on their mind. Public money ... your money. Meanwhile, amidst the growing rubble, homo economicus is isolated and alone. He or she is told they have only two choices, both of which are deeply false. Are you going to be part of the wrecking class or the wrecked?

Funeral flights

The economics of extraction opportunistically feeds off the public, the state, small businesses and whatever else it can get its greedy little hands on. None of this has to do with risk or creative destruction, which was supposed to fuel the dynamism of post-industrial capitalism. It's now more about opportunism, preying on living revenue streams – you and me – that have little choice but to participate. This model of plunder is now a basic facet of big business, with scandals like the one involving Sir Philip Green in 2016 and the British Home Store (BHS) retail chain debacle appearing in the media with increasing frequency. Here is another example. Remember the days of bereavement flights, discounts for passengers who have no alternative but to travel given the loss of a loved one? It was once considered common decency to provide a generous discount since no business ought to profit from such misfortune. Not anymore, however. Welcome to the dark lands of extractive capitalism that will capitalise on absolutely any type of hardship in order to enhance the bottom line. When Michael O'Leary, the CEO of budget airline Ryanair, was asked about funeral flights, he publicly stated:

The best yields (fares) are VFRs (visiting friends and relatives) going to funerals ... They book late because they don't tend to have much notice, and they tend to be price insensitive because they have to travel ... We don't care whether you're (travelling for) business, leisure, or visiting friends and relatives. All we want to know about our customer base is that they've booked and we have their credit card number.[34]

If you tried to leverage this type of 'yield' among friends or in your neighbourhood, they would probably call you a psychopath. But it's now perfectly fine for businesses to behave in this manner. Economic reason demands it.

O'Leary's statement surfaces the parasitical tendencies that many large businesses follow today. Personal debt is another good case in point. Retail banks used to serve a fairly traditional social function. When I tell my undergraduate students that bankers in the 1970s were conservative, rather gentile Justice of the Peace-like characters, they are shocked and often don't believe me. Their version of the banker is wild, greedy and devoid of any sense of responsibility, like something out of *The Wolf of Wall Street*. And the caricature is fairly accurate. Even retailing banking has reinvented its identity and seeks to opportunistically exploit the desperation of people and the deep pockets of the state that often picks up the tab. Take the recent case of Virginia firm Kaleo, which sells a delivery system (called Evzio) for an opiate overdose antidote. Heroin and painkiller use has reached epidemic levels in the USA following the recession. In 2015 alone around 33,000 people died from overdosing on opiates. In light of this growing demand, Kaleo simply increased the price of its product from $690 to $4500. Overnight. Health officials were at a loss: 'There's absolutely nothing that warrants them charging what they're charging.'[35] But they're missing the point. In the lucrative age of funeral flights, it apparently makes perfect business sense to raise the price.

A similar callous capitalisation on desperation – the raw material capitalism now feeds off – is evident in higher education (which Margret Thatcher, Tony Blair and Theresa May all received free of charge, by the way) and the upward social mobility that many believe it secures. There is little doubt that individual debt is perhaps the defining facet of how capitalism functions today. A recent study found that it alone costs the UK taxpayer £8.3 billion every year to assist problem debtors with mental health, employment and housing needs.[36] This is not only an economic issue but a social and existential one. The problem of debt needs to be resolved soon before it's too late. But that looks unlikely in a country such as the USA, where a person like Betsy DeVos was nominated as Secretary of Education in January 2017. Her husband is heir to the billion-dollar Amway Empire. And her brother founded Blackwater, the notorious security firm accused of violating civilian human rights during the Iraqi war. DeVos is known to be a staunch opponent of public education. When she was grilled by Senator Elizabeth Warren concerning her credentials for the role, this was the exchange:

Warren: The Secretary of Education is responsible for managing a trillion-dollar student loan bank … the financial future of an entire generation of young people depend on your department getting it right. Now Ms. DeVos, do you have any direct experience running a bank?

DeVos: Senator, I do not.

Warren: Have you ever managed or overseen a trillion-dollar loan program?

DeVos: I have not.

Warren: How about a billion-dollar loan program.

DeVos: No, I have not.

Warren: Ms. DeVos have you ever taken out a student loan to help pay for college?

DeVos: I have not.

Warren: Have any of your children …?

DeVos: They have been fortunate not to.[37]

In the end, Betsy DeVos was confirmed as Secretary of Education in February 2017.

BANG ... you're homeless

The impact of these draconian (post-) neoliberal tendencies is the reason why so many feel the future has been brazenly hijacked in front of them. For the 15- to 30-year-olds I have spoken with, the idea of a fulfilling job, home ownership and even societal progress feels like a distant memory, part of an era they've heard about but never experienced. This is not to romanticise the past, of course. But in relative terms, we have seen a major deterioration on almost every socio-economic indicator in this respect. These trends of intergenerational inequality (which simply reflect the wider economic inequality sweeping across Britain, the USA and many other countries) has had a devastating impact on class mobility. It has halted so suddenly that a new class classification had to be invented to describe some people ... NEETs (Not in Employment, Education or Training). Society has basically given up on them and they've understandably given up on society. A psychologist recently set up a Reddit site called 'What led to your becoming a NEET?' and invited people to anonymously share their thoughts. There were some very sad responses, but all were intelligent and self-conscious about their predicament. This reply really stood out for me:

I'm 22 years old and I'm a NEET. Why? I guess [it] is a lack of emotional intelligence melt with financial crisis and the rising of exponential disruptive new technologies. The world is changing very fast and it seems there's no security: you can't trust no path, no option. You could spend a lot of energy doing something with a future reward and BANG you are homeless, underemployed, poor, sad, depressed ... There isn't mental feedback, or at least, enough of it. The other problem is education. Why education hasn't changed [since] Bismarck times? It's just pure bullshit unable to engage creativity and far away from new technologies and capabilities. I hate the educational system and I will destroy it if I can. It's just about have an A and not about knowing yourself neither your talent. And that's the point: I'm a NEET because I don't find my element or maybe be I'm too much afraid to know it. Till that moment I will stay at home waiting for Basic Income and financial apocalypse: it's hard, but I'm trapped by fear.[38]

Apologists for neoliberal capitalism like to refer to young people as 'aspirants', go-getters who are enthusiastically entrepreneurial in their worldview. What bullshit. More like *desperants*, a blend of desperation and depression.[39] However, their sense of entrapment, fear and pointlessness is no pathology (one NEET in the survey above mentioned how his or her parents concluded he must have autism). It's merely a *rational response* to the new, concrete realities currently being encouraged by the present political and financial plutocrats, steering our age into a new darkness. That's why it's probably best to simply stay home. For instance, it is common knowledge that the best jobs now go to those born into the right families. Skill and ability increasingly play less of a role. I worked for three years at Cambridge University as a lecturer and was constantly amazed by an immovable, ironclad expectation of entitlement among the student body. For sure, as Thomas Piketty found in his excellent study of inequality, inheritance is today becoming *the* predictor of a person's wealth during their lifetime.[40] Just as it was once in the Gilded Age and Belle Époque. Of course, we're not seeing the return of the traditional aristocracy, a point well made by Mike Savage and his team concerning class stratification in Britain.[41] No, the new plutocracy that rules today represents 'dark money', remote and pitiless wealth-hoarders who'd be more at home in *Blade Runner* than *Downton Abbey*.[42] Their offspring get the best of everything, of course. For everyone else, education is now eye-wateringly expensive and personal debt has mired millions in repayment schemes that will erode their income for years to come.

Numerous other travesties have become the norm in this dying period of late capitalism. The shift wasn't sudden, which might have inspired people to take to the streets in protest more than they have. No, first a moral boundary was tested (e.g., cutting care for the elderly). Then another (e.g., radically increase train ticket prices). And another. Over time people get used to it. Here's another good instance. Along with the big banks, the housing/accommodation industry (i.e., construction firms and the private rentier class) have systematically exploited poor town planning policies in Western cities. This coalition of corporates and investors intentionally underinvest in new housing to keep demand at ultra-high levels, often buying land to simply sit on it and watch its value increase (i.e., land banking), lobby the government to privatise state-owned housing and so forth. As you can imagine, with such a mismatch between supply and demand, the profit margins are extraordinary. Accommodation costs in London, Sydney, New York and many other large cities could easily be classified as a social catastrophe, especially for the young, working poor who have been completely frozen out of home ownership.[43] Things are not much better for those who got in before the 'big freeze' and put down a deposit on the mortgage, as we see in the USA, which is experiencing a largely unreported 'eviction epidemic' on a scale not seen since the Great Depression.[44] As a result, Third World-style slums are popping up everywhere in the land of the free.[45]

This overriding sense of the future being cancelled or closed down among young people – and even those in their 30s and 40s – inevitably shapes their politics, what is thought possible and impossible. For them the world has taken a great leap backwards. Millennials have been conspicuously left behind, earning 20 per cent less than the rest of us, stuck in a morass of debt, playthings of unscrupulous landlords and facing a radically dire job market.[46] In the UK, workers born between 1981 and 2000 are less well off than pensioners, and are the first generation to be poorer than their parents.[47] Being trapped and going nowhere in a feudal-like class structure closes down any image of the future, rendering the present eternal, static and deadening. Perhaps this is how the establishment have got away with the travesty of post-2007 capitalism, a period in which elites have dramatically increased their wealth and position in the global power hierarchy.[48] Without a vision of the future it is difficult to resist the present effectively. When I look at my three-year-old son today, it's not with a sense of hope as it ought to be but anxiety about what he might have to endure. There is very good reason to believe that his will be no ordinary future.

On being Uber-screwed

This ongoing degradation of everyday life is no more evident than in the world of work, which will be explored in some depth in the pages that follow. Employment is today one of the leading causes of distress for a simple reason; it has become connected to everything else in life and one's fortunes are entirely dependent upon it. For those of us who are not part of the global elite or transnational criminal class, paid work is the only way to obtain money. And, of course, everything today is linked to the curse of cash. Even phoning a governmental tax office to ask how much you owe incurs a charge. This hyper-commercialisation creates a vicious cycle that is difficult to escape. It is no surprise that after the global financial crisis and the austerity economics that followed, job satisfaction levels around the world dropped to historic lows, perhaps marginally better than those in the Victorian age, of which we can only speculate.[49] It's important to distinguish this unhappiness with its past manifestation in the workforce, say in the 1990s. What employees dislike the most today are not those 'subjective gripes' so frequently mentioned in the mainstream business press and self-help industry as they prescribe more mindfulness, work/life balance, wellness, exercise, etc. On the contrary, the source of discontent is generally material and basic. Pay levels have stagnated for most over the last 20 years.[50] Job security, conditions and benefits have been significantly pared back.[51] Managerial authoritarianism, even in relatively well-paid white-collar jobs, has returned to the office with a vengeance. It is almost as if capitalist culture has taken a giant step towards a Marxian version of itself, becoming the reality that critics once only imagined it to be.

The malaise affecting working people today is different compared to previous generations in other ways. Many have discovered that having a job has increasingly become a path *into* hardship rather than out of it. Because almost all of the costs of living are now firmly placed onto the individual (rather than equally distributed through progressive taxation policies) it suddenly becomes extremely expensive to be a full, normal participant of the workforce. The high price of commuting, rent, childcare and all the other things we need to get by in an over-privatised social universe means that in-work poverty is rife in the UK, USA and elsewhere.[52]

Take the recent case of Angela, who cares for her unwell husband in Devon.[53] Because of a new policy initiative, she was forced to find work by the Department for Work and Pensions. But when Angela finally found a 25-hour-a-week cleaning job, she lost her carers allowance, income support, free school meals for her children and discounted school bus fares. She still looked after her husband, of course. Angela rightly observed, 'going through the online calculators, I'll probably be worse off ... You do wonder why you bother. But I don't feel as if I've been left with any option.' No wonder millions are now wondering what exactly the point of work is. Governments in the USA and UK spend billions on in-work benefits in order to top-up low pay, which is a direct result of corporations (and their army of subcontractors) unwilling to fairly remunerate employees. In effect, the taxpayer is subsiding big business as they openly rip-off anyone they can.

This is one method for keeping wages low and profits high in the present era, which has nothing to do with the free markets espoused by the Chicago School of Economics. For example, a National Housing Federation study in Britain found that housing benefits – paid to people who cannot afford their rent – resulted in private landlords pocketing around £9.3 billion in 2015.[54] This amount had doubled since 2005. Back at the ranch, workers who can be classified as 'precarious' had grown to 7 million by the end of 2016.[55] Meanwhile, Google got away with paying just €47 million tax in Ireland on €22 billion sales revenue. That's a 0.21 per cent tax rate.[56] Generous corporate welfare like this means you and I have to pick up the slack to fund society either directly (e.g., outrageous train ticket prices) or indirectly (e.g., income taxes, etc.). Here we can note how the extractive logic of a moribund economic paradigm aims to suck the wealth out of society more generally, leaving a dry and depressing husk for everyone else. As an aside, when justifying low corporate tax, dim-witted politicians and business lobbyists often mention the threat of 'capital flight'. That amounts to little more than an idle threat, however. Research suggests that the rich seldom divest when taxed at more civilised levels.[57]

Clearly employers and the governmental apparatus have formed a united front in their management of the labouring economic subject in this respect. Hence, the emergence of firms currently defining the future of work – Uber, Deliveroo, Taskrabbit, Lyft and the like.[58] The business model succeeds by placing almost all the burden of employment onto the individual worker and, if possible, the consumer. Some herald these platform businesses as the cutting-edge of technological innovation with all the apps involved. But they're mainly a form of social regression, especially in terms of economic exploitation and the widespread disempowerment of the workforce. Emerging 'blockchain' technology, wrongly praised too as a more transparent and democratic approach to platform capitalism, doesn't change this fact.[59] It will probably make it worse. Rather than reap the rewards of a sharing economy, participants time and again find themselves being short-changed and having trouble making ends meet. The website Indeed.co.uk is a forum that allows people to review their employers. This one was posted by 'Slave Labour', a user who worked for the delivery service Hermes:

At first, everything was great with 4 hour shifts and a decent amount of money after removing costs such as fuel. About two months in and I found myself doing over 100 deliveries for 50 pound and working from 8–6. They allow no time for holidays, do not pay for extra rounds without constant hounding and offer no incentive or help on 'double volume' bank holidays. The management of the company is abysmal and I would strongly recommend that anyone does not work here ...[60]

Why is individualisation – the Uber attitude exemplified – such a problem when it comes to jobs and employment? Doesn't it increase flexibility and allow people to craft their jobs more around their own particular lifestyle? No, that's California Dreamin ... which is actually where this awful business model was invented. The sober reality is very different in most cases. Collectivisation is crucial for building and protecting workers' rights since we have nothing else to sell but our labour power. Getting together is therefore essential. The so-called sharing economy ironically kills that ethos. That's what is was designed for. The resulting desperation sees individuals (and their families) not only on their own, but permanently preoccupied with the present. This is how history inevitably dies and along with it the future, which is why even the most modest challenge to the status quo today is automatically dismissed as hopelessly utopian. In light of these depressing facts, one commentator recently summed up the conclusion that best fits our predicament: fuck work.[61]

Sugar Daddy economics

In fact, that specific sentiment is perhaps more apt than we think. Take a case that is seldom mentioned in the media. Sex work. Prostitution has always been part of the informal economy. As a result, workers have found it difficult to gain the rights enjoyed by the rest of the employment sector. Protection. Fair treatment. Equal pay. But as the 'oldest profession' became increasingly legitimate, following important struggles spearheaded by activists, workers started to unionise and certain benefits were secured. However, a new business model has recently changed all of this, revolutionising the industry. A businessman (armed with an MBA from Sloan Business School) has developed extremely popular apps like WhatsYourPrice.com, MissTravel.com and SeekingArrangement.com. It allows rich men (or 'Sugar Daddies') to contact girls (or 'Sugar Babies') directly, under the veneer of dating. A contribution is haggled over and the rest is history. Needless to say our MIT graduate – Brandon Wade – is now a multimillionaire.

Once again we hear platitudes about the wonders of technological innovation and the sharing economy in relation to this business. But clearly there is a dark reality driving it and no wonder some describe Wade as an 'e-pimp'.[62] I think this is probably how it operates. With the rise of indebtedness among young women, including university students, sex work becomes a last resort for those seeking a middle-class standard of living.[63] But the WhatsYourPrice.com business model understands that the label 'sex worker' is distasteful and off-putting to the would-be escort and client alike. So now they're just people like you or me who agree to receive payment (or even rent in cities with a housing crisis like London) in return for a certain experience.[64] Of course, all of the employment rights of the regular sex worker no longer apply. This is dating, not work. We're talking about a potential friend or companion, so there's little recourse to employment law if something goes wrong. Nor does the government have any ability to regulate this activity, especially with respect to the health and safety issues. The consumer is completely in charge, just as neoclassical economics asserts they should be. It's easy to see the cold economic rationale at play here. The 'Sugar Daddy' contribution (i.e., payment for sex) slowly undercuts the formal wages and conditions of those who have collectivised and are employed by an agency. As a result, the hard-earned wins of the normal, protected sex worker now begin to look like questionable 'fringe benefits' compared to what 'Sugar Babies' receive. For the WhatsYourPrice.com escort, everything is casual, flexible and totally negotiable. And this has another significant consequence. The boundary between work and non-work swiftly disappears, along with your free time. Employment becomes a perpetual state of being. Does any of this sound familiar? It should. It's the future of work as we know it if current trends continue. Perhaps coming to a job near you soon?[65]

What's certain is that none of this means the 'end of employment' as some have predicted, given how a job and personal life blend into one.[66] Perhaps the opposite has occurred, the extension of work into the very web of life. WhatsYourPrice.com along with Uber and so forth is characteristic of how economic relationships more generally have been greatly *deformalised* over the last 20 years. There has always been an 'informal economy', of course.[67] But its principles are rapidly becoming mainstream in Western capitalism.

Following the deregulation of the workforce and immense growth of the casual economy, *personal relationships* inevitably come to the fore in commerce. It's interesting that this kind of informality has long been championed by right-wing business advocates, claiming it makes work more human and efficient as opposed to rigid organisations that use rules and regulations.[68] More recently, ex-Tory advisor Steve Hilton and author of *More Human* suggests that big bureaucracy is a recipe for disengagement and alienation, killing creativity and morale.[69] Employers need to embrace the ethos of decentralised humanism. Workers and supervisors can be good friends. Everyone can behave much like they would outside of work. Some London offices have gone the extra mile to blur the line between work and play by providing staff with booze trolleys and cocktail bars.

The being 'more human' philosophy is something of a ruse. The push to deformalise capitalism is connected to the massive disempowerment of the workforce that has transpired in Western economies over the last 15 years. From the workers' perspective, it's obvious. We know that bureaucracy squeezes the life out of a job, rendering organisations grey and dull. But when humanity is unleashed in the office, it's not just the nice, caring and fair stuff that we get as a consequence. Humans obviously have a dark side, which is what many of those rules and regulations were designed to keep a lid on. There's a danger of favouritism creeping into career progression decisions. Not in the boss's good books? Unwilling to down copious amounts of alcohol or run for hours at the company gym with your line-manager? Then you're likely to feel disadvantaged. Moreover, who wants to be totally dependent on a capricious boss who suddenly decides he or she doesn't like you today? No wonder workers at Zappos (an online sales firm boasting no hierarchies or job titles) recently resigned in droves when given the chance.[70] Petty favouritism probably thrives under such circumstances. And the likelihood of a little-Hitler emerging as your self-appointed team leader is fairly high. For everyone else an attitude of silent obedience sets in, keeping on the boss's good side when one can. No doubt this is why 'soft skills' are considered so important in the world of work today.[71] The term might mean 'smiling' and being an effective communicator. But it could also mean sucking cock to get ahead. Literally. There is an ironic twist in the move to personalise the employer/employee relationship. If you are not willing to go along with it, then your days in the company are probably numbered. It looks friendly and personable on the surface, but this environment can end up being *more authoritarian* than old-fashioned bureaucracy, not less. Perhaps this is what the philosopher Gilles Deleuze meant when he joked, 'we are taught that corporations have a soul, which is the most terrifying news in the world'.[72] Deep deformalisation blended with authoritarianism? This is the main reason why even the most ordinary employment relationship today feels like a weird throwback to the patrimonial climate that defined the medieval era.

Toddler world

This is a special kind of the dark age, however, since it has also started to utilise the latest developments in 'big data' and various technological platforms in an attempt to elicit more hours on the job than ought to be humanly possible. Such developments represent a kind of 'cyber-feudalism' at the heart of the twenty-first century economy, darkness that sparkles. Uber is once again at the forefront of this rather disturbing trend. It has enlisted the insights of behavioural economics to design driver-response systems that *override* the natural predilection to curb the hours spent at the wheel so that workers drive until they drop, amassing more profits for the firm.[73]

Behavioural economics likes to portray itself as an alternative, more human approach to economic activity. Rather than positing the quintessential rational decision-maker at the centre of social life, it instead sees someone with limited information, deciding on an intuitive basis and responding to their environment in an emotional manner, often confounding rational expectations in neoclassical economic theory. However, as I will demonstrate in the next chapter, behavioural economics doesn't really displace homo economicus so much as *manipulate* his or her limitations and blind-spots to gain a socio-economic advantage over them. A cheap shot, if you like. That is why I think behavioural economics is more wedded to the pseudo-psychological tradition of mass advertising/deception, as described in Vance Packard's classic *The Hidden Persuaders*, than the discipline of economics per se.[74]

Regardless, Uber has apparently deployed techniques inspired by the authors of *Nudge* and other books in the area to squeeze more labour time out of its workers.[75] It specifically wants to have enough drivers on the road when demand is high and be willing to move towards 'surges' in customer demand when they occur, say on the other side of town. Complex algorithms organise the demand/supply data. Then come the psychological tricks derived from videogame interfaces and behavioural economists to do the rest. For example, local managers will often masquerade as females when texting drivers to stay on the road because it is proven to be more effective. 'Sure, no problem Laura', one might imagine a driver replying to a request to undertake one more job. Or the company might use 'loss aversion' tactics. When a driver is about to logoff the on-board app doesn't tell them how much extra money they can make if they stay on the road. It's the projected loss that is highlighted. As an Uber consultant schooled in the dark arts of behaviour science puts it, drivers 'dislike losing more than they like gaining'.[76]

The author of this *New York Times* report decries the manipulation and brainwashing involved. Uber is not only economically exploitative but devious as well. However, what really ought to spark outrage in the reader is the sheer childishness of these management tactics. They're inspired by kid's video games after all. So obvious and clunky are they that a driver would have to be sub-intelligent to fall for them, which is why they don't of course. What Uber is in fact perfecting here is the infantilisation of the workforce, an old ruse in the realm of employee relations. Perhaps this explains a recent incident involving Uber CEO Travis Kalanick. The executive was filmed arguing with one of the taxi app's drivers after they challenged him about low wages. Like an irate parent, it's almost as if Kalanick is scolding his man/child driver for daring to bite the hand that feeds him. Perhaps it's not surprising then that toddlers are all the rage in the business world at the moment, with CEOs like Paul Lindley stating with no irony, 'I would encourage everyone to "grow down" and see life through the eyes of a toddler.'[77]

What is left of darkness?

Workers in the so-called 'gig economy' have been putting up with a lot. For example, it was recently revealed that couriers at Parcel Force – a British delivery firm – could be penalised £250 a day if they call in sick.[78] This was to cover the cost of finding a replacement driver. One UK Mail courier was even charged £800 after being incapacitated by a car accident.[79] In August 2016 Deliveroo workers finally fought back. The company wanted to pay its riders on a per-delivery basis rather than an hourly one. We can easily imagine SeekingArrangement.com doing the same too – the Sugar Daddy only pays for the actual fuck or just the orgasm, not the foreplay or anything else around the 'delivery' of the desired service. After much bad press, the CEO of Deliveroo eventually backed down. In October 2016 London Uber workers successfully fought a court case regarding their status of being independent business owners and/or contractors. For all intents and purposes they were permanent employees, and deserved the same rights. The judge agreed. The company appealed the ruling, but similar struggles have occurred elsewhere around the world, including India.[80]

Many have called these small victories a blow against the gross deterioration of jobs in the present age. It is, but does it really signal a reversal of the underlying expectation of having workers *pay* for the privilege of being employed? I don't think so. As a politician fighting the cause of these independent contractors pointed out, Uber's workers are difficult to organise because 'they are not in the same workplace and there is not the same unity of cause. There is always somebody who will do it if you don't want to.'[81] What's more, the individualisation of employment over the last ten years has made the task of reversing these inexorable trends exceedingly difficult, since *rent* (paying to work) is now a basic feature of the employment system more generally. That means the very structure of employment, ownership and control has to change. And that implies so much more, of course, than fighting to be recognised by Uber as an employee.

Given how things have moved so far to the right, there is no room for half measures or tweaking around the edges. Not just in relation to work but the entire economic system that now stands before us as a mounting wreckage that we're told is normal. The Left is often chastised for not coming up with an alternative in these dark times that are illuminated only by an anti-sun. The accusation is not true. There is an alternative and it's obvious to everyone. One that is simpler, fairer, more innovative and efficient than the convoluted behemoth drowning us, the 99%-ers, in a swamp of manmade misery. The democratic and collective ownership of the means of life. Genuine self-determination and the radical de-privatisation of the public sphere. For even though the oppressive totality of economic regulation today feels complete, with us vacuumed-packed inside it, we must recognise one important fact. This system cannot reproduce itself without parasitically drawing on what it isn't, namely, us. The best way to sum up the present predicament is to restate the old dialectical observation by T.W. Adorno when he noted, 'the power of the relations of production ... is greater than ever, and yet at the same time they are, as objectively anachronistic, everywhere diseased, damaged, riddled with holes. They do not function by themselves.'[82] The continuing endorsement of homo economicus as an ideal human being is capitalism's last ditch attempt to have us carry the system, personally cover for it and fill in the holes as they appear. But now he and she too is being eaten up by the insurmountable contradictions that the myth of endless accumulation involves.

2

Wreckage Economics

By the time Aaron Swartz hanged himself in 2013, federal prosecutors had prepared a punishing case against him.[1] The 26-year-old had been arrested by Massachusetts Institute of Technology (MIT) police and US secret service agents in January 2011. He managed to gain access to the MIT library via its 'Open Campus' programme, which invited students from other colleges to use its facilities. Swartz had found an electrical closet which allowed him to attach his laptop to the network. JSTOR is a very large digital repository that universities subscribe to in order to access research papers. This was Swartz's target. Having hacked the system, he downloaded around 4 million articles over a period of days.[2]

MIT staff suspected something was amiss and planted a secret video camera in the closet. Swartz was filmed checking his handiwork and swiftly arrested. Middlesex County Superior Court charged him with breaking and entering with intent, grand larceny and unauthorised access to a computer network. Then they dropped the charges so that federal prosecutors could step in. They added nine more felony charges to the indictment.[3] With Carman Ortiz acting as lead prosecutor, Swartz now faced a possible 35-year prison sentence and a $1 million fine.[4] He was offered a plea bargain of six months in a federal corrections facility, which he declined.[5] Swartz was rapidly running out of money and his friends were now being subpoenaed by the prosecutors.[6] But by then it was too late. On 11 January 2013 he took his own life in a Brooklyn apartment.

Maths for militants

Aaron Swartz was a child prodigy. His breath-taking intelligence was noticed from an early age. According to his father, when Swartz was three years old 'he taught himself to read and we were flabber-gasted'.[7] For a school assignment he designed an ATM machine and wrote a program that solved a popular maths puzzle.[8] At the age of 13 Swartz won the ArsDigita Foundation Prize. He enrolled at Stanford University but soon dropped out to find investors for his own projects.

Swartz was involved in a number of businesses that created web application frameworks and content management systems. He was pivotal to the success of Reddit and his own firm (Not a Bug) was acquired by Condé Nast Publications, which owns *Wired*. From 2008 onwards, however, Swartz became interested in activism, especially around open access issues. He penned the 'Guerrilla open access manifesto', which paints a gloomy picture of the way freedom has been extinguished on the web:

> Information is power. But like all power, there are those who want to keep it for themselves. The world's entire scientific and cultural heritage, published over centuries in books and journals, is increasingly being digitalised and locked up by a handful of private corporations. Want to read the papers featuring the mostly famous results of the sciences? You'll need to send enormous amounts to publishers like Reed Elsevier.[9]

Swartz calls for 'sneaking through holes and climbing over fences' to liberate information so that it can be shared publicly.[10] To help achieve these aims he set up the DemandProgress collective. He was also involved in the Progressive Change Campaign Committee, an organisation that intervenes in mainstream political debates. Sharing information was key to Swartz' political activism.[11] In 2006 he managed to access the Library of Congress' bibliographic database. It was swiftly uploaded to OpenLibrary. Luckily the data was not copyrighted.[12] In 2008 he hacked 2.7 million federal court documents from an organisation called Public Access to Court Electronic Records. Until then the site was charging 8 cents per page to access these public records. They were swiftly uploaded to Public.resource.org. Spooks from the FBI investigated and found there were no grounds for prosecution. Swartz wryly noted how the investigation displayed 'the usual mess of confusions that shows the FBI's lack of sense of humor'.[13] In 2011 Swartz helped design DeadDrop.[14] This allowed sensitive documents to be downloaded by journalists while keeping the sender's identity anonymous. Versions of the software are now used by the *New York Times* and *Guardian* newspapers, and have been central for enabling major whistle-blowing cases to reach a public audience.[15]

Great firewall of America

In 2012 Republican senator Lamar Smith introduced the Stop Online Piracy bill. The official purpose of the bill was to enact legislation that would 'promote prosperity, creativity, entrepreneurship, and innovation by combating the theft of U.S. property, and for other purposes'.[16] The bill was immediately attacked by open access campaigners, including Aaron Swartz. He said the proposed laws would allow government and big business to 'shut down whole websites. Essentially, it stopped Americans from communicating entirely with certain groups.'[17] As far as he was concerned, the bill represented 'a great firewall of America', an 'Internet black list' that enabled online censorship on a massive scale.[18] Moreover, he averred, the Stop Online Piracy Act would constitute a basic violation of the First Amendment. According to Swartz, this was a turning point in history as far as the net was concerned. Would the wonders of interconnectivity be used for sharing information or locking it up behind paywalls?

> There's a battle going on right now, a battle to define everything that happens on the Internet in terms of traditional things that the law understands. Is sharing a video on BitTorrent like shoplifting from a movie store? Or is it like loaning a videotape to a friend? Is reloading a webpage over and over again like a peaceful virtual sit-in or a violent smashing of shop windows? Is the freedom to connect like freedom of speech or like the freedom to murder?[19]

Following a fierce campaign by Swartz and many others, including Google, Wikipedia and 7000 other websites closing their webpages on 18 January 2012 in protest, the bill was postponed.[20] Lamar Smith stated this what not the end of the matter: 'The committee remains committed to finding a solution to the problem of online piracy that protects American intellectual property and innovation ...'[21]

As we read in the quote from the 'Guerrilla open access manifesto', academic publishing and the paywalls that exclude the ordinary public was a major concern for Swartz. And he had good reason to lament the situation. Academic publishers have captured the *perfect* market – for big business at least. In many universities, faculty are paid by the public (via taxes) to research important issues. This publicly funded research is then submitted to journals that are owned by large multinational corporations. These firms then sell the journals back to the university at increasingly extortionate rates, with little access to anyone outside the university system. Elsevier and Wiley-Blackwell use a classic 'middle-man' business technique. It's not about creating value but capturing it, generating anything between 30 per cent and 40 per cent profit margins through monopolistic practices.[22] In 2012, Harvard, one of the richest universities in the world, said it was being forced to scale down its journal subscriptions because of these costs. Its Faculty Advisory Council noted that the university spends $3.75 million per year on subscriptions, with some journals charging $40,000 a year for subscription.[23]

It's in this context that Aaron Swartz illegally downloaded journal articles from the JSTOR repository. About 8000 institutions around the world subscribe to JSTOR. It is interesting to note that when JSTOR discovered the breach, they swiftly arrived at an agreement with Swartz. He would return the stolen data and that would be the end of it. When the prosecution process escalated, JSTOR sought to distance itself from the investigation and released a statement:

> The criminal investigation and today's indictment of Mr. Swartz has been directed by the United States Attorney's Office. It was the government's decision whether to prosecute, not JSTOR's ... Our interest was in securing the content. Once this was achieved, we had no interest in it becoming an ongoing legal matter.[24]

MIT on the other hand prevaricated. After Swartz' death, the family complained that prosecutors had been totally over the top. They directly linked the aggressive and bullying tactics of the United States Attorney Office and Aaron's awful death: 'Aaron's death is not simply a personal tragedy. It is the product of a criminal justice system rife with intimation and prosecutorial overreach. Decisions made by officials in the Massachusetts U.S Attorney's office and at MIT contributed to his death.'[25]

What is wreckage economics?

The sad case of Aaron Swartz is symptomatic of a new type of economic environment that has swept the world during the last few years. What I call wreckage economics pertains to policies enacted by business and governments that have proliferated in the aftermath of the 2007–08 economic crisis. When it comes to the (mis)management of social value, the practitioners of wreckage economics have a very different mentality concerning how wealth is to be accumulated compared to earlier models.

First, the emphasis is on capture or enclosure of community-based resources and economic activities, since the public sphere is now the last pool of value that hasn't been sapped dry by the corporate takeover of society over the last 20 years. The examples are seemingly endless. Taxable wealth is hoarded in shell companies in Panama. Copyright and intellectual property law is deployed to hijack public inventions and creativity. Just think of Apple in this respect. The company that most think epitomises the dynamism of capitalist enterprise poached many of its ideas directly or indirectly from governmental funding, including the iOS platform, click-wheel navigation, voice-user programs' (or SIRI), multi-touch screens and so forth.[26] In the heyday of the dotcom boom and subsequent decline in the early 2000s, Michael Perelman noted in his excellent book *Steal This Idea* that 'creative capitalism' is largely a myth. The IT revolution relied on sources beyond the profit-making centres that commercialised them, a finding that no doubt resonated with Aaron Swartz: '73 percent of the main science papers cited by American industrial patents in two recent years were based on domestic and foreign research funded by government and non-profit agencies. Even IBM – famous for its research prowess and numerous patents was found to cite its own work 21 percent of the time.'[27]

This parasitical logic of big business has only intensified after the economic crash, especially given corporate investment in infrastructure and R&D halted almost overnight.[28] The increasing reliance on unearned income – either from simple rent on assets or riding on the back of the public sphere – now typifies this present smash-and-grab era of capitalism. In a 1995 interview, Steve Jobs hits the nail on the head when reflecting on his early forays into computers, which he called 'blue boxing'.[29] Jobs and a friend discovered how to manipulate 1970s telephone dial-tones. This enabled them to make free international calls with a gadget called 'blue boxes': 'We were young. But we learnt you could build a little thing that could control a billion dollars' worth of infrastructure around the world ... there would have never been an Apple computer without blue boxing.'[30]

Second, these rituals of capture are violently policed and defended by big business and the state, using tactics like those targeted at Aaron Swartz. Activities that would have once been dismissed as bohemian transgressiveness (hacking, protests, etc.) are today met with a disproportionate level of force. This spectacle of power (especially with the help of well-publicised individuals being made an example of) soon becomes an expectation that seeps into everyday norms, repressing the basic currents of human sharing that took millennia to evolve. In only a short number of years, the notion of the public good has been totally erased from collective consciousness. It is difficult to imagine an environment in which a scientist like Jonas Salk could ever be taken seriously. When he announced the discovery of the polio vaccine a journalist inquired about the patent. Who would own it? Salk famously replied, 'There is no patent. Could you patent the sun?'[31] Business commentators have calculated that Salk turned his back on $7 billion as a result of this decision.[32] When common sunlight is finally privatised by some faceless corporation, we will have aggressive technocrats like Carman Ortiz ready to jail anyone stupid enough to be inspired by Salk's civic spirit.

Third, and related to the above socio-economic shifts, there is now a strong disdain for anything remotely democratic in this era of economic pillaging. Never has the state and business displayed such open hatred for democracy. Governments avoid it like the plague, reducing it to a shallow spectacle, as in 2016 with the European Union (EU) referendum in the UK and the US presidential campaign. No one is more disempowered than an audience forced to enjoy a fiction not of its own making. In 2013 the right-wing New Zealand government received a petition signed by enough people to trigger a referendum concerning the sale of state assets. Public discontent about privatization had become a fully-fledged social movement. The voice of the people, however, was irrelevant. The Prime Minister openly declared that he planned to ignore the result if the referendum ever took place.[33] People soon forgot it was even an issue as the energy companies were partially privatised. A few years later the same government actively promoted an absolutely pointless referendum on the New Zealand flag. And what about the corporate sector? They're now pulling the strings behind the scenes on an unprecedented level, using events like Devos and APEC to undermine the will of ordinary people.[34] Indeed, leaked documents from the proposed Transatlantic Trade and Investment Partnership (TTIP) reveal the level of hatred that the ruling elite has for basic democratic rights.[35]

And fourth, wreckage economics entails practices that seek to both perpetuate a socio-economic paradigm that is already on life-support (e.g., quantitative easing, zero-deposit mortgages, easy credit) and generate revenue from the very same crisis by capitalising on its negative effects. *Social disequilibrium* is an opportunity to exploit for profit, seen most evidently with currency trading, management buyouts, but which has now been extended into a general economic principle. Whereas the global ruling class was nearly wiped out in the 1930s depression, this time around they have actually made massive gains to their wealth through various modes of capture, enclosure and monopolisation or oligopolisation.[36] According to Credit Suisse's 2014 *Global Wealth Report*, the richest 1 per cent presently own 50.1 per cent of all household wealth, an upward trend that has increased since the 2008 financial meltdown.[37] Crisis conditions call for new forms of profiteering, including byzantine levels of secrecy (it took a leak for us to find out about the anti-democratic small print of the TTIP), governmental collusion, asset sweating on a societal level and, above all, an ultra-strong repressive state apparatus that inspires fear in anyone silly enough to mess with the programme.

In sum, wreckage economics is the position of an elite that has become detached from democratic accountability, protected by a phalanx of amoral technocrats and thugs, systematically intent on sucking the life out of the public sphere while prattling on about jobs and growth. In this depressing age of synthetic austerity, business and governments no longer appropriate wealth in the same manner they once did. Just as criminals in an impoverished neighbourhood can't use armed robbery because the wealth pots are dry, thus resorting to extortion to create a steady income stream, present-day capitalism has restructured everyday life around the prolonged sweating of the social body. And of course the threat of force is always near, especially for those who embrace the most advanced facet of modernity – knowledge sharing – and take it too far, challenging corporate entitled and the regime of money. With the horrible death of Aaron Swartz we see an exemplar of crisis capitalism more generally, in all its terrifying tactics and dismal outcomes. While Swartz won an important battle (defeating regressive legislation) he clearly lost the war. To speak of wreckage economics, then, is to observe how the dominant institutions of our time consolidate their power in a society that is literally wrecked ... and carefully document the causalities that follow.

Utopia's dark whisper

Aaron Swartz enacted a grim dialectical closure of the rich possibilities that the information age once presaged. This closure is indicative of the deep disappointment and political frustration that accompanies the emergent matrix of wealth accumulation today. Swartz' ideals regarding the liberating powers of technology and its intrinsic propensity for sharing represents one side of what some have called the Californian Ideology.[38] In many ways, Swartz' problem was that he failed to synthesise the various contradictory components that define this ideology. That is, to be both politically radical and an ardent capitalist. In their classic 1995 essay on the topic, Barbrook and Cameron explain how high-tech capitalism, associated with Silicon Valley and the Bay Area, was the product of a strange amalgamation of late 1960s anti-authoritarianism and the economic individualism of the post-Reagan years. In 1969 the students who were attacked by state troops at the People's Park were hostile to the culture of capitalism. By the 1990s, however, some had been able to combine the ethos of flower power with the market individualism that Reagan so adored. In a revised version of the thesis, the authors argue that a loose alliance of writers, hackers, capitalists and artists from the West Coast of the USA have succeeded in defining a heterogeneous orthodoxy for the coming information age: the Californian Ideology. This new faith has emerged from a bizarre fusion of the cultural bohemianism of San Francisco with the hi-tech industries of Silicon Valley.[39]

Steve Jobs and Bill Gates are perfect examples of this ideology. In one interview we see how Jobs is able to approvingly quote Marx and the importance of market libertarianism in the same breath.[40] More recent examples include PayPal's Peter Thiel (who once said he aimed to form 'a new world currency, free from all government control and dilution – the end of monetary sovereignty' and subsequently made a fortune in the process, supporting Donald Trump's presidency bid to boot).[41] And then there is Steve Hilton, the creator of the UK Conservative government's disastrous 'Big Society' policy, who wears tie-died t-shirts and manages a start-up in California. As an aside, Hilton's easy-going air seemed to rapidly evaporate in a BBC radio debate I had with him in 2015 about why bureaucracy is sometimes a good thing (how could a large organisation like the BBC run without it, for example?). He became visibly incensed, which was fairly amusing given his peacenik credentials.

Swartz clearly struggled in this regard. His last years were a failed synthesis, unable or unwilling to embody the Californian Ideology fully. Sure, on the one hand he was entrepreneurial. Swartz became rich when Not a Bug was acquired by Condé Nast Publications. And on the other hand he had strong social justice convictions regarding resource sharing and open access. Unlike other flower power capitalists, however, he took the liberating potential of the internet *too seriously*. His views ended up defying the basic tenets of corporate private property, especially in the copyright saturated industries of high-tech capitalism. It appears that Swartz decided to pursue the romantic, hippy side of this disingenuous, yet powerful dualism and forget about the punitive realism of money and finance. A clash with the neoliberal power structure was inevitable as the dialectical dance between commercial selfishness and democratic openness became a showdown that Swartz could never win.

Technology to the rescue? Not quite

This is where Paul Mason's otherwise fascinating book *Postcapitalism* becomes a little confused.[42] The emphasis on the emancipating powers of technology is too exaggerated, as is often the case with many techno-optimists. He suggests that we are on the cusp of an open access revolution that will overcome capitalism, heralding a new mode of production based on the principles championed by the likes of Swartz (whom he does not mention). According to Mason, there is now a massive and irreconcilable contradiction between the forces of production (new technologies that promote sharing, peer production and counter-capitalist practices of open access) and the relations of production (based on private property, paywalls and the enforcement of laws that Swartz aimed to challenge). Mason places great emphasis on endogenous technological change (first posited by Paul Romer), claiming that because information is infinitely replicable, with a margin or reproduction cost of zero, the price mechanism is eroded since it can no longer be based on scarcity, supply and demand and so forth. Songs on an iPod don't degrade with use and those same zero-marginal cost processes will soon infiltrate physical goods too as they acquire digital components. In this environment, firms must (a) simply invent a commodity's price and (b) create a monopoly to shore up its value. As far as Mason is concerned, such structures are swimming against the tide, swiftly becoming obsolete as a new economic dawn arrives.

The assumption that this dialectic between the forces and relations of high-tech capitalism will be resolved by the sheer momentum of peer innovation and online sharing is refreshingly optimistic, but perhaps a little misguided. For example, take the following prediction:

> alongside the corporate response, we are seeing the rise of non-market production: horizontally distributed peer production

networks that are not centrally managed, producing goods that are completely free, or which – being Open Source – have very limited commercial value … Non-market forms of production and exchange exploit the basic human tendency to collaborate – to exchange gifts of intangible value – which has always existed but at the margins of economic life. This is more than simply a rebalancing between public goods and private goods: It's a whole new and revolutionary thing. The proliferation of these non-market economic activities is making it possible for a cooperative, social just society to emerge.[43]

No doubt Swartz authentically symbolised this potential. But the operative word here really is *potential*, which is very different to a dialectical synthesis or even tendency. One must remain extremely cautious about seeing in Linux Open Source or the bohemian cooperatives dotted around Shoreditch the beginnings of a new transition to a better society. Why so? First, we should not place so much faith on technology or at least its digital variant without appreciating the wider cultural influence of the Californian Ideology and the Gates Empire. On a global level, banks, oil and guns still rule the roost, with iPads and FaceTime fairly far behind. Let's not forget that US nuclear weapon systems still use 1970s-era floppy disks. Second, the friction between the potential of free social relations and the actualised brutality of private property today forms the *animus* of wreckage economies. In other words, these tensions drive many of the revenue streams in a hollowed-out post-industrial society, from micro-finance, co-production and other moments of enclosure that allow the social commons to be systematically stripped by various business models associated with the so-called 'new economy'.

It's crucial to remember that wreckage economics is about capture, not innovation, production or even growth. Homo economicus is stretched on a rack between the ideals of freedom and the draconian realities of late capitalism, still naively believing those ideals are realisable via the gadgets and networks that have been thrown up by Silicon Valley. Perhaps the most important reason to doubt the possibility of such a transition (as described by Mason at least) takes us back to Aaron Swartz. In many ways the zero-marginal cost tendency of the techno-liberation movement is not really that damaging to private enterprise. In fact, since the price of production is reduced to zero we could see why capitalists of all creeds would love the prospect. Apart from the initial capital investment costs – many of which can often be crowdsourced for nothing or shifted to other organisations like the state in the case of academic publishing – all other revenue is pure profit. The profits are literally endless.

We should not believe for one minute that multinational firms are embarrassed by this outrageous income, as Mason implies, perhaps even backing down in shame. No, these institutions instead tend to react like an outraged monarch, displaying egregious aggression to preserve their right to extract wealth unhindered, since the profit margins are so lucrative yet based on such flimsy grounds. Just like in the medieval period, social violence becomes a kind of visual metanarrative as firms enlist the law and its punitive agents to maintain the universal right to loot the commons for nothing. Aaron Swartz learnt the hard way what big money means in this brave new world of wreckage economics. The networked and connected civic order that was created out of the tools of the IT revolution are but a hypostatised, sad memento of a democratic future that never was.

Money ... behind enemy lines

Societies that have adopted and committed to policies I call 'wreckage economics' have done so in the wake of the global meltdown of 2007–08. But it's not as if things were rosy before this major recession. Even if we judge neoliberal reason by its own standards – growth per capita – the deregulation of entire economies in the USA and UK from the late 1970s onwards was a failure. For example, Cambridge University scholars Ken Coutts and Graham Gudgin studied growth patterns before and after the rise of Thatcherism in the UK: 'Those who believe in the free market economy must be able to show that economic performance after 1979 was better than it would have been under the "corporatist" economic policies of earlier decades.'[44] Rather than improved growth, they found the exact opposite. Between 1949 and 1979 growth rates stood at around 2.6 per cent. From the rise of Thatcherism in the late 1970s to the 2007–08 global credit crunch, that figure fell to 1.7 per cent. From then on the UK has been sitting on 0.2 per cent. Economic liberalisation simply did not deliver the goods. With wreckage economics, we see an escalation of commitment (in an attempt to recover sunk costs that only get worse) to a dead-end economic ideology.

The expansive development of shareholder capitalism is a good case in point. Even the Bank of England has blamed this corporate model on low growth and productivity rates, since the pressure to pay dividends to shareholders means little is invested in the economic sustainability of the business itself.[45] In 1970 about £10 per £100 of profit was paid to shareholders. Today it is closer to £70 per £100 of profit, allowing the rot to set, eroding both physical and human capital. In this manner, according to the Bank of England's chief economist, firms are literally 'eating themselves', leaving us to clean up after the extraction process has done the damage.[46] But the feeding frenzy never pauses, even when things go terribly wrong. Indeed, the logic has spread. The principle of short-term shareholder capitalism has become the basic operational template for large swathes of economy and society. Governments swear by it given that politicians generally only have a few years to plunder the common good before departing to their well-paid corporate board position.

Wreckage economic policies are both a response to and deepening of the very different vision of economic propriety that has encompassed Organisation for Economic Co-operation and Development (OECD) countries (and beyond) for the last ten years. Perhaps the watchword of 'austerity' and 'living within our means' is the most pronounced manifestation of wreckage economics, with a touch of xenophobia and anti-immigrant sentiment thrown in for good measure. It is bizarrely ironic that the academic justi-fication for austerity was Reinhart and Rogoff's paper 'Growth in the time of debt'.[47] Their calculations suggested that any economy with a GDP-to-debt ratio of 90 per cent or more will contract drastically and this ought to be managed by debt reduction to kick-start growth. A PhD student later found an error in the Excel spreadsheet. The growth formula was wrong. Such economies just grow at a slower rate than economies with lower debt ratios.[48] A miscalculation had set the ball rolling on an erroneous economic experiment in many OECD countries.

It is astounding how the idea of austerity ever gained mainstream traction given that it was imposed on the 99%-ers so shortly after the big bank bailouts. That the public ought to pay twice – first for the initial recklessness of the financial sector and then again in the long withdrawal of public spending following the 'belt tightening' process – is plaintively peculiar.

In particular, the family budget/state budget analogy has profoundly influenced how many people think about the economy. The comparison is bogus, of course. My personal debt, be it a mortgage or credit card bill, is nothing like fiscal debt, which operates on very different principles.[49] That's not to say sovereign debt, for example, isn't a problem. However, the way central banks create and administer money, bonds and so forth is nothing like the real debt I must pay each month to avoid having my car repossessed. Unlike a consumer with a credit card, the Federal Reserve in the USA, for example, can purchase public debt and use it to influence economic growth. Debt is sometimes good for stimulating economic activity. Central banks might issue currency, whereas you and I can't. Government bonds often have low interest rates, something a normal family can't orchestrate, and government uses taxes to strengthen its capacity to spend and invest. In a number of ways, debt can actually generate spending income for governments. Whereas for us it lowers our ability to spend because real wages drop.[50]

Austerity sucks

If state officials do treat a country's accounts as if it was a family budget that requires tightening, then they rapidly run into major difficulties. For sure, a number of austerity-led governments have pursued policies that defy basic economic reason, making many wonder whether some secret desire to prolong dropping living standards was the real agenda. Even deeply conservative and pro-capitalist technocrats have raised red flags about the viability of austerity wisdom. For example, in 2013 the IMF argued that governments rethink the idea of fiscal restraint given the low growth it was perpetuating.[51] Similarly, in a 2016 report studying the global effects of austerity, IMF economists Johnathan Ostry, Prakash Loungani and Davide Furceri argued that:

- The benefits in terms of increased growth seem fairly difficult to establish when looking at a broad group of countries.
- The costs in terms of increased inequality are prominent. Such costs epitomise the trade-off between the growth and equity effects of some aspects of the neoliberal agenda.
- Increased inequality in turn hurts the level and sustainability of growth. Even if growth is the sole or main purpose of the neoliberal agenda, advocates of that agenda still need to pay attention to the distributional effects.[52]

The report continues to demonstrate that the focus on debt reduction through taxation/spending cuts has been a lethal combination: 'episodes of fiscal consolidation have been followed, on average, by drops rather than by expansions in output. On average, a consolidation of 1 per cent of GDP increases the long-term unemployment rate by 0.6 percentage points.'[53] The same message was issued by the OECD in 2016, singling out governments that had seemingly shot themselves in the foot by strangling demand and productivity. As its chief economist stated,

Given the significant downside risks posed by financial sector volatility and emerging market debt, a stronger collective policy approach is urgently needed, focusing on a greater use of fiscal and pro-growth structural policies, to strengthen growth and reduce financial risk.[54]

In other words, more than anything else austerity sucks the life out of the economy and its inhabitants. Quantitative easing (gilt-edged securities, bonds, etc.) is a good example, which risks fuelling yet another debt bubble. Indeed, current economic wisdom practised by most of the OECD represents a kind of slow and painful suicide. And this is the considered opinion of some of the most conservative, pro-market institutions in the world, organisations that still consider Milton Friedman, Margret Thatcher and Ronald Reagan heroes of the modern age.

Corporate warscapes

Privatisation is yet another feature of wreckage economics. Of course, the sale of state assets is not particularly new in the UK, Australia, New Zealand and many other countries around the world. The twin attack of neoliberalism and globalisation in the 1980s saw a spike in the rate of state asset sell-offs. The programme had a clear ideology. Competitive firms operating in a free market are better organised than public ones, avoiding waste and delivering superior customer services. The idea helped justify a huge amount of public goods being transferred into private hands.

George Osborne, the UK Chancellor of the Exchequer until June 2016, sold more state assets than any minister since the Thatcher era. During five and half years in office he sold assets worth £3.37 billion and was lining up another £20 billion in 2016 before being ousted.[55] Is this push to privatise society a mandate championed by everyday people? No, of course not. A 2015 UK poll found that a large majority were against this new wave of sell-offs, even among Tory voters.[56] For example, with regards to the Land Registry, 16 per cent supported privatisation while 70 per cent disapproved, including many Conservative voters.[57] In the end, this is not about expressing the will of the people but the corporate capture (typically large offshore institutional investors) of organisations that have benefited from years of taxpayer investment. Now they are given away at bargain bin prices.

What makes this policy a kindred spirit of wreckage economics more generally is not that the services being privatised often consist of natural monopolies that ought to be treated as basic public good.[58] Placing these assets in private hands, including water, transport, energy and so forth has been a hallmark of the privatising process for some time now. And there was always something rather parasitical about the trend, as for example the UK government's pledge to underwrite pensions liabilities (with a 'crown guarantee') to make assets more attractive to buyers. British Telecom was privatised in 1984 on these grounds. But then wreckage economics rears its ugly head. Years after being sold BT successfully argued in court that if it goes bust then the 'crown guarantee' also applies to the 300,000 plus employees who joined *after* the date of privatisation.[59] The initial blow to the taxpayer becomes an ongoing relationship of extortion. Profits are privatised whereas liabilities are socialised for as long as possible. As of May 2016 British Telecom's pension deficit was about £10 billion, a 50 per cent increase in 18 months.[60] What gives this latest round of privatisation a worrying air of self-destructiveness is the way in which public wealth has been so blatantly transferred into private hands *while defying* the very principles of neoliberal economics that were initially used to justify the sale. It reveals both the anti-democratic corporatisation of the public sphere and, just as importantly, the sheer arrogance of the ruling elite, openly brazen in its unjust self-enrichment.

Miserable miracles

Take the privatisation of Royal Mail, the 500-year-old British institution, for example. The application to buy shares opened on 27 September 2013 and the company was listed on the stock exchange in October 2013. The government retained 30 per cent ownership, employees received 10 per cent and the remaining shares were sold, raising £1.98 billion. The minster in charge of the sale claimed, 'the aim is to place the shares with long-term investors, we are absolutely confident that will happen'.[61] And Royal Mail should 'start its new life with a core of high-quality investors who would be there in good times and bad'.[62] On the day of the sale the value of each share immediately jumped 38 per cent and six months later was worth 87 per cent more than the original asking price.[63] Clearly the initial governmental asking price was grossly undervalued, meaning that a number of large institutional investors and pension funds (who had been granted priority purchasing rights) had made a miraculous profit.[64]

So what on earth had happened? The government told a 2014 parliamentary committee that the threat of strike action had lowered the initial asking price since it introduced risk into the mix.[65] But something else was amiss. The committee wanted to know why stocks that were now trading at 530 pence (p) per share were so grossly undervalued (they were sold at 330p). It was revealed that one of the investors prioritised by the government to have automatic purchasing rights was Lazard Asset Management. The state officials responsible for the privatisation were receiving advice from Lazard's corporate advisory arm, Lazard & Co, which received a fee of £1.5 million for its services. It strongly advised against raising the floating price over 330p since it might frighten off buyers during an uncertain period. Lazard & Co even recommended a floatation price of 212p, while other banks were suggesting 510p.[66]

So the Initial Public Offering (IPO) went ahead at 330p. Lazard Asset Management swooped in, purchasing 6 million shares at 330p and sold them 48 hours later for 470p. They made a £8.74 million profit.[67] The so-called long-term investors didn't end up staying around for very long. Out of the 16 firms given priority purchasing rights, 6 sold their shares immediately and another 6 sold within a few weeks. Taxpayers lost £750 million in one day.

According to the head of Lazard Asset Management, nothing was untoward about its dealings because the two arms of the firm didn't talk to each other.[68] The governmental minsters involved had no regrets either. The minister of finance even stated that the sale was 'very successful.'[69] In 2015 the remaining 30 per cent public share of Royal Mail was sold. What has transpired since the sale is now almost a textbook case of what privatisation really means in the dark shadows of corporate control. Pension benefits of workers are now in the process of being cut.[70] In 2015, around 5500 redundancies were announced and its CEO Moya Greene received a £1.5 million pay packet, a 13 per cent increase compared to the previous year.[71] And, of course, the price of postage stamps has risen above inflation.[72]

Royal Mail is a sad but vivid example of how privatisation operates when conducted using the principles of wreckage economics. The idea is to undermine and then bleed the public sphere, with little long-term interest in the actual asset being purchased, nor its workforce or the community that relies upon it. Slash and burn is the basic business mentality here. Another example might reinforce the point. The British 40 per cent ownership in Eurostar, a train service that travels from London to Paris under the English Channel, was sold in 2015 for £757 million. The then Chancellor of the Exchequer stated that this represented a 'fantastic deal for UK taxpayers that exceeds expectations'.[73] However, a report by the National Audit Office found that the British public had previously invested £3 billion in Eurostar, and the sale price represented a significant loss.[74] In fact, the government had been advised that the share value of Eurostar would increase significantly from 2016 onwards because infrastructure investments were coming to fruition. Dividend payments over the next ten years would be in the region of £700 million. But given the 2015 election was coming up, the government rushed to sell the asset quickly. The National Audit Office stated that selling Eurostar despite the potential undervaluation was 'primarily driven by the desire to sell prior to the 2015 general election'.[75] The healthy revenue stream that ought to have been the public's given their investment is now enjoyed by

London-based Hermes Infrastructure and Canadian pension fund Caisse de dépôt et placement du Québec.

Ten easy steps to oblivion

The NHS represents a special example of how wreckage economics has gripped the UK. Mention the infamous Lorenzo patient record computer system to any health official and you will see them wince. It was described by one observer as 'one of the worst and most expensive contracting fiascos in the history of the public sector', in which the projected £6.4 billion budget swelled to around £12 billion and is still struggling to get underway to this day.[76] When Accenture pulled out of a £2 billion contract, the National Programme for IT (NPfIT) could have fined them 50 per cent of that figure or £1 billion. Instead it only charged them £63 million. As London GP Youssef El-Gingihy notes in *How to Dismantle the NHS in 10 Easy Steps*, Director-General of NPfIT Richard Granger previously worked for Andersen Consulting, which later became Accenture.[77]

Apart from the increased costs, outsourcing has raised wider concerns about patient safety. Now that a particular social service is being run on a profit-making basis, any overhead reductions automatically enhance the bottom line. The financial temptation to sacrifice safety to boost profits in this manner has been difficult to resist for some. For example, a whistle-blower leaked an email to a newspaper in 2012 revealing how the contracting giant Serco was putting patients at risk.[78] The local health authorities in Cornwall had contracted the multinational to manage a call centre whose role was to answer out-of-hours calls to GPs. Tele-operators assess whether the caller warranted an emergency 999 service (i.e., an ambulance). However, Serco had replaced medically trained staff with call centre operators who had little medical training. Given their lack of expertise, caller referrals to the 999 emergency service rose fourfold. Staff didn't want to have blood on their hands if they got it wrong. Serco then sent an email to operators in an effort to reduce emergency referrals:

Please be aware that once the disposition screen for a 999 response is reached, we have three minutes in which to close the call and phone South Western ambulance service trust ... If the call remains 'open' for longer than this three-minute window we fail on our KPIs (key performance indicators). If you do not want/cannot close the call immediately ... please click back to the previous screen and 'change answer' as this in essence stops the clock.[79]

Resetting the clock was widely used to provide the impression that contract conditions were being met. For example, on 25 February 2012 a call was logged at 9.34 am. It was then 'triaged' at 3.37 pm. But the home visit by the GP then planned was not achievable in the expected time frame. Instead of missing the target (3.37 pm) the case was 'retriaged' with a call at 3.12 pm, completed at 3.16 pm. A new target time of 9.16 pm was then allocated to the visit, it is alleged.'[80]

A similar incident occurred in 2015 at G4S Public Services which deals with police 999 calls. The firm took over the £200 million contract to manage the police's back-of-office services.[81] Certain targets were promised. Workers were required to answer 92 per cent of calls within ten seconds. When call handlers in Lincolnshire fell behind this target they made false calls to manipulate the figures, with 724 in total carried out over a three-month period. Jack Dromey, a politician dealing with policing issues, offers an unambiguous conclusion: 'Time and time again G4S have let down the public. This case raises serious questions about the ability of G4S to play a role in vital and sensitive areas of policing. At a time when police forces are under growing pressure, this is a reminder of the importance of crucial emergency services being in public hands.'[82]

Herein lies a key problem. Outsourcing one service can have a domino effect, creating further need for private sector involvement. As Tom Crewe notes in relation to councils in the UK,

every time a service is outsourced, experience and understanding are lost, weakening supervision and creating gaps that in the future will need to be filled by more private-sector support.

The inability of government departments to manage or even understand these contracts has created a thriving secondary industry in public sector consultancy, parasitic on the growth of the outsourcing market.[83]

Crewe goes on to point out that around £600 million of public money has been transferred to KPMG, Deloitte, PwC and Ernst and Young in this manner over the last three years, a 17 per cent increase compared to previous years. Does outsourcing really create better quality services and save the taxpayer money? Probably not.[84] Conducting a major study on this subject, Christopher Hood and Ruth Dixon compared running costs of public sector contractors to 'customer' satisfaction over a 35-year period of reforms.[85] Using a variety of metrics and measures, they found that the cost of managing central government rose significantly in real terms, from £15 billion to £30 billion between 1980 and 2012. While customer satisfaction dropped significantly. Outsourcing led to 'a striking increase in running or administration costs in real terms, while levels of complaint and legal challenge also soared'.[86]

Hell earnt

Despite all of the right-wing fanfare about competition in open and free markets that we hear on an almost daily basis, capitalist reality has seldom conformed to the principles of competitive enterprise. The anarcho-capitalist myth is still going strong (especially among some variants of the alt-right) but has little basis in the real world of wreckage economics. For one of the defining features of this mode of the production is the centralisation or concentration of capital. Not its dispersal. That is why competition is the *last* thing a proper capitalist wants. A firm would rather capture a customer base – especially if demand is inelastic, meaning the customer requires the product/service no matter what the price is – and monopolise the sector.

This is why the multinational corporation loves the state. It simply sees large wads of cash that can easily be sucked away with few of the investment and management costs typical of other business ventures. In the UK and USA, this has been particularly nasty because it is tantamount to taxpayers funding their own asset stripping. When the British railway system was privatised between 1994 and 1997 it was supposedly in the name of competition. Of course, as James Meek points out in his book *Private Island*, the outcome was the opposite, a disaster and perhaps even deadly (given accidents like Hatfield) for the average citizen.[87] Railtrack, the pre-privatised version of British Rail, was estimated to be worth £6.5 billion. In the end it was sold for £1.95 billion, with over a £1 billion in debts written off to help the transfer along.[88] The government assured the public that services would be improved in private hands, as John MacGregor, then Secretary of State for Transport argued, due to the 'harnessing of the management skills, the financial disciplines, the entrepreneurial spirit and the 25 efficiencies of the private sector, and the removal of the constraints of public sector ownership and its monolithic structures'.[89]

That statement was made in 1992 to soften up the public who largely remained unconvinced. Now let's fast forward to the present, the era of wreckage economics. Railtrack – the then privatised owner of infrastructure and maintenance – doesn't exist. It had to be reacquired by the government following the 2000 Hatfield disaster. Network Rail, its replacement, now dishes out taxpayer subsidies to a handful of private companies to run the lines. Private investment has stagnated.[90] To rub salt into the wound, some ticket prices have increased between 151 per cent and 245 per cent since British Rail was privatised.[91] The average age of regional trains is 24 years old (and 19 years old in London).[92]

Privatisation of the railways was turning out to be a bad joke. Take this example. In 2009 East Coast Mainline was in deep trouble. National Express, the private owner of the franchise, dropped the contract because of falling revenue. The government had no choice but to renationalise the organisation. It was then managed by the state-owned Directly Operated Railways. It did very well over a five-year period, making healthy surplus payments back to Treasury and providing a much improved service.[93] Despite this, the government re-privatised it in 2015, selling it to Stage Coach and Virgin. One observer correctly warned that this was a 'costly mistake ... By taking the East Coast out of public ownership the government is passing the profits to Stagecoach and Virgin shareholders, instead of using the cash to reduce rail fares and improve services for passengers.'[94]

An efficient allocation of scarce resources neoliberal capitalism certainly is not, especially when it comes to transport and almost every other public good it has pirated. Just look at the London worker who gained notoriety in early 2016 for sitting in the cupboard with buckets and mops because the train was overcrowded.[95] He paid £6000 a year to commute between Ipswich and London five days a week. Not being able to find a seat he decided to innovate, 'in the evening the train I catch, the 18.30, is usually so full there's no space. I found this little spot some time ago and I use it quite often. No one seems to mind but it isn't great.'[96] With first class carriages often empty, plus an overall lack of investment in infrastructure, we can see why homo economicus, worn out by a long day at the office, might take his chances with toxic cleaning fluids rather than stand the whole commute home. In July 2016 Southern Rail passengers finally snapped and staged a protest, chanting 'Southern fail' and handing out leaflets reading 'Commuter Hell'. Not long after, the Go-Ahead Group, the railway's parent company, recorded a £100 million profit in 2016, up by 26.8 per cent compared to previous years.[97]

Modelling worthlessness

The ideology of competition and its benefits is no more popular than in neoliberal arguments about the labour market, especially executive pay and bonuses. Amazingly enough, this is so even after the scandals that have incited shareholder revolts concerning the massive pay packets. According to the High Pay Centre, the average CEO-to-worker pay ratio in the UK in 1980 was between 13:1 and 44:1. In 1998 the average FTSE CEO pay packet was 47 times greater than the average British worker. In 2013 the ratio was 174:1.[98] In the

USA the figures are even more disturbing. Between 1936 and 1976 executive pay didn't change a great deal. But from the late 1970s onwards the ratio between CEOs and workers rapidly increased. In 2015 top CEOs earned 300 times workers' pay, according to the Economic Policy Institute.[99] They also note that the real pay of CEOs increased by 937 per cent between 1978 and 2014. Workers only received a 10.9 per cent increase over the same period.

An economist at the Adam Smith Institute – a right-wing think-tank based in London – was recently pressed on the issue and asked whether executives like Bob Dudley at BP really deserved a £14 million per year salary: 'Do CEOs in general create the sort of value that justifies giant pay packets that they get and in practice *they do*.'[100] This rationale is based on the idea of supply and demand, and market competitiveness. According to management writers Ray Fisman and Tim Sullivan, the argument goes like this.[101] It's not that some CEOs are amazingly better than you and I, or even their peers in other industries. But if they can add even a few percentage points of advantage to a firm vis-à-vis others in the job market, they will end up getting paid a great deal more because those small percentage points translate into multibillion dollar amounts for the company over time. Well, that's the argument mainstream economists would like us to believe at least.

There has always been some controversy around the issue of executive pay. But the ethos of wreckage economics enters the fray when pay is conspicuously detached from performance and utility. What any particular individual contributes in precise terms to the value of an organisation (i.e., marginal product) is notoriously difficult to measure. However, in some ways it doesn't really matter because 'use value' is no longer the point. The old days in which your pay was linked to the number of hours you clocked up, the skill required and the societal worth of the job are gone. Other factors play a bigger role in determining how much you are rewarded today. For example, the revelation that London dog walkers are paid considerably higher (£32,356) than the national wage average (£22,044) tells us much about how employment operates within the wreckage economics paradigm.[102] Not only are dog walkers paid more, but they work only half the hours of the average employee. Indeed, the task of walking a millionaire's dog through Hyde Park is considered more valuable than an NHS nurse (starting salary £20,700). It is clear that the relationship between jobs and pay is now governed by a new principle.

This disconnect between work and remuneration is obvious when we hear about the gargantuan salaries awarded to business executives and senior public servants. Does job market competition determine these eye-watering figures? Such obscene salary packages cannot reflect increased effort because no one can raise their productivity levels by that much. Neither can these salaries be put down to market scarcity of skilled individuals. It's not as if the pool of able executives suddenly dried up in the last ten years. As the Economic Policy Institute stated in relation to the 937 per cent increase CEOs received since 1978: 'growth does not simply reflect the increased value of highly paid professionals in a competitive race for skills (the 'market for talent'), but rather reflects the presence of substantial "rents" embedded in executive pay'.[103] Neither can these pay packets be linked to company performance given the 2008 financial crisis. Executive remuneration has trebled over the last few years despite the double-dip recession and the banking crisis. For example, BP made a $6.4 billion loss in 2015, suffered 7000 job cuts and saw its shareholder value (and dividend) decrease by 23 per cent.[104] However, CEO Bob Dudley's salary increased 20 per cent in 2015 to £14 million. In the era of wreckage economics, occupational worth appears to have very little to do with performance, social importance or market competition. It doesn't help that leading business schools such as the one at Harvard University appear to encourage this 'winner take all' ethos (even when you're *failing*) among its graduates.[105]

So something else must be going on, more about the privilege and power around the job than the actual job itself. Pay rates are probably determined most by your location on a rather steep employment hierarchy. And that in turn reflects the wealth you *already have*. At the apex of this hierarchy are senior executives and public officials, selected from the same group of elite schools and families. These individuals receive so much money that they do not really need to work. They easily join the ultra-small group of unearned income holders, the rentiers and idle rich that control good parts of Britain, the USA and the Global South. Then you have the second tier of employees who hold very well-paid jobs that service the rich. The third tier consists of the 99%-ers and they make up the rest of the jobs pyramid. It has engendered its own hierarchy of 'good jobs' and 'bad jobs'. Some of these are crucial to society: midwives, street cleaners, postal workers, health inspectors. Others are 'crap jobs' that have proliferated in the service sector, but are still considered infinitely preferable to entering into the government-run hell called the unemployment industry.

Abolish restaurants

Labour market competition is not causing the 'crap jobs' revolution that has characterised wreckage economics in the years following the long recession. Deskilled and underpaid work is not an inevitable outcome of economic efficiencies, as if it was somehow neutral or apolitical. This is all about institutional power and its belligerent quest for self-preservation. The extractive tendencies of the dominant business model today too easily find their way into everyday managerial practices. In the current climate, employers no longer even need to hide their sense of entitlement or mission to cut pay, training and health/safety expenses that would have otherwise been an obligatory employee benefit in a previous era.

This became evident in a scandal that embroiled London restaurants in 2015. The large chain Pizza Express (owned by a Chinese multibillion dollar private equity firm) was revealed to be charging employees an 8 per cent levy on tips left to them if the customer paid by card. One employee said in a letter to their trade union,

I have worked at Pizza Express for 15 years. After all this time I'm still only paid the national minimum wage of £6.50 an hour. So you see my colleagues and I are heavily reliant on customer tips to top up our low wages. I work hard and am good at my job, but when Pizza Express thinks it can get away with taking a percentage of our hard-earned tips left on a card, I get upset.[106]

But Pizza Express was not alone. It was revealed that restaurants like Zizzi and Ask Italian also charged 8 per cent. The Latin American chain Las Iguanas forced waiters to pay back 5.5 per cent of their sales at the end of the night.[107] The worst offender was Harrods. It was recently reported that they swiped 75 per cent of the waiters' tips at its restaurant.[108] This is basically a 'right to work' tax. One waiter understood the idea: 'Over five shifts in a week is a substantial loss of my tips. Sometimes it works out as if I am paying to work.'[109] The policy clearly takes Milton Friedman's famous adage ('there's no such thing as a free lunch') to an entirely new level.

Labour unions strongly reacted to these 'wage theft' tactics, but wreckage economics makes no secret about despising the very existence of unions. In the wake of London Tube driver strikes in 2015, for example, the UK government proposed the Trade Union Act. If passed, it would be illegal to strike unless there was a 50 per cent turnout on any particular issue. And 40 per cent needed to motion a strike for it to proceed. Some Tory watchdogs were worried, however.[110] Didn't the proposed law contravene the Human Rights Act on labour liberties? What's more, the irony that the very government proposing the bill was elected in 2015 with 36.1 per cent of the vote was not missed. The bill was passed into legislation in May 2016.

It seems that the only competition occurring in this type of labour market is between firms and how far they can extort their employees with impunity. One recent study has even suggested that employment systems today bear a remarkable resemblance to 'villainy', more associated with the methods used during Feudalism to tie a peasant to a lord of the manor.[111] Like the peasant, employees today on a zero-hour contract must pay rents to gain access to the very institution of work. There isn't any guarantee of income. And a good deal of work is done for free, around the formal labour process

in order to give a good impression to the employer. This is a sort of
plantation neoliberalism.[112] No wonder people in their 20s in the
USA, UK and Europe have seen their living standards lag behind
all other age brackets.[113] The average 20-something is now poorer
than retired people. Matters get worse if people decide to raise a
family in a city like London. A 2016 study revealed that the cost
of raising a child to 21 years old is about £270,000, representing
a 65 per cent increase compared to 2003 figures.[114] Childcare will
cost £70,000, a 78 per cent increase. As a result, it's easy to see why
a vast informal economy of unpaid labour inevitably emerges to
pick up the shortfall. A survey by Age UK discovered that around
417,000 people in their 80s are now providing unpaid care to family
and friends, sometimes up to 35 hours a week.[115] With an ageing
population and grossly underfunded state services, the elderly
are stepping in to rectify a care deficit. But as a spokeswoman for
Age UK correctly points out, 'They can't do it all on their own and
we shouldn't take advantage of their determination to do right by
those they love.'[116]

Investor vandalism

Because this way of making money creates such a mess the wealthier
practitioners of wreckage economics understand the importance
of having an escape route to the Bahamas or Fiji, leaving others –
you and me – to deal with the fallout. Billionaire Sir Philip Green
exemplified this art of escape when the retail chain British Home
Stores (BHS) when into receivership in April 2016. It was formed
in 1928 but by the mid-1990s was suffering from poor sales.
Green bought the company in 2000 for £200 million and took it
off the stock market, making it a private firm. In March 2015 he
sold the business to Retail Acquisitions for the sum of £1. Retail
Acquisitions was led by Dominic Chappell, who had gone bankrupt
three times in the past.[117] By the time it faced receivership, BHS had
debts running up to £1.3 billion; £571 million of this was pension
liabilities for its 11,000 workers who risked departing with nothing.

So far, the story sounds fairly standard for a firm hit hard by the recession. However, it was discovered that after Green bought BHS he started to bleed the faltering firm. For the 13 months it owned BHS, Retail Acquisitions received more than £25 million in payments from the beleaguered company. Over the course of Green's ownership of BHS (15 years) he and his family were paid £586 million in loan repayments, interest, dividends and rental fees.[118] This money was paid to Arcadia, a company held in Green's wife's name located in low-tax Monaco, thus dodging a £130 million tax bill on dividends.[119] In 2005, the Arcadia Group paid its shareholders (technically Green's wife, thus himself) a massive £1.2 billion dividend from pre-tax profits of £253 million. The arrangement avoided the £300 million dividend tax that the Greens would have otherwise been liable for.[120]

As far as BHS' pensions go, in 2001 the fund was running a £5 million surplus. By 2016 this had slumped to a £571 million deficit. It did not help that when these figures hit the headlines Green was about to take ownership of a new £100 million superyacht. Angela Eagle, the shadow Business Secretary, summed up the nature of wreckage economics very well when discussing the case in Parliament: 'In this situation it appears this owner extracted hundreds of millions of pounds from the business and walked away to his favourite tax haven, leaving the Pension Protection Scheme to pick up the bill.'[121] One can only imagine what employee morale was like as BHS floundered, the pensions black hole was revealed and pictures of Green on his yacht in the Mediterranean appeared in all the newspapers. An anonymous online diary by BHS workers gives us a clue. There was talk that Sports Direct's Mike Ashley might bail out BHS. Ashley was also in the news (prompting another parliamentary commission) concerning the gross maltreatment of his workers:

TUESDAY 21 JUNE: As if that uncertainty wasn't bad enough, an article has appeared online claiming that there's a chance that up to 80 stores might still be 'saved' by Mike Ashley of Sports Direct fame/infamy. God help us all if that turns out to be true.

I can't help but wonder why BHS seems to be so irresistible to all these overfed, self-serving clowns. First Green, then Dominic Chappell and now, perhaps, this rambling bullyboy? What kind of terrible crimes could BHS staff have committed in their previous lives to deserve that?[122]

Welcome to the dark economy in which profits are made without producing anything. Although Sir Philip finally agreed to cough up £363 million in March 2017 following a long pursuit by the pensions regulator (88 per cent of what employees are owed), the debacle more generally revealed how bad capitalism had become. The asset sweating logic behind wreckage economics is the new normal, defining almost every aspect of power in society. And its machinations are often slow and prolonged, easily slipping beneath the radar if there isn't a major scandal to reveal it. Such a corporate exercise in extraction (think of a quack dentist pulling out a good tooth) means the elite must cushion themselves at a safe distance as the economy is wrung dry. Hence the present importance of mega-yachts among the rich capitalist class, equipped to silently sail away in the night.

Orphan bonds

We see precisely this new mode of accumulation in Aditya Chakrabortty's excellent investigation of the iconic UK chemist chain Boots.[123] John Boot established the store in 1849 in Nottingham. His son Jesse Boot took over the store and expanded its presence nationwide. Jesse Boot was a keen philanthropist and gave generously to found University College at Highfields, which later became Nottingham University. He sold the company to a US firm in 1920 and during the recession it was taken back into British ownership in 1933, with Jack Boot (John's grandson) at the helm. By the 1970s and 1980s Boots was a prominent presence in much of the UK and an essential part of the NHS since the public relied on it for prescriptions (totalling £2 billion a year and a third of Boot's annual income) and out-of-hours advice.

In 2006 the company was bought by Alliance UniChem and renamed Alliance Boots. It was then acquired by the private equity firm KKR, a deal forged by the tycoon Stefano Pessina in 2007. The company's gold-plated final salary pension scheme – one of the first to move into bonds back in 2000 – was terminated in 2010, even though it was running a healthy surplus.[124] According to Pessina, this was done to 'help protect the business from the effect of pension funding volatility'.[125] In 2012 KKR sold a 45 per cent stake to the American company Walgreens, and the rest in 2014, creating Walgreen Boots Alliance, with Pessina acting as CEO. By October 2015 Walgreen Boots Alliance's net sales had markedly increased to $103.4 billion with earnings of $4.2 billion. However, it was with the private equity takeover in 2007 that the business becomes driven by wreckage economics. First was the instrumental use of debt, a typical move by private equity firms:

To buy Alliance Boots, Pessina and KKR had invested £2.5bn of their own money – but they borrowed almost £9bn from Barclays, the Royal Bank of Scotland, Citigroup, JP Morgan, and Merrill Lynch among other banks. The borrowed billions were then shoved onto the balance sheet of Boots UK Ltd – and those banks jumped to the front of the queue for repayment out of the profits made by the company.[126]

KKR received its income in the Cayman Islands and Stefano Pessina is based in Luxembourg. Alliance Boots moved out of Nottingham to Zug, Switzerland, a low-tax zone popular among global capitalists. By now the climate in the store was very different to the old Boots we used to know. The budget cuts, use of performance targets and the insistence that chemists act as salespeople had taken its toll. Because of staff layoffs (which looks good on the quarterly reports), pharmacists were now 'self-checking' the dispensary because there was no one else to help out. Moreover, staff experienced new pressures to make money, including the prevalence of the Medicine Use Reviews (MUR). The NHS had set up a programme whereby pharmacists at stores like Boots would give medical advice. It was aimed to alleviate the burden faced by GPs. The NHS pays Boots £28 for each MUR consultation. This is when management told pharmacists they now had a 'non-negotiable' target of 400 MURs per year. An email from an area manager drove home the point:

> I personally don't want colleagues to feel 'brow-beaten', but we do need to deliver our targets of 400 MURs per store this financial year for two reasons:
> 1. Delivering 400 MCUs is a measure of Excellent Patient Care
> 2. The company can make £28 profit for each MCU, so each one we don't deliver is a lost £28.[127]

One pharmacist who received the email had worked at Boots for 30 years. He describes his employer as 'Big Brother, a giant profit-seeking monster. There's such a culture of fear.'[128] It appears that Boots had basically been economically captured and bled dry. In particular, the use of debt and years of short-term investor extraction had left the firm financially hollowed out and with very low staff morale. When asked how he felt about Boots, one staff member said, 'All the company cares about is profit, figures, services. They are not interested in patient safety, appropriate staffing levels, training time for staff, appropriate breaks etc. Each day I am worried about making a mistake due to the enormous amount of pressure I am constantly under.'[129]

(Anti-) Sun in Panama

How is it possible to make large amounts of money when your company is saturated with debt? It seems the global business network has discovered a big advantage of debt, which doesn't apply to you or me of course. The reason is *tax* or rather its avoidance. Wreckage economics really shines here. For us, without people and institutions making a fair contribution to funding society (i.e., taxes) we would have no public sphere, life-saving discoveries, democratic institutions, museums, justice courts, libraries and the list goes on. Unfortunately, multinational corporations don't care about any of this, although they're happy to opportunistically feed off that public sphere whenever they can. But in the end, the multinational firm simply aims to reduce its costs and maximise profits. A key cost to be neutralised is tax liability. Today there are some easy, legal ways for a household name company to enjoy huge revenues in the UK, for example, yet pay zero tax. This is not because the UK is a tax haven like Panama, but it does little to discourage what is now a feeding frenzy in tax avoidance.

Let's use some fictional examples to describe how this is so. Imagine a very successful US coffee company called XYZ who aims to gain global domination of the market. It is very popular in the UK, generating billion pound revenues over a number of years. Corporation tax in the UK is 20 per cent. But that is paid on *profits*. Using transfer pricing methods, the US HQ decides to set up a subsidiary in Holland because of their favourable tax regulations. It's this subsidiary that now deals with XYZ in the UK, charging a significant fee to use the iconic XYZ brand. These fees along with other expenses including salaries and rent exceed XYZ UK's annual revenues. The Dutch-based firm shifts these revenues back to the USA. The UK branch ends up paying no tax because technically it's making a loss. In the meantime, its global shareholders are very happy with their dividend and the CEO is a multimillionaire. Another way to artificially depress profit figures is to mire the local subsidiary in debt, perhaps as operating and investments costs for setting up in a new country. The interest payed on the debt by the subsidiary is transferred to a tax-sheltered HQ. This nullifies the profit margin of the local firm, and the taxman is powerless.

Transfer pricing – where a company literally trades with itself via subsidiaries or shell companies – is used for tax avoidance because most governmental tax agencies focus on declared profits within its jurisdiction rather than direct sales or revenue. Economics textbooks tell us that trade involves an open market in which a 'fair price' is reached between competitors. In reality, however, this arrangement is typically a fairly closed system that seeks to externalise costs onto you and me. It's been estimated that up to

80 per cent of global trade is conducted between business entities owned by the *same* parent company.[130] This is how the infamous 'Double Irish' arrangement operates allowing Google, for example, to pay €47 million tax in Ireland on sales of €22.6 billion in 2015.[131] The trend is not a minor one. A major international investigation by Tax for Justice analysed data from the Bank of International Settlements and the International Monetary Fund (IMF), finding that between $21 trillion and $31 trillion moves around the global economy in this manner.[132] In 2016 the EU's competition watchdog went after Apple for doing a 'sweetheart deal' with Ireland. The firm's tax rate was 0.005 per cent in 2014. Apple appealed and adopted a truculent stance against the EU authorities.[133]

In terms of public confidence that the taxation system is on our side – which has perhaps reached an all-time low – there is a growing suspicion that the rich can almost *systematically* get away with paying little or no tax. For example, the UK governmental tax authority, HM Revenue and Customs (HMRC), said it was now closely scrutinising wealthy tax avoiders, especially those who had outstanding income tax bills but simply didn't pay up. After a few years a parliamentary commission found it was a joke. The rich were getting rather cosy treatment. The tax taken from the average wage earner rose by £23 billion since the government set up a special unit to 'crack down' on the wealthy in 2009.[134] Amazingly, the tax take from top-percentile earners actually dropped by £1 billion over the same period. The deepening scepticism among the general public isn't helped by the way the HMRC itself has been financially squeezed by austerity policies. For example, since 2010 the 26,000 staff who deal with personal income tax has been cut to 15,000. The lack of resources becomes evident for those who call the tax helpline. Call waiting times have tripled since 2014. And remember, you have to pay to use this service. A report by the National Audit office found that the average wait time to receive tax advice was 47 minutes. They estimate that phone charges and wasted time cost callers a total of £97 million during 2015–16.[135] For these frustrated people, sitting on the phone racking up an expensive bill while reading newspaper reports about the Panama

Papers and the latest corporate tax avoidance scheme, a sense of impotent betrayal becomes a basic everyday emotion. Now wreckage economics is in full swing.

Pony meat

Let's extend our analysis of this kind of profit-by-pillage model of corporatisation. In the commercial relations between firms and suppliers, and firms and customers, two forces govern in the run-down economies of neoliberal capitalism. Extreme *deregulation* on the one hand and strict *normalisation* on the other. We might think these two forces are contradictory. But it's the way they work together that has unleashed the madness of twenty-first century commerce. Let's take extreme deregulation first. Governments are lobbied to simply let firms monitor themselves apropos ethical codes and risk management. This was one of the key arguments behind TTIP, which would see massive deregulation around public assets, environmental law, health and safety and worker protection. One key clause even allowed corporations to sue governments if they decide to change regulations in the future, which tends to happen a lot in democracies.

However, the business world's track record concerning self-regulation is pathetic according to a major 2015 study.[136] It states that 'the impacts of most voluntary schemes are limited, and that the efforts of responsible businesses are often undermined by the failure of such schemes to attract widespread industry participation and compliance'.[137] For example, when the UK horsemeat scandal made the headlines in January 2013, many blamed the ruthless profiteering of seedy suppliers. Tests revealed that beef products being sold in supermarkets, such as burgers and microwave ready-meals, sometimes contained as much as 100 per cent horse meat. Investigators traced the meat to a Romanian slaughter house. It had been labelled as horse meat, but on its way to the Netherlands and then the UK, was repacked as beef. However, what the scandalous reports didn't highlight as much were the agencies responsible for testing the products we eat every day in the UK, the Food Standards Agency (FSA) and Department for Environment, Food and Rural Affairs (Defra). Between 2013 and 2015 the FSA's budget was cut by £22 million. Staff levels have also been reduced.[138] Some claim the agency simply cannot do what is required to monitor foodstuffs, and it's easy to assume that more unscrupulous supply chain networks will take advantage of these gaps in monitoring. Who knows what we are eating now? This everyday uncertainty and paranoia is one of the major cultural outcomes of wreckage economics.

So how does the other force, strict *normalisation*, fit into this deregulated world? This force relates to how commodities have become 'superficialised' in an unregulated supply chain, with deviating goods simply discarded. That would be great if it applied to supermarket ready-meals. But the situation is more sinister. Take vegetables, for example. Everyone knows that appearance has sadly become the only thing that matters, not the taste ('Hello? Where are you?'), horticultural processes or labour conditions under which they came out of the ground. This means that in the UK, for example, tonnes of food is simply binned because it doesn't look correct. A 2015 report witnessed '20 tonnes of freshly dug parsnips consigned to the rubbish heap in a Norfolk farmyard – purely because they didn't look pretty enough.'[139] This is enough food to feed 100,000 people. Supermarkets reject these unsightly vegetables because they fail the 'cosmetic standard'. Around one third of all produce grown in the UK is left to rot for this reason.

But isn't the fussy consumer to blame? According to farmers interviewed in the report, that's not the case. We don't care if a carrot or potatoes looks a little funny, but supermarkets do. One farmer noted, 'when it suits them, the supermarkets start selling it [funny looking produce]. In years of poor harvest, the cosmetic standards are relaxed, and the farmers are asked to bag up the ever-so-slightly bendy or blemished produce that would normally be rejected. Of course nobody even notices.'[140] This normalisation occurs in parallel with deregulation because both processes resist *depth* when it comes to the products and services that are consumed. A rich red beef burger made from pony meat and a perfect looking, yet tasteless tomato exist on the same economic register.

Zoo city

Innovation is perhaps the centrepiece of neoliberal ideology. Capitalism unleashes creative destruction in technology, organisational forms and commodities that simply cannot be compared with other modes of production. Even Karl Marx spoke of the relentless revolution of the forces of production, and we saw earlier how commentators like Paul Mason and many others place great hope in the emancipatory potential of new inventions in info-technology. According to Milton Friedman too, innovation was one of the key reasons why capitalism ought to be defended against centralised systems of governance:

> the great achievements of civilisation have not come from government bureaus. Einstein didn't construct his theory under order from a bureaucrat. Henry Ford didn't revolutionise the automobile industry that way ... there is no alternative way so far discovered of improving the lot of the ordinary people that can hold a candle to the productive activities that are unleashed by the free-enterprise system.[141]

For sure, 3D printing, artificial intelligence, breakthroughs in neuroscience, driverless cars and ecommerce can sometimes make our age seem like the most dynamic ever. But I want to suggest that innovation is anathema to the everyday practices of wreckage economics. Sometimes by design, but mainly because the social formation that crisis capitalism erects is counter-conducive to innovative thinking. Even the IMF understands this. Austerity economics, in particular, depresses growth and investment, undermines labour freedoms and thus tends to kill new ideas rather than encourage them. The IMF's Vitor Gaspar and Ruud De Mooij point out that fiscal spending on R&D is vital if a culture of inventive creativity is to thrive.[142] Since the private sector tends not to invest in R&D (because it's too risky or expensive) innovation is now 'highly dependent on government policies. We find that a little government support can go a long way in boosting innovation and growth.'[143] Unfortunately the austerity-led state has placed such spending at the very bottom of its priority list. That then encourages commercial cartels to block new entrants who might actually come up with something exciting and new. Suddenly the twenty-first century sparkle of cutting-edge capitalism doesn't look so bright after all.

One of the most damning analyses of corporate capitalism's tendency to stagnate rather than innovate is by Robert Gordon.[144] Growth spurts usually coincide with major innovations, especially when industrial activity intersects with high modernism. In his analysis of US data from the 1890s to the present, Gordon discovers that economic growth (or growth of total factor productivity) has probably already peaked and may never return. Between 1891 and 2007 there was an average growth rate of 2 per cent per capita of income. This hits a high in the 1960s and 1970s and then steadily declines, with a predicted growth rate of only 0.2 per cent to 2100. He paints a fairly gloomy picture of the future in this respect:

Doubling the standard of living took five centuries between 1300 and 1800. Doubling accelerated to one century between 1800 and 1900. Doubling peaked at a mere 28 years between 1929 and 1957 and 31 years between 1957 and 1988. But then doubling is predicted to slow back to a century again between 2007 and 2100.[145]

After the first industrial revolution – based on the steam engine and railroads – came the second in the 1880s. The combustible engine meant no more horse-led carts, which clogged the cities with huge amounts of manure. As a result, the land could be used for producing crops rather than horse fodder. Electricity, running water and sewers then catapulted standards of living. But growth and innovation today has drastically slowed down, even according to some basic measures:

Until 1830 the speed of passenger and freight traffic was limited by that of 'the hoof and the sail' and increased steadily until the introduction of the Boeing 707 in 1958. Since then there has been no change in speed at all and in fact airplanes fly slower now than in 1958 because of the need to conserve fuel.[146]

The info-tech revolution looks like a massive breakthrough. But is it? The mainframe was invented in 1942, the personal computer (and microprocessor) in the 1970s and honed in the 1980s, and barcodes in the 1990s. However, the innovative impact has not been as influential as we would like to think:

Inventions since 2000 has centered on entertainment and communication devices that are smaller, smarter, and more capable, but do not fundamentally change labor productivity or the standard of living in the way that electric light, motor cars, or indoor plumbing changed it.[147]

To make his point, Gordon plays a thought experiment to challenge the idea that the last 15 years have been characterised by amazing, innovative zest. Imagine you are in 2001, the year the dotcom bubble burst. You have two options. First, you can get everything up to that year, including clunky versions of Google and Amazon, but also running water and toilets. Or you can get everything after 2001, including iPhone and Facebook, but you have to forego all pre-2001 inventions. It's not hard to predict the option most of us would choose. The death of innovation is intertwined with the way growth has flatlined, driven by social inequality and changing demographics. Many seriously believed that artificial intelligence would have relived us of life's worries by 2017. Instead we might be entering into a new kind of post-modern dark age.

Candy Crush capitalism

It is telling that since the 2000s most innovations have focused on entertainment and communication devices that have very little collective social impact compared to the modern sewer, for example, which led to a life expectancy rate three times higher than it was in the nineteenth century. Perhaps one reason for this focus on cheap gadgets designed to bemuse (and only bemuse) is due to the types of frameworks being used to understand innovation in the corporate era.

Take the massively popular concept of 'disruptive innovation' first broached by Harvard Business School professor, Clayton M. Christensen.[148] The phrase sounds like a form of innovation that will overturn the status quo, but in an interview on the subject, Christensen admits he might have been mistaken when using the word 'disruptive'. The concept actually has less grandiose meanings. Most firms create inventions that are too far ahead of their customers and way too expensive. They're often developed off the back of governmental funds, as with Silicon Valley, and thus still carry a heavy price tag. A disruptive innovation replicates that technology from the bottom of the market, creating a less expensive variant and then slowly cornering the industry. According to Christensen, it's all about the *individual consumer* owning and using the product.[149] Think here of the young Bill Gates' ambition to transform the mainframe computer into a personal gadget used in all homes.

Since the mid-1990s, Christensen's theory has become extremely popular and endorsed in many industries. Perhaps this explains Gordon's pessimistic reading of capitalism since 2000. What could have been a major civic innovation in the realm of energy, for example, which is expensive, collectively used and vital for improved standards of living was instead channelled into a mindless Candy Crush Saga videogame, Pokémon Go, the OKcupid dating app and Snapchat. Christensen happily dubs this the democrati-sation of technology. It might also be a form of proletarianisation. Who knows what wonderful alternative futures we might now all be enjoying today if Facebook hadn't arrived on the scene.

Factories of fear

Major changes in the sphere of employment might also account for stalled innovation in the shadow of wreckage economics. There has been much debate about whether the capitalist labour process fans the flames of creativity – typically using monetary incentives – or smothers it. Pop psychologists like Daniel Pink and Malcom Gladwell argue that financial incentives are generally detrimental to problem solving and imaginative thought. That's because workers begin to focus on the metrics (money and time) rather than the task itself. But that space of relaxed, unpressured creativity that Pink and others recommend modern managers foster has *never existed* in the capitalist workplace. And probably never will. This is why Andre Gorz is correct when he contended that the very social relations of production (labour versus capital) are what really stunt creative new ideas from emerging. Based on his research of flexible labour markets he pointed out that 'where it is relatively easy to take on and lay off temporary workers and to employ a very low-cost work force, as in Britain and France, technical innovation is less rapid'.[150] Such flexible labour relations has now subsumed a good part of the workforce in wreckage economies. Knowledge accumulation and organisational learning never get a chance to flourish under these conditions, since employment today merely means sacrifice (for the individual worker) and 'stretch and extract' (for the employer, institutional shareholder or private equity firm).

One of the most likely workplaces that we might expect to be the glowing hub of innovation are universities. And true to the wreckage economics credo, they too have been systematically restructured in a manner that makes *fear* (of unemployment, students, bullying administrators) the leading emotional experience. According to Stefan Collini, higher education establishments in the UK have been colonised by a 'business analogy' in which research and teaching careers are increasingly indexed to the functional needs of business (often couched in vague terms such as 'impact').[151] In the US context, Randy Martin observes the 'technocratic takeover' of universities, systematically restricting academic freedoms and generating a massive retinue of part-time, hourly-paid instructors, prompting some to relabel the university a kind of Taylorised assembly line or 'Edu-Factory'.[152] It's not simply that universities have been forced to act like businesses, embracing an environment defined by satisfaction surveys, key performance indicators and budgetary restraint. The problem with universities in the UK, USA and elsewhere is worse than this. They are simulating an image of business which is so exaggerated that, ironically, not even the private sector would recognise it.

Recently at one British university, for example, the Vice Chancellor initiated a policy ominously called 'Raising the Bar' or RTB. It aimed to yield precise metrics for an equally scary policy entitled 'Expectations for Research Performance'. All of this was implemented with little staff consultation. The university union listed some of the words that frustrated faculty used to describe the system:

Heavy-handed. Appalling. Vulgar. Absurd. Unacceptable. Wrong. Inappropriate. Ridiculous. Divisive. Reductive. Abominable. Bullshit. Neoliberal. Aggressive. Disgraceful. Erosive. Punitive. Scary. Perverse. Disastrous. Crass. Unjust. Outrageous. Concerning. Dreadful. Facile. Simplistic. Stupid. Irrational. Egregious. Shameful. Ignorant. Useless. Ill-thought. Harmful. Idiotic. Brutal. Contemptuous. Reductionist. Unhealthy. Demeaning. Discriminatory. Detrimental. Unworkable. Irresponsible. Corrosive. Unproductive. Anti-academic. Anti-human. Insane. Crushing. Draconian. Foolish. Quasi-Stalinist. Negative. Toxic. Unilateral. Offensive. Inequitable. Noxious. Witless. Managerialist. Distressing. Obscene. Uncollegial.[153]

Staff at another university were ordered to 'love students' and toil to keep them satisfied. The directive was backed up with punitive performance measures. This is on a backdrop of vice chancellor pay packets rising by almost 14 per cent over the last five years, while staff have seen their incomes decay.[154] I spoke with a member of faculty employed at this university. He told me that at the end of a speech, a senior manager showed a PowerPoint slide with a smiley face and the caption, 'not just happy students but fans'. I'd heard that phrase somewhere before. But where? I gazed out the window of the central London pub. By chance was a Metrobank branch across the road and then the penny dropped. *Fans Not Customers* is the title of a book penned by the bank's primary investor.

Universities were once leaders of innovation, not simply because of the large funding streams they received. It was also the time and space to study, experiment and be curious that allowed wonderful new ideas to emerge. That inspiring environment also represented an important ethos, a kind of brave amateurism that has always been at the heart of great inventions. Universities of yesterday were lucky to have somehow blended that ethos into their institutional DNA. Now it is being systematically purged in the hyper-corporate, PR-saturated but ultimately forlorn hallways and lecture theatres of the Edu-Factory. Indeed, where the ethos of the customer ultimately leads was perhaps exemplified in 2016 by Faiz Siddiqui, an Oxford graduate.[155] He didn't receive the top grade, which he claimed was due to the poor teaching quality. So he sued the university for £1 million.

Hate the internet

It's suffocating conditions like these (today found everywhere in the neoliberal enterprise and the political establishment that helped spawned it) that Aaron Swartz was rebelling against when he entered an MIT basement to make a stand for open access. Perhaps he could foresee what the wreckage economy meant in relation to the potential of the 'internet revolution', including knowledge sharing, creativity and public enrichment. But I think he was also looking further than just info-capitalism and the high-tech sector. Democratic society as a whole and its shared future was in danger. The forces that Swartz aimed to resist might very well result in our entire lifeworld being punitively commercialised and destructively privatised. The beautiful movement of the human imagination closed down forever by corporations and governments fastidiously wedded to anti-social, capitalist values. In the figure of Aaron Swartz, therefore, we see homo economicus reach its fateful conclusion in the high-tech era, accelerating its own ideals to the point of no return.

Swartz was undeniably a victim of bullying. However, his life and death also reveals a coming epoch in which the limits of capitalism are turning upon themselves and morphing into something terrible. It is happening on many levels, but it is especially evident when the ideological missives issued by power (e.g., the importance of entrepreneurship, the knowledge society, etc.) are murdered by its own will to perpetuate private property as an army of zombie accountants claw over the next state asset to be sold. Free market zealots have no answers. They merely call for a 'return' to the pure ideals of competitive enterprise to correct the situation, chanting that if we only had more Milton Friedman then the system would stabilise. For them the present setup is not *capitalist* enough. Of course, in the last instance it *never is* and that systemic deficit becomes a perverse excuse among the technocratic elite for squeezing the working poor and middle class even more. In the meantime, leaders of industry enjoy a state-funded socialism because they understand that pure capitalism is an impossible abstraction that is meant for the masses to toil with, out there beyond the perimeter. A similar problem dogs liberal critics who call for a return to Keynesianism. It isn't that capitalism has become corrupt and deviated from its underlying principles.[156] No, the corruption has simply risen to the surface, especially given how the countervailing force of the labour movement has been obliterated.

On this score, the Left also runs into problems. Some suggest identifying tendencies or ideals in the growing wreckage and accelerate them in the hope of creating a clean break and a more democratic, free society. Holland's concept of 'free-market communism', a blending of Friedrich Hayek and Karl Marx, is a case in point.[157] As with Paul Mason, discussed earlier, the argument misses how these internal potentials operate as a kind of *functional limit*, a deceptive lure that binds us closer to the carnage. These limits do not represent capitalism's 'breaking point' but play a proactive role in generating the endless social 'noise' that keeps a moribund economic paradigm alive ... for now. Jarrett Kobek puts it best in his 2016 novel *I Hate the Internet*: 'the illusion of the internet was the idea that the opinions of powerless people, freely offered, had some impact on the world. This was, of course, total bullshit ...'[158]

Paul Mason passionately argues that the end of capitalism is nigh and the high-tech forces of liberation cultivated over the last 15 years might work as a platform for post-capitalism.[159] But after the rise and fall of Aaron Swartz it is difficult to see this. The trends that both Mason and Swartz found hopeful have been captured and punished by large institutions that have consolidated their extraordinary power since the global financial crisis. The self-destructive shockwave caused by this restoration process has now become a driver of a different kind of economic vision. It represents a system that no longer produces but only extracts. And as we enter a new dark age that spurns true innovation, favours a dreadful economic polarisation among the classes and widens what Naomi Klein calls environmental sacrificial zones, it might be true that we're witnessing the birth of post-capitalism.[160] Not the one Mason envisages, but a lonely winter of mankind that will require more than the internet to save us.

3

Why Homo Economicus had to Die
... Over and Over Again

Dawn Amos was a 67-year-old woman from Essex in the UK. She had been suffering from a chronic lung disease for some time and found it difficult to breathe. Dawn received a weekly allowance of £55.10 or £82.30 as a sickness beneficiary, depending on her care needs. Her husband – a self-employed window cleaner – said his wife couldn't even walk to the end of the garden on bad days.[1] But this was not the only worry Dawn and her family faced. The Department of Work and Pensions (DWP) had decided to take a proactive stance on getting people like Dawn back into the workforce. The minster in charge of the scheme even suggested work might cure the illnesses afflicting the unemployed:

> There is one area on which I believe we haven't focused enough – how work is good for your health. Work can help keep people healthy as well as help promote recovery if someone falls ill. So, it is right that we look at how the system supports people who are sick and helps them into work.[2]

On 17 November 2015 the office responsible for Dawn Amos' allowance reversed an earlier decision concerning her benefits and fitness for employment. Based on current treatment, test results and current symptoms, the letter informed Dawn, she was now able to rejoin the workforce. She was now fit for work. This meant she was no longer eligible for an Attendance Allowance that funded her care.[3] The subtext of the letter was fairly clear. Dawn Amos better dust off her CV and hit the streets to find some way to cover the financial shortfall. However, when the DWP letter arrived at the Amos household, Dawn was not there to receive it because there was a problem. She was dead. Dawn's husband explained, 'She had stopped breathing and I was doing CPR while I was on the phone to the ambulance.'[4] At the hospital her condition deteriorated. On the day the letter arrived, Ms Amos' husband said, 'we had to turn her [life-support] machine off'.[5] Regarding the government's suggestion that Dawn was healthy enough to hold a full-time job, he continued, 'how ill do you have to be? Our garden is 40 or 50ft and she couldn't walk down it without having to sit down at the bottom.'[6]

It was reported by government sources that between December 2011 and February 2014 around 2380 people died after being found fit for work and losing benefits.[7] In May 2016 the Scotland police announced they were considering a criminal investigation into the health and safety of the 'Fit for Work' scheme after claims it could be linked to a spate of suicides.[8] This would be tantamount to the wilful neglect of public duty by an official. At the time of writing, the scheme remains an integral part of the pervasive 'ideology of work' being propounded by the government in the UK. But in true parasitical form, some companies have spotted an opportunity to make money even here. Private subcontracting firms Atos and Capita received £507 million between 2013 and 2016 for adminis-tering 'fit-to-work' tests.[9]

Got a letter from the bank the other day

Toby Thorn's mother was very proud of him. Only a few years ago he had unexpectedly dropped out of high school. But she convinced him education was the only way to get ahead in life – he had to persist. So he returned to school and worked hard, graduating with good grades. He then found a job as an IT apprentice for Barclays Bank, earning £21,000 a year.[10] Unfortunately his office was closed down and outsourced to India. So Toby and his mother looked at the possibility of a university degree in computer science. Toby

gained admission to Anglia Ruskin University in Cambridge. His mother said,

> I used to tell people that he didn't go to school, but look at him now: he's at uni, he's sorted his life out. He even had his first girlfriend, who was one of his housemates. He shyly told me about that. I said, 'Do you still play on the computer?' and he said, 'No, no, just a little bit.' I naively thought this was it – I didn't have to worry about him anymore.[11]

But sadly it transpired that Toby's mother did have to worry about him. On one occasion she received a letter saying that he hadn't paid the rent. She was the guarantor and promptly settled the bill. By then he had slowly drifted away from his studies and would have to re-sit his second year. This time Toby's mother would pay

89

the rent directly to avoid any nasty letters. On 10 July 2011 a police officer knocked on Anne Thorn's door. Toby had killed himself. A suicide note was written on the letter from the bank – Barclay's ironically – regarding his debt and that no more funds would be available. He was £3000 overdrawn and had a £5000 student loan. The suicide letter read, 'Thank you to all my friends. I appreciate your support. Later, ANON.'[12]

The coroner said that Toby had certainly suffered from depression. However, his indebtedness was obviously a contributing factor given the evidence. In England and Wales there has been a 50 per cent rise in the number of students committing suicide, with debt being cited a significant factor.[13] A spokeswoman for the Nation Union of Students stated that today 'being a student is a stressful time … finance and debt problems are adding increasing pressures. When you're paying that much for your education, coming out with a good mark matters even more.'[14] High-profile deaths attributed to student loans have also been reported in the USA. For example, Jason Yoder incurred a $100,000 debt studying at Illinois State University. He committed suicide after he failed to find a job. His mother said that even when preparing for her son's funeral the debt collector agency constantly called about the outstanding sum.[15] According to the US Department of Education, 36 million Americans have outstanding federal loans and 11.3 per cent of those registered in 2009 have already defaulted.[16] The student loan bill currently stands at a breathtaking $1.26 trillion.[17]

The neoliberal state has tried to tackle the issue in two ways: privatisation and coercion. In the UK, successive governments have warned students that their debt will soon be handed over to private financial institutions. It did so again in February 2017, despite a public outcry.[18] And in addition to this, because 44p in each £1 lent remains unpaid, the state has resorted to more punishing repayment conditions.[19] In New Zealand, student loan defaulters living overseas are being arrested on the border after visiting the country. When the then Prime Minster John Key (an ex-banker) was asked whether it was fair that he received his education for free and a graduate in a similar position now has a NZ$60,000 debt, he replied, 'if you've got a chance, go to university don't worry about the student loan, that is the least of your problems'.[20] Of course, there is no way the New Zealand government can arrest the thousands of defaulters who are living abroad. The point is to scare people into contacting the Inland Revenue Department to set up repayments. Nobody wants to miss their mother's 50th birthday because they have an old unpaid student loan. Nevertheless, a recent report found that many defaulters are simply avoiding the country of their birth for this very reason. For example, a woman living in Australia borrowed NZ$6500 over 20 years ago and phoned the tax office after reading about the arrests. She learnt that the initial loan had ballooned to NZ$30,000 and was ordered to immediately pay $20,000. She simply hung up:

> I went into complete shock, I was petrified and shocked that over the period of 21 years my loan had increased 4 times the amount I borrowed ... to tell my family I cannot come home for a tangi [celebratory meal] is shameful. Will I be arrested at the airport? How will I pay my mortgage if I'm detained in New Zealand, what will happen to my children?[21]

Game over

Forty-nine-year-old Rodney Jackson worked at Val-Fit, a steel fitting firm based in Houston, Texas. The company suffered a major downturn in business following the recession and Jackson was sadly laid off after one year with the firm. Described by neighbours as a quiet man who kept to himself, reports said that Jackson was severely disappointed when he was fired, especially given the difficulty job seekers faced in Texas. But Jackson was not going to leave quietly. Instead he walked to his car in the parking lot and reached for a handgun. Jason S. Yanko, his supervisor, attempted to stop him entering the building but it was too late. Jackson shot his manager several times and killed him. He then went on the run, sparking a manhunt before eventually turning himself in.[22] A co-worker explained his surprise on hearing the news. The incident was

> disheartening because whatever it was it wasn't worth that. It's not worth it. Let it go. If you get laid off, you get fired, move on and get you another job. It may be hard but nothing is fair these days so you go out and do what you have to do to make a living.[23]

According to the US Bureau of National Statistics, 10 per cent of management deaths in the USA are due to homicide. The probability of a boss being murdered on the job is only slightly behind being accidently struck by a foreign object.[24] This deep-seated vitriol towards management has permeated popular culture with films like *Horrible Bosses* and online games such as *Whackyourboss.com*.[25] Business advisors typically tell managers that layoffs are best conducted in a humane and sensitive manner (for example, be friendly and respectful, provide information, offer extended severance pay, etc.). However, matters do not always go so smoothly. That's why a vibrant industry has arisen that provides 'employee termination security' to prevent violent retaliation by ex-workers. One anonymous employee fired from Chevron describes his experience on a blog:

> Ex-Employee. I'm not a troll but a former employee who was let go after 27 years of unblemished service. The layoff process was humiliating and embarrassing to all who endured. Armed security guarding the 'layoff communication rooms' was particularly embarrassing. Personally – I am ashamed of the treatment during the process for the company who is admired for its people, partnership and performance. Clearly – the Chevron Way concept is purely lip service for the benefit of the investor community.[26]

A spokesman for PRMG Security (whose corporate motto is 'Confident in Crisis') describes the protocols they follow: 'As they [the terminated employee] are being escorted to clean out their desk or locker, and then out to their car, they usually ask what we are there for. I always reply professionally and tell them that management wanted to have employee termination security as a precaution.'[27]

Built to burn

Dying while deemed fit for work. Suicide in the shadow of debt. Redundancy and murderous revenge. Each of these three rather disturbing cases tell us what the dominant economic model for the last 20 years really stands for today. What has come to be known as homo economicus – or economic man – is in serious trouble, even in terminal decline. Illness, debt and violence are not just exceptions to the rule. They are symptomatic of how the ideology of homo economicus now operates in the current economic atmosphere of precarity and crisis. Dawn Amos, Toby Thorn and Rodney Jackson are extreme cases no doubt. But they also signal an underlying essence of what all economic actors today must approximate and endure in order to survive. This is why even the healthy ones somehow look sick too, especially in countries that have been directly or indirectly inspired by Chicago School economists like Gary Becker, Milton Friedman and others. As the dismal science articulates its final iteration before certain oblivion (the discipline of economics is undoubtedly dying), its practical outcome is now about returning human life to dust, a social dust that is paradoxically lived over and over again in the form of a crippled mode of existence.

This is not simply a story about an economic paradigm misfiring or short-circuiting. What was once conveniently considered a miscarriage of economic man – illness, self-harm and unpredictable violence – is now clearly its fullest embodiment, what we risk becoming if we take the ideals of homo economicus seriously and follow its prescriptions to their conclusion. These unalloyed principles of 'economic man' represent a new set of truths inside crisis capitalism. Dawn Amos' ordeal typifies the new *truth of work*. Be ready to submit to it 24/7, regardless of your health and wellbeing. Toby Thorn expresses the *new truth of debt*. It consumes everything and transforms a simple economic contract into a deeply disturbing way of life that can last forever. And Rodney Jackson expresses the new *truth of power*. Capitalist force doesn't cloak itself in niceties anymore but arrives raw and ready to eject you when your exploitation is no longer needed. Revenge is at the forefront of workers' and ex-workers' minds. This twisted tripartite – work, debt, violence – might seem like personal failures for those who suffer them. But I argue that they represent the unadulterated expression of what homo economicus today has become, especially since it needs to undermine its own ability to act in order to be valid. When she crashes and burns, it is merely fulfilling a mission, the dark underside of the economy that is seldom mentioned by politicians, business leaders or university professors.

Too ill

We can observe these 'designed to fail' tendencies being played out as the authorities attempted to push Dawn Amos out of her sick bed and into work. For them, the assumption that one must be well in order to be gainfully employed no longer applies. It is tempting to probe the logic. From this point of view, perhaps illness might even make an individual *more* eligible for work than those fit and well. This demented normative stance towards the infirmed is epitomised by that special, bullying letter from a faceless technocrat, arriving to be read by someone already deceased. A ghost at the scene of their own final humiliation. This sums up what the so-called work ethic currently means for everyone entangled in 'total economics', whereby every fibre of the social body is subjected to fiscal and monetary scrutiny ... just as the Chicago School said things ought to be.

Too sad

Toby Thorn was an ordinary middle-class kid who believed he could live what I call the British Fantasy: do well at school, go to university in a picturesque town, find a romantic partner with whom he could enjoy long Sunday brunches in the summer, land a well-paid job and perhaps start a family, with doting grandparents babysitting every second Saturday. This narrative is endlessly proliferated by BBC television shows and smug baby-boomers writing for the *Telegraph*. One wonders whether it really existed. Regardless, the 'good life' narrative truly became a lie in the 1990s, when higher education in the UK was ruthlessly commercialised and personal indebtedness became a basic fact of life. Of course, the poor never entertained such aspirations. Ironically, they were perhaps lucky in this small respect. But the middle classes were hit hard since their misinformed, idyllic expectations clashed with the brutal new reality of economic power that has obliterated the old ways. The blow was particularly felt by their children in the post-2008 horror show. These 20-somethings have realised it was all pretty much a confidence trick. University and work are not a path to economic security. Perhaps they are the opposite.

What Howker and Malik call the 'jilted generation' have borne the brunt of the neoliberal assault on the democratic distribution of economic resources. The ladder has been pulled up and millions have been left behind.[28] For those lucky enough to have parents who accumulated capital before the 'big squeeze' occurred, they're able to get interest-free loans from the 'Bank of Mum and Dad'.[29] For the less fortunate a personal debt trap awaits because now the *future* itself has a price on its head. And someone has to pay. Rather than being classified a ghastly act of irresponsibility following the global meltdown, cheap credit virtually became the leading business model for banks seeking to profit from the aftermath of the subprime debacle. Personal indebtedness is a widespread norm because average public expenditure has been shifted onto the individual, regulated by our own yearning to have a decent standard of living, one that is increasingly unattainable without a credit card. Of course, 'fiscal restraint' policies rub salt into this wound by simultaneously hiking taxes (unless you're a large corporation based in Luxembourg), redoubling the financial burden that the average working person or student must bear.

In 2014 the Financial Control Authority (FCA) released a report in the UK accusing banks of not only opportunistically exploiting economic desperation, but actually encouraging debt servitude: 'Why are card issuers providing the means, in some cases, for the most indebted consumers, to escalate their way into further debt?', the chief executive of the FCA asked.[30] The answer is profit seeking, of course. A large swath of the British population are now considered survival-borrowers. Banks and parasitical payday lenders circle like scarcoptic vultures, making a killing out of the sheer volume of fees and fines that inevitably accumulate. Yes, easy credit might still be the norm. But the halcyon days of *friendly credit* are long over. Banks are getting nasty as they too feel the pinch with diminishing profit margins and government fines. That's why the bigger ones now engage in predatory and even deceptive lending practices. For example, when I recently purchased a jacket at a London department store a retail assistant asked if I would like a loyalty card, which would entitle me to a discount. I said, sure. They obtained my details and returned five minutes later with a card. I inspected it and quickly recognised an activated credit card instead from a well-known bank. The cost of the suit had been charged to it. I was already in debt! The next hour was spent angrily lecturing a manager about the legalities of lending practices. He looked bored. A group of non-English-speaking tourists slowly gathered around us, trying to figure out if something was amiss with their new loyalty cards too.

Too angry

Nothing justifies the actions of Rodney Jackson and the murder he committed at Val-Fit. However, his violent response to being laid off is indicative of the profound frustration and desperation that currently infuses the workforce in many countries today. Jackson's experience of work was clearly very pessimistic, especially when he was tossed away like an orange peel as the economy dipped. But his actions were not only in response to the ghastly future of insecurity that awaited him, being churned through the dehumanising unemployment industry and imploring employers for any work they can offer. No, his actions were also a kind of reprisal or revenge. He was getting his own back, albeit in an extremely criminal and destructive manner.

But there is more to this. Jackson's disproportionate reaction is somehow connected to the more brutal turn in management over the last few years. The typical employer today no longer seeks to generate happy workers, which was fashionable during the excesses of the 1990s when businesses could afford to worry about employee wellbeing. In the era of wreckage economics, things are different. It's almost a badge of honour to enforce low wages and economic anxiety, just so workers fully understand their rightful place in the economic order of things. One writer for *Forbes* even argues that fear is now a legitimate management technique.[31] This deflates those false promises of industrial democracy propagated by super-tanned Californian gurus like Tom Peters. Management in the era of austerity will never pander to workers, but it might frighten them: 'contemporary management and leadership theory focuses on consensus, collaboration – the democratic "flat" style – rather than the top-down, "do as I say" style. Be comfortable with, not afraid of the person in charge. The problem is: fear as a tactic to get others to do your bidding … works'. Upping the ante in this way will inevitably attract like-minded responses from the workforce.

A 2016 job satisfaction survey by the Chartered Institute of Personal Development (CIPD) in the UK tells us how bad things have got.[32] Job satisfaction has reached a two-year low. Most of us do a rough job satisfaction calculation every day. We ask ourselves, typically on that long and dreary commute to the office, is this job giving us more than it takes? If the answer is yes, then we're generally satisfied. The CIPD survey found that more are saying *no*. In fact, one in four UK employees want to leave their jobs as soon as possible.[33] What might be causing this malaise? One basic driver is money. Capitalism tends to react to crises by supressing wages, keeping people under the thumb in case things get violent. The average US worker, for example, was paid less in 2014 than they were in 1973.[34] Combine this with the legitimation of aggressive management tactics and the never-ending reminder that you are expendable, it's easy to see why some workers resort to extreme measures to get even. Bosses and co-workers are usually the target. It appears to have become an epidemic in the USA, inspiring a controversial videogame series called *Postal* (after the phrase 'going postal'). Gamers play 'Postal Dude' who snaps and goes on a murderous rampage that is not too dissimilar to those that have swept the USA in real life. At the time of writing, there have been 14 mass shootings in 2016 alone, with over 100 deaths.

Born to lose

How did economic causalities like Dawn Amos, Toby Thorn and Rodney Jackson and many others ever emerge? While it took some seismic shifts to accomplish with no modest amount of violence, our society is now built around the ideological abstraction of the 'economic human' or homo economicus like no other: self-reliant, self-interested, singly focused on economic gain, the organic seat of bearer of 'human capital' and ultra-rational in its conduct. Homo economicus represents a model of social being invented mainly by economists. This template is then used to understand and manage the state, marketplace, employment sector and even (according to Chicago School economist Gary Becker) the family and crime. It enforces a very specific way of being together and apart.

While this prescription for human behaviour has origins in John Stuart Mills, Adam Smith and Pareto, the 'dollar-hunting animal' truly comes into his own with the rise of neoliberal capitalism and its focus on individualism and enterprise. Following the works of Hayek and Becker among others, people no longer approximate *homo reciprocans* (reciprocal man) or *homo politicus* (political man), nor rely upon the baseline of *homo biologicus* (biological man). Instead they obey the monetised principle of pure utility, articulated through the moral matrix of rational choice, endless accumulation and egocentric competitiveness. Money and work therefore become central institutional forms in societies that are organised around homo economicus. They are the key drivers for maintaining and spreading the message of utility maximisation, especially its individualistic variant. None of this sounds very remarkable. However, we often forget how overcoded our world has become by money. It has crept into almost every facet of social being and taken on a mysterious life of its own, calling the shots as if it were some ghost in the machine of modern life. Perhaps that is the paradox of late capitalism. The cold cash nexus was meant to radically demystify mankind and purge it of providence. But in doing so it has become a magical deity in its own right, one that you don't want to anger or offend.

But all is not what it seems when it comes to understanding precisely how homo economicus (mis)functions in our society today. When one thinks of economic man in his or her purist form, Wall Street bankers and money-obsessed property developers tend to spring to mind. And needless to say, this image probably has strong gender connotations. In the popular imagination, such be-suited individuals exemplify a life dedicated to constant accumulation. However, today the stereotype is misleading. In many ways the rich don't need to worry about embodying the ethics of homo economicus because the institutional environment is always conspicuously weighted in their favour. Norms of reciprocity and collective entitlement (even at the expense of economic rationality) are more important to 1%-ers than the cool, individualistic instrumentalism preached by the Chicago School of Economics. The template of homo economicus is primarily designed for those outside the inner circle of the ruling class, perhaps even intended for those who will benefit least from a money-obsessed cultural agenda. In this sense, extreme capitalism is primarily for those *without* capital, while the political and financial elite enjoy a softer socialistic existence in which homo economicus would seem out of place and unwelcome. Economic man is a prescription for those who are least able to live up to its ideas.

What interests me is the 'living gap' (*diastema* or purposeful disajustment) between the pure abstraction of homo economicus and its systematic failure as a bearer of economic interests. Two facets are noteworthy. First, the miscarriage of homo economicus creates an example for others to try harder to avoid the same fate, resulting in the 'life or death' climate that neoliberal societies use to govern the work ethic and social order more generally. This process might play out within an individual too. Rather than the incapability to embody economic man properly lead people to reject it, the opposite can happen. An even stronger attachment to the impossible ideal, an example of what Lauren Berlant calls 'cruel optimism', whereby the more we're hurt the more we desire to stay in case things get better.[35] And second, another economy has stepped out of the shadows to capitalise on homo economicus in turmoil. The debt industry is the most obvious example. So is the self-help movement and mass incarceration, which are billion dollar businesses in the USA in particular. Vast security/ policing complexes are built upon the probabilly that another Rodney Jackson is out there somewhere. It turns out that worry, desperation and an abiding sense of disappointment among the wider population is good for business.

The unhappiness industry

Hence, the prevailing mood in the large metropolises of the West. No longer cynical (for who can be bothered), but morbidly melancholic, shot through with other-directed nihilism. These feelings are not just a by-product of crisis capitalism. In many ways unhappiness and unwellness is a sort of informal industry in the prolonged era of austerity. We are constantly reminded about our potential abandonment by society (the threat of *not* being exploited), spend massive amounts of money on ineffectual and self-defeating forms of escape that only take us closer to the void (look at England's obsession with over-drinking, for example) and build community cohesion, whatever is left of it, out of fear and self-reproach (e.g., Brexit, Trump, etc.). The focus is on unhappiness or at least mild depression rather than joy, which a resurgent political Right has systematically encouraged over the last few years. This is not to say that books like *The Happiness Industry*, *Smile or Die* and *The Wellness Syndrome* do not make excellent points.[36] They suggest that happiness and wellness is being sold to us on an unprecedented scale, tactically bombarding everyone with diets, self-help exercises, mindfulness manuals, fitness gimmicks and so forth.

Despite the obvious class bias here (I'm not sure if the global poor have never heard of the happiness industry) there is also a fundamental problem regarding the somatic mood that has prevailed in the wake of the global financial crisis. These studies suggest that neoliberalism uses the discourse of happiness and wellbeing to control us. But is that really the case? One could argue the contrary. In many ways sadness dominates the language of the world economy. Feelings of unhappiness and unwellness are the informal tone of governments who have embraced the ludicrous notion of fiscal restraint, especially as they harm the citizenry through public and civil neglect. For example, a 2016 report by the Centre for Crime and Justice Studies argues that the UK's government's 'light touch' on business regulation has resulted in what they term *social murder*.[37] State-funded bodies charged with independent inspections have seen their budgets drastically cut. We are now supposed to trust the business world to regulate their own behaviour. The outcome? – 29,000 deaths a year due to polluted air; 50,000 people die every year due to injuries and health-related issues sustained in the workplace. And food poisoning causes 500 deaths a year and a further 20,000 being hospitalised.[38] Not much happiness here. A whole raft of industries have, of course, stepped in to earn plenty of money from this pain and sadness. No doubt multinational pharmaceutical firms, for example, are eager to sell recuperative opportunities to those physically wounded by unregulated corporate capitalism.

However, even in light of this unhappiness industry, it might be argued that at the cultural level happiness is everywhere being forced down our throats. But it depends on your perspective and what you choose (or not) to see. For me, the explicit narrative of belt-tightening economics (which our politicians tell us will last generations) trades in shades of permanent wintery greys. Almost every policy announcement by the state and its semi-lobotomised think-tanks encourage a profoundly pessimistic outlook on life, including monotonous speeches by dim-witted politicians warning how 'the storm clouds are gathering'. Indeed, as homo economicus deteriorates in all the major cities of the world, wellness indexes (such as warnings about responsible levels of alcohol) are not used to curb bad behaviour or spark feelings of guilt. No, if the pre-diabetic and overworked banker looks to the wellness/happiness industry at all, it is to calculate if she has reached an adequate level of hedonism and self-harm. Without the health warnings, there would be no way to tell. They reside in the post-rationalisation culture of painful truths. The unscrupulous city trader no longer lies to himself. He knows what type of person he really is. And that sense of disillusionment becomes addictive. Evermore extreme 'truth telling' rituals are required to capture what one has authentically become.

That's no zombie ... it's worse

If economic man represents a perpetually failing way of life, following economic models that have been proven all but dead, then it is easy to see why the metaphor of the semi-dead/semi-living *zombie* has become so popular among critics. Books with frightening titles such as *Zombie Economics, The Strange Non-death of Neoliberalism, Dead Man Working, Monsters of the Market* and *Zombie Capitalism* all point to how the ideas of neoliberal orthodoxy have died, been disastrous, yet are still being lived by us today.[39] John Quiggin's *Zombie Economics* perhaps stands out because it so persuasively deconstructs each tenet of neoclassical economics, including assumptions about rational actors, market equilibrium and pricing signals. The Chicago School has bequeathed entire generations with ideas that are fraudulent at best and socially injurious at worst.

No doubt neoliberal dogma has been proven wrong but still walks among us in a semi-dead fashion. But we have to remember that capitalism has always exuded such qualities, noted as early as Marx's description of the exploitation of workers as something resembling a vampire. Derrida demonstrated in his reading of Marx that the theme of hauntings and ghosts runs throughout much of his analysis of the capital accumulation process.[40] So in some ways, neoliberalism is perhaps simply an extension of a more general zombie-like mode of production, which actually might be more worrying.

However, the current use of metaphor runs into other problems. It assumes that the economic power structure (such as the wreckage before us) has to have recourse to rational and truthful ideas in order to govern. But that is not necessarily the case. No government in the West adheres to its own proclamations about the virtues of free markets, competition and so forth. The USA is the highest subsidised economy in the world with import levies that clearly contradict free market principles (no one seems to remember that Ronald Reagan was the most protectionist US president in the country's post-war period). The UK sells natural monopolies like water, rail and mail to multinational investors who can't believe how lucky they are to be able to extract rent without competition. And even when once robust ideas around monetary and fiscal policy openly fail, as publicly admitted by Alan Greenspan (in relation to the US subprime crash) and IMF chief Christine Lagarde (in relation to economic austerity in the UK), it doesn't mean that institutional power holders will change their course of action.[41] For in some ways none of this is about ideas, rationality or even economics for that matter, but political dominance regardless of whether the theorems work or not. Power is hardly ever rational in that classic Kantian sense and it would be irrational to expect it to be. And finally, the zombie motif implies that we have all been taken over by a deadly virus, sleep walking through life, guided by deceased ideological forms, like the half-dead/half-alive people in *The Night of the Living Dead* (Romero's brilliant critique of consumer culture). But that cannot be. The built-to burn tendencies of homo economicus as it is currently being imposed on the global poor, and the hollowed-out middle classes of the West actually need a high quantum of life to function.

Therein lies the contradiction. Without fully breathing people there is no oxygen for homo economicus to burn as he flunks another Fit for Work assessment, on the job drug test or car repayment. No, it is not us who are the zombies. We are more like the fully alive and aware characters in the TV series *The Walking*

Dead. In other words, *witnesses* to a semi-dead and dangerous world peopled by hostile 'walkers' and relentlessly trying to evade the enemy. Whole capitalist industries flourish on this flight mechanism that has become a way of life for the multitude. It's euphemistically termed the 'sharing economy'. Uber, Blabla Car, Nubelo, Amazon Mechanical Turk, YoupiJob and many other similar firms tap into the 24/7 rhythms of the informal population who are struggling to avoid hostile forces. Airbnb, for example, exploits otherwise non-commercialised housing and spaces of rest. This is not a case of friendly city neighbours openly stating 'what's mine is yours' but the reverse.[42] Uber-parasites mopping up spaces of life that were once beyond the remit of commercial exploitation, reshaping you and me into another dead commodity, a logic that produces little and simply extracts economic value from others. Hershel cautions us in *The Walking Dead* to this effect: 'You walk outside, you risk your life. You take a drink of water, you risk your life. Nowadays you breathe and you risk your life.' Entering into the scrapped back world of 'life' poses so many economic threats. So it is watched from a safe distance. As a result, we become witnesses to a life that isn't so. What passes for 'living' is but a reminder of its own absence. Isn't that an apt definition of a ghost? A living audience who is present at the site of its own non-being.

Why is behavioural economics so creepy?

It could be objected that the recent popularity and diffusion of behavioural economics might challenge or displace the supremacy of homo economicus in many spheres of society. Decision-making psychologists such as Dan Ariel and Richard Thaler have recently shaken up the world of mainstream economics – or at least that's what they say – with books like *Nudge, Predictably Irrational* and *Misbehaving*.[43] These writers build on a classic 1979 paper by Daniel Kahneman and Amos Tversky that analyzed how people's perceptions of risk can have a major influence on their economic reasoning.[44] Economic actors don't really behave as the self-interested maximisers that neoclassical economists imagine us to be, especially in theories such as expected or rank-dependent utility theory. We don't even act like this when presented with complete information. Rational choice is only one aspect of the emotional and cognitive architecture informing our decisions in the sphere of commerce, frequently flying in the face of linear econometric models.[45] The famous ultimatum game is a useful way to explain the counter-intuitive findings of the approach. Two people are sitting in a room and I give one of them £100. I instruct her to give a portion of this £100 to the second person. They can choose any amount. But there is one catch. If the second person rejects the offer then the entire £100 is confiscated and they both leave with nothing. According to models based on rational utility, whatever the second person is offered – be it 10p, £1 or £10 – they ought to accept. After all, they started with nothing. However, the experiment finds that most will reject any offer below £40, because it's unfair.

Behavioural economics (and behavioural finance) has become so acclaimed that in 2010 the UK government set up a Behavioural Insights Team (also known as the Nudge Unit, which clearly has sinister connotations) to apply the idea to statecraft and population management.[46] According to its website, the Nudge Unit has a mission of '1). making public services more cost-effective and easier for citizens to use; 2). improving outcomes by introducing a more realistic model of human behaviour to policy; and 3). wherever possible, enabling people to make 'better choices for themselves'.[47] But what exactly is meant by better choices and by whose standards? In the USA, the government funds the Social and Behavioural Sciences Team, which similarly applies behavioural economics to a disparate range of conundrums, including college fees, form filling, micro-loans to farmers and difficulties experienced by low-income families.

Does this focus on the economic irrationalities of individual choices displace homo economicus as the dominant template for human action today and cast doubt on my arguments thus far? No, I don't think so. Behavioural economics surreptitiously extends the idealisation of economic man by assuming that the unpredictable qualities of human life might still be accounted for within the present economic context of crisis capitalism and its warped assumptions about justice, fairness and the good life. Even one of the founders of the perspective, Daniel Kahneman (along with Amos Tversky), admitted that 'theories in behavioural economics have generally retained the basic architecture of the rational model, adding assumptions about cognitive limitations designed to account for specific anomalies'.[48] But I would go further. Behavioural economics represents an attempt to recoup or reappropriate the in-built failures and anomalies of homo economicus, redirecting them into the same set of capitalist coordinates that incited them in the first place. It is no coincidence that Richard Thaler titled his book *Misbehaviour* since exactly that is being remodelled into a revenue stream. That's what makes behavioural economics fundamentally creepy. Perhaps a little closer to the mark in this respect are economists George Akerlof and Robert Shiller when they draw on this perspective to demonstrate how we're systematically duped and misled by big business.[49] The problem is they see this 'phishing' as an isolated facet of commerce. What if it went to the heart of neoliberalism itself, making it one terrible confidence trick?

If the juggernaut of neoclassical economics paved the way for the predominance of capitalist values by crowding out all others, then the clearing that emerged, marked by human disorientation and bewilderment, is the playground of behavioural economics. Kahnemania enters into this barren social clearing created by an immoderate adherence to neoclassical orthodoxy and continues to see this as the only *reality* in town that people must adapt to in various ways. To really take on neoclassical economics and econometrics we need to question the very ontological certainties it is wedded to and speak about capitalist *unrealism*. A world that should not and cannot exist with fidelity outside of the 1 per cent in fact. Behavioural economics still favours the language of the untouchable rich, still presupposes that the 'dollar-hunting animal' is what human life is all about. In this way it actually relies upon the achievements of right-wing stupidity in order to define itself. Think about it another way. Behavioural economics would look positively alien in pre-1976 Britain or the USA. It can only gain traction on what is left of society after monetarisation has dominated all social spaces, that interminable numbing-by-numbers encouraged by Thatcher and her present-day acolytes.

When Richard Thaler was asked about Thomas Piketty's renowned analysis of economic inequality, he said that he realised what the problem really is with neoclassical economists of the Chicago School type. They don't give tips.[50] After reading *Capital in the Twenty-first Century*, Thaler said he concluded we should 'all leave a bigger tip'. Doesn't that perfectly sum up the political vacuity of this approach? Or what about this example. One of the first tasks that the Nudge Unit were given by the Tory government was to get more ordinary working people to pay their tax bill.[51] No, not deal with tax evasion by Google, Amazon, Starbucks and other multinationals operating in the UK. Nor flush out the users of tax havens in Panama and Jersey, where the UK elite hide their megabucks from democracy. Instead the Nudge Unit was asked to devise a method for getting the overtaxed working poor to pay up.

The solution was as simple as it was manipulative. Rather than send John Doe, a struggling window cleaner from Manchester, another menacing letter from HM Revenue and Customs outlining the ghastly fines he will accumulate, John receives a different kind of message. It states that 95 per cent of his close neighbours had paid *their* taxes on time. So shouldn't you pay too, John? Peer pressure, guilt and shame are persuasive drivers of action. The reverse psychology behind these mind games that seek to nudge the poor (for some reason, it's never the rich who are nudged by behavioural economists) are designed to extract a surplus (in this case, probably from John's new credit card) while placing the responsibility for the ensuing impoverishment onto the same failed economic actor. The dark logic is captured in a classic Rodney Dangerfield joke: 'A guy stopped me in the street the other day, you could see he was down and out. He asked me for some money to buy a bottle of booze. I looked at him: I know your type. You tell me you'll buy a bottle of booze then go and get food instead … no way, I'm not giving you a cent.'

Daddy Entrepreneurs

Until now we've been highlighting the losers in the economic game of life that is neoliberal capitalism in decline. But what about the winners? I have claimed that the last place you will find anything remotely resembling homo economicus is in the corridors of corporate and political power. Is that true? Don't the distinct qualities of the 'dollar-hunting animal' demonstrate precisely those who can work the system to their advantage, the successful captains of industry and dynamic entrepreneurs who stand apart from the rest due to their commercial acumen? This 'great man' thesis is very popular, often involving rags-to-riches fairy tales as billionaire businessmen and women try to justify their bizarre levels of wealth. According to this story, they've built something from nothing, taken risks that paid off and inspired faithful followers to work hard for them. Homo economicus perfectus, to the point where some even suggest these business geniuses must possess a special gene that makes them innately great compared to the rest of us.[52]

Of course, in reality neoliberal capitalism bears little resemblance to this glowing narrative concerning the innovative, creative individual who gets rich, like something out of a bad Ayn Rand novel. Pre-existing wealth, class privilege, familial connections and sheer luck are often more decisive than innate skill. Take business leadership, for example. A 2015 study has convincingly debunked the myth of the extraordinary corporate leader.[53] Markus Fitza selected 1500 of the largest US firms and tracked their financial performance from 1993 to 2012. His question was simple: how much of a corporation's performance can be attributed to its CEO, namely his or her skills and abilities? Fitza expected the 'CEO effect' to be significant since these individuals have much influence over the firm and are rewarded accordingly. Using a complex modelling technique called variance decomposition the study produced some rather surprising results. The 'CEO effect' was so low that a firm's performance could largely be put down to chance, external events and trends beyond the control of the leader.

It might then be argued that over the long term, say 10 or 20 years, negative and positive chance events could be cancelled out in the study, making the expected 'CEO effect' more discernible. However, the average tenure of a US CEO is only four years. The implications of the study are important. The fetishism of leadership that has gripped business schools, political discourse and so frequently used to justify wealth in the popular imagination has been a hoax. Most importantly, according to Fitza, 'if we do not want CEOs to be rewarded or punished for luck, then understanding their true contribution to company performance should be an important part in determining the level of their compensation'.[54] A comparable study in the UK had similar results. Researchers at Lancaster University focused on England's top 350 biggest firms. Between 2003 and 2014 these firms increased their value (returns on investment/capital) by only 1 per cent. Executive pay over the same period increased by 80 per cent, most of which was ironically performance related.[55]

The same sort of misguided 'business talent' mythology that justifies perverse executive salaries also surrounds the much idolised entrepreneur. However, these so-called self-made men and women rarely hark from a humble background. Titans of commerce like Donald Trump and Gina Rinehart encourage the image of coming from nothing. But they could be more accurately called 'Daddy Entrepreneurs' in that they have had a good deal of help along the way, including family wealth, inheritances and trust funds. This is what makes Australian Gina Rinehart, one of the richest people in the world, so amusing. She claims 'there is no monopoly on becoming a millionaire. If you're jealous of those with more money, don't just sit there and complain – do something to make more money yourself'.[56] Rinehart actually inherited her billions from her father, iron-ore magnate, Lang Hancock. Hancock in turn was born into one of Western Australia's oldest land-owning families.

Wealth has perhaps always functioned in this manner. But as John Maynard Keynes famously argued, modern capitalism was meant to 'euthanise' the old, unproductive rentier-class. It didn't quite turn out this way. That's why this latest phase of capitalist development represents a major step backwards. As Thomas Piketty decisively demonstrated, non-earned income is now a cornerstone of the contemporary class structure, much as it was before the arrival of the welfare state.[57] Decrepit neoliberal economies now begin to look more Victorian or even feudal than a modern social system. For example, in the UK a 2016 study revealed that those holding the most influential jobs in the public and private sector have been disproportionately educated at Oxford or Cambridge University, indicating elite family backgrounds.[58] The findings were summed up: 'Just 7% of the UK public attended private schools, which compares to 71% of senior judges, 62% of senior armed forces officers, 55% of Whitehall permanent secretaries and 50% of members of the House of Lords.'[59] Social mobility appears to be pretty much dead in Britain. The key factor that determines your probability of becoming a judge or CEO is not intelligence, skill or aptitude. It's your family wealth, social networks and the private members club you belong to.[60]

Monkeys in the boardroom

Surely the instrumental and calculative workings of the stock market is the true crucible of homo economicus victorious, with traders only succeeding if they are smart enough to out-think everyone else? Well, that's the impression we are given by popular culture and Finance 101 business school lectures. In the reality TV show *Million Dollar Traders*, people from all sorts of backgrounds (a retired soldier, teachers, students, IT experts, pensioners) are hired for two months to see if they have what it takes to become a profitable trader. Each is given the sterling equivalent of $1 million and either sink or float in the unforgiving world of finance. The hedge fund manager who has put up the cash, Lex van Dam, interviewed thousands of applicants before deciding on the final eight. To qualify for a place he asked people only two questions. 'Would you screw someone to get ahead?' and 'what is 32 x 32?'

The first question presents a moral trap. Does Lex want me to say yes or no? We never find out.

But the second question is the decider for Lex. The answer is 1024 but only a few are smart enough to crack the calculation on the spot. The ideology of the show lies in the idea that financial capitalism is built on meritocracy. Anyone good at maths can become a rich trader. These people will have a natural intuition for how the market works, like the Christian Bale character in the film *The Big Short*, who grasps small tell-tale signs that no one else notices, bets *against* the booming US housing market just before the subprime crash hits, and makes millions in the process. Once again, homo economicus perfectus.

However, the idea that the stock market is managed by exceptionally gifted experts has recently been challenged. To determine whether luck or expertise governs profitability, Andrew Clare, Nick Motson and Steve Thomas examined US stock data, particularly the market capitalisation-weighted index between 1968 and 2011.[61] They were inspired by the infinite monkey theorem first popularised by mathematician Emile Borel. If millions of monkeys tapped away on typewriters for infinity at some stage they would randomly reproduce one of Shakespeare's great plays. So Clare, Motson and Thomas designed a computer program that simulated about 10 million monkeys playing the stock market (i.e., totally random and incoherent trading) to see how real traders compared to their primate counterparts. They found that

> many of the ten million monkeys managed to outperform the Marketcap index and the other alternatives ... which produces a terminal wealth value of just under $5,000 ... Half of the monkeys produced a terminal wealth value greater than $8,700; 25% produced a terminal wealth value greater than $9,100; while 10% produced a terminal wealth value greater than $9,500.[62]

It appears that monkey economics outclasses trained traders on almost every level. Chance and random events that lead to positive wealth outcomes are erroneously put down to the shrewdness of investors who in reality are no better than random monkeys. Homo economicus as the king of Wall Street? No as it happens. Not even the jungle.

Smash and grab

We are told that economic man – as opposed to all of the other ways of being – fits seamlessly into societies based upon free markets, individual self-interest, competition and private enterprise. Since *pure capitalism* is the social backdrop, it would be wrongheaded to conduct our lives in any other way. Herein lies the problem. This isn't pure capitalism. We live in a society that Milton Friedman would not recognise in any of his theories. In fact, almost all of the tenets of free market capitalism are missing today, which is one reason why homo economicus has become such a ruinousness endeavour. The normative prescription for how to conduct one's life no longer matches reality. This is how wreckage economics ends up wrecking real life people. And the disjuncture between the ideal and the real world has only grown following the 2007–08 crisis.

For example, we are taught that open markets allow the best companies to succeed, weeding out those that are inefficient or neglectful of customers. However, corporate revenue streams today are mainly generated through rent and capture of public goods. The UK economy exemplifies this logic, which has little to do with 'free markets' or anything remotely resembling neoclassic economic models. Look at Thames Water. It holds a monopolistic grip over much of London's water supply. Customers (i.e., all of the captured citizens of London who need water) must simply pay whatever they charge. Sold off in 1989, generations of public and taxpayer investment was appropriated in one swift deal. Water bills slowly and surely increased in a big way. The only real winner is the Australian investment bank Macquarie, aka the 'vampire kangaroo'. They sold their stake in 2017 for £1.5 billion. During its ten year reign Macquarie paid enormous dividends to shareholders, underinvested in the business and hiked household water bills. Who needs the mafia when you have businesses like this lurking in your neighbourhood?

James Meek has perhaps done the most to catalogue the irresponsible irrationalities and hypocrisies of privatisation in the UK (and the chapter on water-supply is particularly painful to read).[63] The so-called post-capitalist society that Peter Drucker predicted would result from privatisation – we would all be shareholders and thus owners of capital – turned out to be only partially true. Post-capitalist for sure, but in a negative sense that companies like Thames Water are free to behave like premodern landlords:

> the simplest way to understand the way the water set-up works in England is to think of it as a form of buy-to-let scheme, with us, the customers, as tenants paying water bills, like rent; the shareholders as landlords, owning the water companies; and the company staff, like a property management agency, collecting the rent and maintaining the property ... but if we don't like the property, the management agency or the landlords, or we think the rent is too high, we don't have any choice. We can't move to a different property or a better run one, we're stuck.[64]

As I write, outside my London flat an army of emergency service personnel are trying to contain a massive flood caused by burst mains pipes. Thames Water's system is so rundown that three such incidents have occurred across the city in the last week.[65] While homo economicus is judged by the quality of the deals he brokers, in terms of water supply in London he is no longer a customer (who can pick and choose) but a captured prisoner of a distant corporation that charges extortionate rents. So in the end what does that make homo economicus? A self-contradictory non-entity. That's the point. It's very clear Thames Water and the many other similar corporations presently preying on the UK population have nothing to do with the ideals of economic man so glorified in discourses of population management. If it wasn't for all the faulty plumbing that make leaking ceilings a perennial feature of London accommodation (property maintenance is the last thing on a private landlord's mind given the gross undersupply of housing), homo economicus would have burnt out long ago. For that is what he built for.

Cyber-feudalism

When we think of capitalism, we mainly think of the *production* of things. Commodities, services, experiences all have to be produced before they're consumed. However, this type of capitalist activity takes time, investment and a paid workforce. Companies at the vanguard of the present, feudal-like world economy are not really keen on that. Is there an easier way to make profits? Yes, so it happens. Rather than produce goods and services, better to enclose them, making use of the means of production that people already are. That would keep costs down. This is the business model for so-called 'platform capitalism', be it the Uber, Deliveroo or YouTube.[66] These organisations seek to commercialise the informal economy and rent it back to the community.

The worst aspects of the business model were exemplified in the recent fracas about one of YouTube's most popular shows, *React*. It was set up by the Fine brothers Benny and Rafi as a bit of fun. Subscribers post videos of friends and family reacting to a new experience for the first time. *Kids React* and *Elders React* are particularly popular. The idea, of course, was on YouTube long before the Fine brothers' came along. They simply collected and repackaged it into a show driven purely by user content. This is why its 14 million subscribers were so surprised when the Fine brothers decided to trademark *React* content. They also announced that *React* was to be restructured using a license arrangement, effectively reinventing the brand into a business. Viewers 'reacted' with hostility as millions cancelled their subscription.[67] That same spirit of vehemence ought to be directed at Thames Water and many other corporations that are nothing but rentiers of public goods.

The pattern is the same throughout the post-industrial economy. The couplet of capture and rent of de facto common resources drives the profit margins for many firms, even ones we believe have created their own value from scratch (e.g., Microsoft, Apple, etc.).[68] But the monopoly status that these larger firms establish has another downside. Once a market is cornered there is little incentive for progressive innovation. In terms of natural monopolies such as the London water supply, assets are simply rundown. If there is investment, it is typically derived from debt guaranteed by the state so that shareholders will never lose.[69] Where the rentier monopolies are orchestrated, as in the IT sector, innovation is killed by shutting out competition and predatory patenting activity. Consumers are then irreversibly wedded to substandard products and services. Perhaps the only area where technology is truly cutting-edge pertains to tools of repression and control. For example, many of the leading IT breakthroughs used today have derived from the sizable investment made by the Israeli Military, including the legendary 'Unit 8200'.[70]

But it's the innovations that aim to capitalise on the failures gathering around homo economicus that are truly striking. For example, US subprime car loans reached about $145 billion in 2014.[71] Technology is rapidly advancing in this sector. New software is installed in the latest model cars that allow it to be remotely disabled if a customer is late on their repayment. 'Starter Interrupt Devices' perhaps exemplify Gilles Deleuze's dark prediction about societies of control. Like the silent killer drone, the process of disabling the ignition is remote, dehumanised and automatic. No repo-man will be knocking on your door in a threatening manner. You simply can't start the car until you pay. All it takes is one click to disable the vehicle. A lender at First Castle Federal Credit Union in Louisiana even bragged, 'I have disabled a car while I was shopping at Walmart'.[72] Cars have been disabled only moments after a loan default. There is an inevitable class bias operating here. Lawyer Robert Swearingen points out that 'no middle-class person would ever be hounded for being a day late ... But for poor people, there is a debt collector right there in the car with them'.[73] But it's not unreasonable to assume that the desperate middle classes will be next. Indeed, in a society built around the automobile, one can imagine this technology being licensed to other institutions such as banks, water and electricity companies and the tax office.

'You're a fat ugly bitch'

According to Michel Foucault, homo economicus is a consumer economic of life as much as a producer. He or she works in order to purchase better life chances and invest in the future. Foucault ignores, however, an important motivation behind this redefinition of everybody as customers. We often think that the state remoulds the public and citizenry into paying customers because it has adopted a 'user pays' mentality to services provision. Commercialisation of health and education, for example, is about individual responsibility. If you benefit from it then you ought to pay. But there is something else just as significant going on here. The push to rescript students, patients, passport applicants, taxable citizens and television viewers (to name just a few) into consumers is also designed to undermine public sector *workers*. It's an indirect anti-worker tactic. As civic institutions are slowly starved of funds and inevitably become substandard, unsatisfied 'customers' blame the service providers (university lecturers, train drivers, junior doctors, border control personnel, police officers) rather than the leaders responsible for these organisations. This gives the managerial elite of these institutions plenty of ammunition to further repress pay and conditions because the primary agent that now matters the most – the end user – is unhappy.

The extent to which this mythology of the customer has been used to weaken public servants in the UK is incredible. When a major hospital fails, sometimes scandalously, the Secretary of State for Health is first to publicly condemn the institution. Workers are singled out as the primary cause. In the pre-customer era, the minister and senior managers in charge would have been held accountable, not their subordinates who're doing their best in rundown organisations. This is how the discourse of customer service can be deployed as a covert weapon against the public sphere. As the budget cuts kick in, the fact that workers inevitably fail is used to justify further cuts while steep management hierarchies absolve leaders of accountability. The beleaguered nurse, court assistant and junior lecturer are therefore hamstrung by the template of homo economicus twice. First as workers who struggle to pay the bills and second as customer service providers who are too stressed and underresourced to meet their customer satisfaction targets. This strategic deployment of 'the customer' happens especially when strike action is threatened. How dare train drivers and mail delivery workers voice their discontent when there are thousands of consumers relying on these employees to silently accept shitty job conditions!

It is surprising how effective this divide and conquer strategy has been, perhaps perfected in the higher education sector. The coming 'Teaching Excellence Framework' (or TEF) in England has been proposed by governmental advisors as a way of ensuring that fee-paying students receive the quality education they deserve. Once again, the voice of the student cum customer is put centre stage, since universities ought to be effective teaching institutions. Who can argue with that? Moreover, it's fascinating how so many themes from the radical Left (e.g., student-centred learning, pedagogical empowerment, student participation, etc.) have been symbolically appropriated by the corporatised university and used to dominate academic labour with Stalin-like vigour.[74]

Of course, it could be argued that this isn't really about the student. It's more about work intensification by a state apparatus that loathes the autonomy academics have accumulated over the last century. Along with the draconian Research Excellence Framework and an increasingly casualised faculty, the old days of a quiet, contented professorial class are long gone.[75] The TEF will probably break what remains of academic self-determination by subjecting, say, a physics professor in her late 50s to the capricious opinions of an 18-year-old. Precisely *because* the outcome will be comparable to internet trolling, its accuracy will probably be cherished even more by university authorities.[76] Think here of the disturbing US website Rate My Professor (including its option to evaluate physical attractiveness or 'Hotness'). The same attitude risks becoming official state policy. Regardless, the aim is for teachers to become customer service representatives of the university, and we all know that the customer is never wrong. Early retirement will begin to look very attractive for many in this coming Edu-factory. Just look at some of these student evaluations that lecturers have received from their students:

'You're a fat ugly bitch.'

'The class was pretty cool, but she needs to get a tan and stop wearing all those Amish dresses.'

'How to improve this course? Teach in a miniskirt.'

'Even though she's a feminist, she listens.'[77]

Yet another grim and disconcerting logic governs the cult of the customer. It kills any democratic input by citizens regarding how organisations interact with the public. Free market zealots from Friedrich Hayek and Steve Jobs once argued that if students became 'service purchasers' who can pick and choose from a range of schools competing in the marketplace, then the good institutions will be rewarded by high demand and the bad ones punished. This was Milton Friedman's rationale with vouchers. He thought the system would give parents freedom to spend their vouchers on the best performing institutions. The idea is also supported by the current US Education Secretary Betsy 'government sucks' DeVos, who also happens to be a billionaire. However, there's clearly something very troubling about the argument. Think about what happens when I become a customer in, say, a supermarket. I have the choice to go to this or that supermarket if I'm lucky, but the bigger players usually price out the smaller stores and geographically diversify in relation to the larger rivals so that only one large provider tends to dominate a neighbourhood. Even putting that issue aside, there is something more sinister happening here. Once cast as a customer I have no say whatsoever over how that institution is run. The same with schools. Class size? Teaching methods? A parent's power to transform their schools is drastically impeded under the system. Commercialised universities provide ample evidence of this too, despite the attempt to create the appearance of participation by encouraging students to comment on how 'hot' a professor is. All of a sudden we have university 'management' who make most decisions and aggressively dissuade involvement from faculty and students. Metrics that ought to measure academic activity in a university become singular ends or 'targets' in themselves, creating all sorts of perverse dysfunctions and unintended consequences as they're enforced by distant technocrats.[78] Even the physical space is designed to curb self-organisation and awareness-raising activities among the student body. No, the customer is not 'king'. They're the pinnacle of anti-democratic disempowerment, which ultimately harms the service quality in the long run ... not enhance it.

Paid to hurt

Homo economicus ought to represent the apogee of human self-regulation and freedom according to neoclassical dogma. But everywhere he is inundated by cumbersome corporate and governmental bureaucracy, more now even than in days of the welfare state. The proliferation of red tape, of course, contradicts the promises of neoliberalism, which apparently only apply to the rich, who do seem to enjoy 'fully automated luxury communism'. In *The Utopia of Rules*, David Graeber notes the amplification of state bureaucracy following the global financial crisis given the inequalities it leads to.[79] An unfair society needs more layers of technocrats to keep a lid on civil unrest. Moreover, because state power is ultimately based on the threat of violence, its army of faceless apparatchiks can safely ignore what Graeber calls 'interpretive labour' when dealing with us. That's the emotional and empathetic work people conduct every day when trying to understand what another is thinking. Basic social interaction hinges on it. When being processed by a bureaucracy, however, interpretative labour is mainly done by the disempowered party as they desperately attempt to figure out a functionary's thoughts and intentions. Bureaucrats are only handling a 'case' or 'file' and have violence to back up their judgements. They don't really care what the other person is thinking or feeling. People become mere derivative *objects*.

Hence, the pitiless official we've all met at some point, devoid of any interpretative curiosity concerning the real person before them. Graeber rightly labels this a form of stupidity. For example, take the following description of complaint to a budget airline. It was written by a man who had missed his flight. He arrived at the airport on time only to be repeatedly given incorrect information by staff he dubbed, 'The child', 'Not So Bright' and 'Vacant'. When he was finally able to coax a middle manager out of the back office, he was simply told 'Check in opens 3 hours before the flight'.

> [**Customer**] 'Why is this our fault, and why should we miss the flight because Ryanair staff have admitted they made errors?'
>
> [**Official**] 'Check in opens three hours before the flight'
>
> [**Customer**] 'Do you acknowledge we have just cause for complaint as we tried to do the right thing and the only reason we are not on the plane is because of communication failures with Ryanair Staff?'
>
> [**Official**] 'Check in opens three hours before the flight'
>
> [**Customer**] 'What colour are my trousers?'
>
> [**Official**] 'Check in opens three hours before the flight'
>
> [**Customer**] 'Do you think economic sanctions on Russia will diffuse the escalating situation in Ukraine?'
>
> [**Official**] 'Check in opens three hours before the flight'[80]

This is a great example of what Graeber means. Power simply issuing empty words with little emotional involvement. However, this theory of the administrative personality is accurate only up to a point. For it risks missing the important role that *sadism* can play in an otherwise impartial bureaucratic encounter. The neoliberal technocrat does sometimes engage in interpretative labour. But not the empathetic and compassionate sort. No, they're instead calculating whether the emotional anxiety inflicted on the 'other' has genuinely met its target. If positive identification (or what Graeber calls 'interpretative labour') is about trying to see one's self in the eyes of another, *negative identification* is about refusing to see yourself in the victim as you paradoxically stand in their shoes to register their pain. This represents an active moral blindness that gains energy from its own self-recognition. Sadism can certainly be a characteristic of the individual functionary, something most of us have experienced. But institution-level sadism is probably more common and easier to achieve since the individual can rationalise their own behaviour via the edicts of the organisation and disavow personal responsibility as they become expert pain-givers.

De Sade at the Jobcentre

In the UK, an ex-advisor employed by the Jobcentre – responsible for assisting the unemployed in their search for work – admitted that she was rewarded for being cruel to her clients.[81] Angela Neville said that the centre was managed through performance targets, and ranked by the government against other offices in England. This meant advisors were under great pressure to force someone with a disability, for example, to attend job interviews. In one incident, a supervisor told her to call a hospitalised client and threaten them with sanctions. For this she received 'brownie points'. She goes on,

> The pressure was incredible. Advisers were actively encouraged to impose sanctions (along the lines of 'sanction of the month') to contribute to the points system that ranks jobcentre offices. It was often for stupid reasons ... And it was happening all the time. A customer maybe would be a little bit late or would phone in and the message wasn't passed on. It was very distressing to have customers literally without food, without heat, without resources and these are unwell [and] disabled customers.[82]

However, unlike her colleagues it looks as if Angela is a failed sadist. This bureaucratic role demands that the advisor engage in a certain amount of 'interpretative labour' to gauge whether the symbolic violence enacted has triggered the necessary levels of distress. Angela clearly could not do this without feeling guilty. In Gilles Deleuze's language pertaining to the *unsuccessful* sadist, she couldn't disintegrate her ego and allow an all-encompassing Meta-Superego to emerge, one that relies on the ego of another person (the victim) to function to say no, a sort of self-censorship by proxy.[83] In other words, Angela couldn't become a monster.

Of course, a proper sadist gains *sexual* pleasure from inflicting pain. Hopefully that is not the case here. By the same token, however, sex (or 'climax') is only the end point in this psychic drama. The first step towards sadism is to imagine or occupy the pain of a vulnerable/dependent person and attach positive affect to that agony. In the Jobcentre case this positivity is garnered from institutional rewards or 'points'. As Jean-Paul Sartre also points out concerning the sadist, they are not simply trying to erase the subjectivity of the victim, but occupy it in order for the aggressor to become both subject and object (both seen from the victim's point of view), which is how pleasure is derived.[84] And there must also be a system of standards or measures to allow the pain to be calculated. Gradations are central here too because 'light and strong' responses are registered by reference to the number of rewards collected by the aggressor. The effective delivery of this type of attack can only be calibrated by way of transferring the master's understanding or 'negative interpretative labour' onto a set of objective coordinates.

In the case of the Jobcentre, the victim's pain was gauged through a points system and targets, which calculated what rewards an advisor and his or her organisation would receive. Airlines, of course, have engaged in the strategy of 'calculated misery' for some years now. One of its key revenue streams is fees from extra-baggage, check-in, failing to check-in online, fast lane boarding and so forth. At the same time, economy class seats have been progressively crammed in, making long haul flights particularly intolerable compared to the 1990s. As Tim Wu points out in his excellent essay on the topic, this degradation of airline travel is designed to encourage us to pay a 'pain avoidance' fee.[85] The airline bureaucrat thus attributes your pain with positive outcomes, much like the sadist who needs to intimately understand the victim's suffering before they can glean any meaningful satisfaction. While 'economy plus' (for seats that used to be 'economy' in the 1980s) sounds inviting, Delta Airways are reportedly moving in the opposite direction, proposing to introduce 'economy minus'.[86] Seats that are barely useable.

Politicians too like to use a bit of sadism. How else can we interpret the announcement by the then Chancellor of the Exchequer (the ultra-austere George Osborne) concerning the government's tax deal with Google. In early 2016, while thousands of working people were frantically filing their income tax returns to avoid late penalties, Osborne announced that he had brokered a great deal with the internet giant. Google were willing to pay £130 million in corporation tax. Effectively a 2 per cent rate for a multibillion dollar firm.[87] The public were not happy at all. Rupert Murdoch even complained that the British people were being ripped off. Given the timing of the 'deal', one has to wonder if it was in part an act of State Sadism, designed to incite a flash of desolate anguish as homo economicus begrudgingly funds her own disenfranchisement via the taxman. One of the most popular books of 2015 was *The Joy of Tax*, an excellent manifesto on how tax is essential for any democratic society.[88] Perhaps the Chancellor of the Exchequer was confused and mixed it up with a famous 1972 book with a very similar title?

Robots of the world ... relax

Under such austere conditions it's understandable why so many turn to technology for answers. While it too has a dark side, its progressive potential for liberating us from our all too human condition and the misery of politics still lingers in the radical imagination. When comedian cum activist Russell Brand was recently asked about the liberating possibilities of technology, he unwittingly touched a nerve: 'yeah, when are all these robots going to get off their fat arses and start doing our work for us so that we can laze around and have more picnics?'.[89] It's a good point.

Shouldn't this dazzling new generation of machines be pulling their own weight by now?

The reason they're not has something to do with the uneasy alliance that automation has formed with employment in the twenty-first century. Therein lies the problem. If we seek to picture a world that is truly liberated from work then we shouldn't dwell too long on the technology side of the equation. But this is precisely what's happening in current thinking. Techno-optimists – proposing ideas such as 'fully automated luxury communism' mentioned above – are vying with a growing number of techno-pessimists who hold a much bleaker view of what lies in store. For example, Oxford University researchers recently released a report suggesting that half of all jobs could be computerised in the near future.[90] A 2017 report by consulting firm PwC similarly predicted that 30 per cent of current jobs will be automated in just the next few years.[91] Innovations like Google's driverless car, for example, will render millions of people unemployed with no new jobs picking up the slack. Jerry Kaplin's *Humans Need Not Apply*, Brynjolfsson and McFee's *Second Machine Age* and Martin Ford's *The Rise of the Robots* predict calamity for everyone who depends on paid employment.[92] We're not just talking about the automation of manual work but skilled occupations that many thought were beyond the reach of robots: doctors, journalists, academics, pilots and scientists.[93]

Both techno-optimists and pessimists tend to fetishise mech-anisation in the era of artificial intelligence (AI) and too hastily proclaim the end of work. As machines imminently threaten to rule the globe, work has not disappeared. On the contrary.[94] Employment figures in the UK and the USA easily demonstrate this. But the jobs that do result tend to be precarious, insecure and underpaid. That's the depressing side of the trend we need to appreciate. Automation might even *deepen* the ideology of work currently gripping our society, not release us from it, fuelling a 'crap jobs' revolution in the USA, Europe and elsewhere.[95]

Take the rise of call centres. They epitomise occupational com-puterisation. It was even predicted back in the 1990s that call centres would completely replace customer service providers of the all-too-human type. But it never happened. There are now 1 million people employed in call centres in the UK and 2.2 million in the USA. The global workforce is huge. The reason why is simple. Customers can't do without a living person on the other end of the phone when they need help to decide if their bank account has been hacked. Needless to say, the pay and conditions are atrocious in this line of work.[96] Another example is airline pilots. The arrival of fly-by-wire and automated flight systems didn't do away with the need to have pilots in the cockpit. Someone's got to be there in case something goes wrong. But the work itself has seen a steady deterioration in pay and conditions, including the introduction of 'pay-to-fly' flexible employment systems where pilots pay for hours when training.[97]

There is another way of looking at it. Let's turn the question around for a moment. Isn't it surprising that more jobs *haven't* been automated given the technological leaps and bounds we have witnessed of late? I think there is a good reason for this. It is now *cheaper* to employ people rather than install/maintain machines in supermarkets, petrol stations and so forth. That tells us how bad the world of work has become. Living, breathing people are undercutting robots. This reliance on labour does not result in the workforce receiving better treatment since what we might call the *sub-automation* movement is made up of hundreds of thousands of workers desperate to earn a wage, however meagre. For example, an Oxfam investigation of employees in the US poultry industry found a workforce languishing in humiliating conditions: 'Workers urinate and defecate while standing on the line; they wear diapers to work; they restrict intake of liquids and fluids to dangerous degrees; they endure pain and discomfort while they worry about their health and job security. And they are in danger of serious health problems.'[98] Cheaper-than-machine labour conditions demonstrate how automation becomes a perverted standard – in terms of cost and maintenance – used to calibrate living labour against, compelling management to find even better ways to beat the machine.

Technological investment in a specific sector can have knock-on effects that encourage work dependency/degradation in other parts of the economy. This is how fully automated ports function. Ports are key relay points in the international logistics network and are heavily protected. In the past, however, teamster unions leveraged this importance to fight big business.[99] Breaking these unions with fully automated ports not only crushes resistance on the dockyards, but also *reverberates its message* throughout the supply chain, which in the USA consists of many thousands of workers dominated by a few large firms.[100] The same applies to fully automated aeroplane loading systems. The wider effects are part of technology's capitalist character and cannot easily be expunged from it once wedded to the ideology of work and inequality.

It is important to note that the 'jobless future' thesis has been around since the dawn of capitalism. Sure, many occupations have certainly vanished because of mechanisation. But steam power didn't end the reliance on living labour and AI probably won't either. What has changed, however, is the way sophisticated technologies are now paving the way for millions of 'crap jobs' to flourish. Even occupations once deemed prestigious are increasingly seen as degrading, stressful and undesirable by those that hold them. Moreover, and at a wider level, even rather mainstream economists suggest the connection between digitalisation and capitalist advancement (using measures like GDP, total factor productivity and economic growth) is not clear-cut. For instance, Robert Gordon compares the impact of the 'digital revolution' to inventions such as washing machines and flushing toilets popularised during the second industrial revolution – in terms of business growth and profitability – and they simply don't compare to those offered by Bill Gates.[101] In this respect, technology is probably not the answer when it comes to envisaging a future that is genuinely free of work. We need to tackle the social relationships behind the deployment of automation. Otherwise, any emancipatory stance that favours full automation risks inadvertently supporting what capitalists have desired all along – escaping their dependency on labour, while tapping the riches of a new generation of impoverished and insecure workers. In the unlikely event that robots did develop AI, they would probably refuse to do the kind of work that millions of humans now must accept to make ends meet.

死亡 ... one last time

Computerized automation is clearly linked to the perpetuation of the work ethic in crisis capitalism. And this normative compulsion to endlessly toil increasingly involves negative consequences for its human carriers. Homo economicus was meant to be the living embodiment of neoclassical theory taken to the utmost limit. It demarks a universal persona that would complement any society regulated entirely by the marketplace. A life calculated on the basis of money and nothing else. Our failure to fully internalise the precepts of homo economicus has probably characterised capitalism right from the start, even back in Adam Smith's day. That failure, however, has become something different under neoliberal capitalism in the post-2007 crisis period. When we speak of economic man, we should stridently resist picturing Wall Street titans and property entrepreneurs in expensive suits. The elite actually enjoy a gentler socialist variant of economic life. No, homo economicus is for everyone else not wealthy enough to fend off a brutal system. And here we get a particularly nasty version of it. Sickness beneficiaries like Dawn Amos who are deemed fit for work. Indebted students such as Toby Thorn who see no way out. Angry, vengeful workers like Rodney Jackson who are fired when the economy tanks.

Homo economicus is now for the losers of late capitalism, a category that has extended deep into the middle classes in only a generation. When coerced to play the game of 'total economics', we must do so against insurmountable odds. The winners have already decamped to the British Virgin Islands and Lana'i, Hawaii. The losers must remain at the table and play ... into oblivion. And you can be sure that when failure does arrive – an unmanageable debt, anxiety caused by overwork, depression – a new breed of capitalists will be ready to jump on your misfortune. They follow a simple business philosophy that is redefining what large-scale commerce means today: profit without risk, capture without producing, capitalism for all but not us.

My point is this. The narrative of homo economics is not just about people making money. Or chasing cash. It's also about those *beaten* by the dollar and crushed by its big government/business representatives. Or even worse, in the *process* of being beaten, a procedure that can last forever. This sense of universality is important. When scholars at the Chicago School of Economics were building their abstract models, homo economicus was intended to be a general principle for life. Every aspect of modern existence could be calculated on a cost/benefit basis. It defined the future. Work, leisure, romantic relationships, family politics had a precise monetary value, potential gains and liabilities. One must choose wisely, even in matters seemingly removed from the realm of commerce. And there's the catch. Once this theorem takes over a living host it cannot be turned off. When things are going well then unending gain is all he or she can see. When they're not, which is more likely, defeat defines one's place in the world absolutely. All perspective is gone. For this reason it's not surprising that between 2007 and 2009 there were 10,000 more suicides than normal in Europe and the USA.[102] As the German philosopher Dietmar Kamper put it, when the horizon disappears what appears is the horizon of disappearance.

Thankfully most do not resort to such drastic measures. Having said that, it's not a world away from how many of us live in the shadows of deep capitalism as it teeters on the edge of extinction. If homo economicus is an impossible ideal applied to the nth degree, it's certainly marked by the quest to endlessly accumulate, just as we would expect with a prototypical entrepreneur. They are never satisfied. For the 99%-ers who do not own the means of production, however, that spirit of gain is inverted into an unconditional, black-and-white universe in which potential loss quietly defines everything he or she does. They're never safe. The alternative to making the mortgage payments on time? Nothing. The car loan payments? Nothing. A possible eviction? Nothing. The same applies to holding down a job and the children's university education. There are no second chances. Failure and demise coincide, which is why the threat of coming death doesn't act as a catalyst for liberation ('you have nothing to lose but your chains') but the exact opposite. Ultimately, this is how an impossible life is lived.

4

The Theatre of Loss ... Work

A few years ago a disturbing story appeared in the media that perfectly summarised what work means for many today: 'Man dies at office desk – nobody notices for five days'. The case was unnerving for one reason mainly. People die all the time, but usually we notice. Are things so bad in the modern workplace that we can no longer tell the difference between the living and the dead? Of course, the story turned out to be a hoax. An urban myth. As it happens, each country has its own variation that still fools people when they periodically appear. In Finland the dead guy is a tax inspector. In the USA a publisher. In other countries a management consultant. We might even embellish the story ourselves. Perhaps the dead accountant not only went unnoticed for five days but was rewarded with a promotion for all the extra hours and loyalty, possibly making vice president. In all variants of the myth the said worker is never a woman, which is interesting for its own reasons.

Isn't it strange that so many of us who encounter this apocryphal story genuinely shrug and mumble 'yeah, that's about right'? Why does it resound so well with our experiences of employment in late capitalist societies today? The most obvious reason for our nonchalance concerning the dead man at his desk pertains to the sheer amount of time that jobs are extracting from our lives at the moment, so much so that people are flirting with death in order to get things done. The dead-man-working narrative reminds us that the otherwise bizarre idea of toiling non-stop for hours or even days on end has quietly become the new normal. Behaviour that our grandparents would have deemed insane is now rather pedestrian. For example, the average British worker spends 36 days a year answering work emails. London workers in particular receive around 9000 emails each year.[1] As a result, work spills over into private time. One recent survey revealed that 80 per cent of employers consider it perfectly acceptable to contact their employees outside business hours.[2] And then there's the commute. Londoners waste 18 months of their lives commuting, which is often expensive and stressful.[3] Overall, this labour intensification, with the aid of mobile technology and new management systems (such as zero-hours contracts), seems to indicate that employers are once again attempting to increase absolute surplus labour by lengthening the working day. For example, a 2015 survey of over 9000 full-time employees from around the world found that few office workers consider the 40-hour work week realistic when it comes to getting their jobs done effectively.[4] Indeed, almost 40 per cent said they had experienced an increase in working hours over the last five years. One third of respondents felt their work/life balance was in serious jeopardy.

The tragedy of human effort

For this reason, paid employment is reflected or echoed in almost everything we do in the present economic paradigm. The obsession runs deep like some unshakable addiction. We genuinely live in a workers' society, and homo economicus has been shaped into an all-too-human vessel to carry its message. The compulsion to work is no longer only contained to office hours. It has seeped into everything else, restructuring our everyday imagination, how we perceive our future and past. Even our sex lives increasingly revolve around jobs given that so many of find long-term romantic partners in the workplace. Along with gender roles and class, work is one of the few ideological memes that are ready waiting for their occupants before they're born. As the French Marxist Louis Althusser pointed out in his essay on the ideological state apparatuses, this is what makes the 'interpellation' process (his name for a particular kind of capitalist indoctrination) so effective. Inside its workings we're mysteriously 'always already' an active ideological product.[5] Every 'before' is but a retroactive reading of the present in an endless recursive curve that ultimately weaves the individual's attachment to his or her cultural environment, much of which is fairly negative but nevertheless powerful. This might sound like tautological reasoning, but it is actually a way of avoiding self-referentiality when it comes to explaining how we are 'made up' by a system that has no outside.

Work probably inhabits this symbolic circle so defiantly because we are constantly told that so much relies upon it. Biological survival. Happiness. Security for you and your family. Perhaps this is why the most fervent agents of preparing the 'not even born' for a life of writing emails are parents. One recent report revealed the emergence of so-called nursery consultants who're hired by mum and dad to train toddlers, imbuing them with social skills that will increase their chances of landing a good job.[6] The disciplinary forces of a cut-throat labour market have entered the crib, it would seem ... along with its prejudices concerning the meaning of life and society.

This cultural fixation with work comes at a cost, of course, which is why the dead man slouched over his keypad seems so apt for capturing the realities of the high-performance work ethic, personified by the individualistic, self-reliant and driven office worker who is now quite unwell. Job-related illness is a growing epidemic in the UK and USA, exacerbated by stress and an overwhelming 'to do' list that never ends. Making matters worse, in times of recession we are more willing to put up with horrible workplace environments, which only adds to the pent-up frustration. According to some research, job burnout is just as bad for your health as chain smoking. Even the long hours sitting at a desk has been blamed on serious illnesses. Sitting is now considered the new smoking.[7]

Only in this warped context would we ever hear about people being 'worked to death' in the corporate sector. In China, for example, death from overwork or guò láo sǐ (their version of Karoshi) has become a serious public policy problem. According to the *China Youth Daily*, around 600,000 Chinese die each year from working too much.[8] Many of these employees do literally die sitting at their desks. It is also interesting to note that much of this deadly excess labour is facilitated by the use of mobile technologies. As mentioned earlier, this has become a massive problem in Western economies as well. It's tempting to suggest that only neoliberal capitalism (in either its faux democratic or communistic variations) could subvert the clever labour-saving possibilities of an invention like email and use it to extend the working day ad infinitum. Let's face it. The tyranny of office email is now so out of control that even the multinational corporation is starting to have second thoughts about its utility. Some French companies, for example, have discouraged its employees from logging on after office hours.[9] In a similar vein, a number of German firms automatically erase incoming emails when an employee is away on holiday.[10] And for good reason. Those last few days of vacation are often ruined by dark thoughts of the overflowing inbox awaiting us on our first day back. Capitalism understands its own contradictions here only too well. The human body's inability to fulfil the glorified ideal of homo economicus without getting sick or making errors undermines the extraction of surplus value. Hence, employers try to temper the 24-hour work ethic unleashed by neoliberal capitalism, a task it struggles with. The 2013 death of Bank of America intern, Moritz Erhardt, testifies to this – he died after working 72 straight hours, which caused a major scandal in London. In fact, capitalism is now taking the task of managing its own self-destructive tendencies seriously. Matsuri Takahashi, a young graduate recruit at the large advertising firm Dentsu, committed suicide after clocking up 105 hours of overtime in a month.[11] Dentsu's president –Tadashi Ishii – took full responsibility and resigned, stating that despite the attempt to tame the punishing culture of overwork in the company the problem was still rife.

Corpse culture

But the 'Man died at desk and nobody noticed' urban legend strikes a chord for another and more depressing reason. Yes, the office should have noticed the man was dead. Five days is a long time. But they also should have noticed that his work wasn't getting done. Nobody did, of course. For that isn't how the modern workplace functions today. Take those 36 days spent on email mentioned earlier. It would simply be impossible to fill every minute of that time with only productive work. The same goes for the long hours put in at the office. Apart from getting the actual task done, which is usually completed in short bursts, there is also a good deal of messing about, chatting, paying the bills, surfing the net, daydreaming and waiting for the day to finish. Most importantly, it is not that we're doing nothing or even doing things unrelated to work (although there might be much of that). No, this frenetic behaviour is more about *busy looking busy*. This is why contemporary employment has something of a ceremonial feel about it, becoming a sort of theatre or spectacle. Not only are we working more now than ever (or searching for it if unemployed) but a good deal of it is unnecessary. We are obliged to *appear* like a worker as much as actually be one, whether we're sweating in a business for nothing (as part of the UK government's 'back to work' programme) or employed in high finance. The research seems to bear out this observation. A study of management consultants in the USA found that 35 per cent employed in this occupation actually 'faked' an 80-hour workweek.[12] For various reasons these individuals *pretended* to sacrifice themselves at the altar of work. They still got everything done. In this respect, perhaps entire occupations might be considered phoney, something David Graeber recently called 'bullshit jobs'.[13] Pointless security guards, 'atmosphere coordinators' (people hired to create a party vibe in bars) and chief learning officers in the corporate world might be classified as such.

Weirdly, the ritual of work is no more observable than among those who *don't* have a job. The irony is indicative of how the template of employment affects almost every facet of life today. Studies of unemployment reveal the sheer labour expended by those seeking a job. In her ethnographic investigation of laid off IT workers in Texas, Carrie Lane describes how these ex-employees continue to act like a quintessential worker, such as displaying leadership skills in their self-help group and replicating all of the trappings of office life in and around the home.[14] These individuals were condemned as 'dead wood' by their firms following the economic downturn, but still maintain an attitude of easy-going confidence, knowing that nobody will hire a disgruntled ex-worker. So they work hard to keep up an appropriate appearance. Lane explains this strange play acting:

> Tech job seekers often said that looking for a new job was their new job. They also said it was the hardest job they ever had ... unemployed white-collar workers created a system of looking for work that shared the form if not the function of professional employment. To this end job-seekers tried to recreate in their unemployment the rhythms of the office.[15]

Here the ceremony of employment is often identical to that of the employed with the exception of the salary, something that studies of unemployment in the UK have also demonstrated.[16] For good reason, we tend to believe that most unemployed people are fairly critical of what has been befallen them, which is often the case.[17] But Lane noticed a significant shift among the ex-workers she spoke with. It appeared that their adherence to the simulacrum of work (acting like a worker) had mysteriously generated a particular political stance towards corporate power which was very different to the views held by workers laid off in the 1970s and 1980s. Unlike previous generations who considered themselves victims of uncaring capitalism and its ruthless cost-cutting creed despite the loyal service provided by the workforce, the people Lane met with were ardent supporters of their own abandonment. In fact, she was shocked by the degree to which they'd internalised the capitalist ethos. These fired workers saw their uselessness in the same manner that the accountants and HR managers who had fired them did:

> when they discuss their lives, layoffs, and careers. And when they articulate their expectations of their employers, families and future, these job seekers expressed a decidedly neoliberal set of values and beliefs ... they believe in the efficacy and justness of the free market; they favor individual responsibility over collective action and support globalisation even when their own jobs head offshore.[18]

Lane sadly labels these individuals a 'company of one'. They believe that their fortunes mimic the logic of the marketplace completely, an existence that is nothing more than a loyal reflection of periodic economic highs and lows. The ceremony of work in the absence of actual work inadvertently transformed these abandoned ex-employees into ultra-orthodox believers of the power structure they were crushed by. This is a significant shift. Not only is the culture of unemployment highly politicised in neoliberal societies (there is something profoundly wrong with you if you're classified as such) but there is also an ideological component to the empty ritual itself. But what exactly?

High-performance idleness

We need to return to the office and the paid workforce to more carefully scrutinise this question concerning work and ideology. That is to say, work's present tendency to signify more than just the economic utility of the job itself. The ritualism of the modern labour process is perfectly depicted in David Bolchover's *The Living Dead*, an account of office life in London.[19] The author was employed for many years in an insurance firm and forged a successful career in this and related industries. He quickly realised, however, that in terms of substantive work outputs he was hardly doing anything. Sure, walking around the building with papers and attending meetings took effort. But didn't actually achieve much. To make matters worse, Bolchover surmised that many of his co-workers weren't doing much either. He then arrived at a scary conclusion. If Bolchover didn't come into the office tomorrow it probably wouldn't make much difference to productivity outputs. He wondered how long he could remain absent from the office or work email without being noticed. So the next day Bolchover simply stayed in bed. And the next day. Cheap wine, football and a three-day growth? The pay check still arrived each month. He claims it took ten months before anybody noticed and began to einquire about his whereabouts.

The account tells us that jobs and work have somehow drifted far away from the principles of utility. It is now a mistake to think of employment as strictly related to biological necessity – as if sending useless emails all day is akin to hunting and gathering. In the wreckage economies of the Western world (and beyond) work has assumed the form of a self-referential rite. As long as the visible cues and triggers are respected (and for Bolchover this was not even necessary given his absence), the organisation runs smoothly. Such 'empty labour' occurs in both high paid and more menial work simply because the optimal point of productivity no longer maps onto the job itself.[20] Its rule over our lives in capitalist culture is thus even more perplexing in this respect. In the meantime, we must find ways to fill those long, empty hours.

According to Bolchover, for example, around 40 per cent of casual drug users get their fix during office hours. We often think of pornography use as something far removed from work – especially given the notable cases of termination that periodically appear in the media. However, it turns out that 70 per cent of internet pornography sites are accessed when people are supposed to be working. One in five workers in the USA have had sex on company time. Sex, drugs, alcohol and simply surfing the internet (Bolchover hardly ever mentions productive (non-work) activities such as writing a political manifesto, for some reason) are not the reasons why the typical working day is increasing (in order to get everything done despite the distractions), *but the opposite*. The doctrine of being in the office all day is so embedded, yet unnecessary and obsolete, we need to do something in order to kill the time until we can finally come home. It is perhaps for this reason why Ivor Southwood claims that his experiences of being both unemployed and employed weren't miles apart:

> from the responsibilities of the Jobcentre customer to the self-marketing duties of the unpaid intern, from the agency worker on permanent standby to the Virtual Assistant in search of virtual clients. The distinction between employment and unemployment seems increasingly arbitrary. While their form differences are maintained by a border-patrolling bureaucracy, in terms of (lack of) content they are approaching a point of convergence. The new privatised version of unemployment is its own job description, person specification and disciplinary framework ... and under the conditions of precarity and short-term insecurity, this work never ends.[21]

Porn for office workers

The phrase 'killing time' is here very apt since Bolchover describes the experience of all this needless labour as something like a living death:

> you don't hear about these people because who wants to boast they don't do anything at work? Their working lives are mindlessly boring, utterly pointless, and without meaning, their abilities are utterly wasted. Their home lives might be happy and

fulfilled but at work they are the people that time forgot. They contribute nothing. They are the Living Dead.[22]

But here is my point. Don't we now have two contradictory accounts of employment in neoliberal society? The first one highlights the massive intensification of labour and marathon-like stints we're expected to put in at the office. This is characterised by stressed out individuals in a constant state of anxiety since the 'to do' list is practically infinite. They drop dead of heart failure in their small cubicles. The second narrative tells us that the opposite might be true. Most employees don't actually do a great deal at work and might even feign stress to keep the boss happy. As jobs become ultra-ritualised it's the hours people put in at the office (or online) that is seen as the 'output' rather than the concrete results those hours achieve, which are frequently negligible. From this perspective, individuals are victims not of unrelenting pressure or lack of time. On the contrary. Their hurt derives from too much vacant time. They're bored to death.

How can we explain the contradiction between these two opposing accounts? Perhaps it is a quantitative issue. X number of jobs are prone to genuine overwork whereas others naturally gravitate towards ritualisation. No, I think something else is happening here. The trouble with the empty labour thesis is that when it portrays jobs as a type of theatre it assumes they're easier and less troubled than real work. After all, being 'zoned out' (to use Bolchover's phrase), watching porn all day does sound rather untaxing. I would argue that, although work might entail a lot of acting, much of it is *deep acting*, whereby the script is followed very closely, almost too closely. And that can make jobs very onerous indeed. Moreover, the conceptual dualism between remunerated inactivity in the office (e.g., 'empty labour' or 'bullshit jobs') and properly active work is a false one. It assumes that real work involves people using every minute in a productive manner. It's a view that is ironically shared by advocates of zero-hour contracts who insist that employees be paid only for the exact work they do (measured down to the minute). We know that's simply a way of transferring the costs of all the background labour that every single job requires onto the individual employee themselves.

So, rather than the theatre of labour being a proxy for 'zoning out' and relaxing doing nothing, perhaps it's the other way around. The act itself (including the face-work deployed to cover up the gaping void at the heart of the modern labour process) is what takes its toll on the health and wellbeing of the workforce. Not a holiday at the office but some kind of grinding hell. In this sense, then, there would be little contradiction between deadly forms of overwork and hours, weeks and years spent pretending to work hard in a role that is basically useless. If that is true, then it makes the situation more lugubrious than we thought. Work is not only ceremonial, something to be performed and observed within a power hierarchy, but the ritual is one that signifies a stressful waste of potential. Beautiful human faculties totally unused but still observable in the shadow form they take of acute anxiety, high blood pressure and an early death, all caused by doing fuck all rather than something meaningful. In this respect, the theatre of labour takes on sadomasochistic or even pornographic elements since the open display of that erased potential is routinely celebrated by the power hierarchy as people arduously strive towards needless expenditure. Organisations congratulate those who are able to master this melding of economic pointlessness and existential sacrifice. It may even provide pleasure for both the observer (power) and the observed (worker) alike as homo economicus finally expires in a garish open-plan office.

Pretend or else!

A thorough critique of work is an important component of any progressive, post-capitalist politics. To refuse work is to reject the myth that organised employment simply derives from a seamless, one-to-one relationship with biological self-preservation. David Graeber ('bullshit jobs') and Roland Paulsen ('empty labour') are right to decry the frenetic dormancy of modern work. It's a sign that something is very wrong about our society's sheer obsession with an activity that could be radically reduced easily. We could all be doing something much more interesting and worthwhile with our time, making love, meeting friends, inventing new technologies, anything but sitting in an office staring at a screen all day. However, it's worth noting that this decidedly left-wing observation has in part been seized upon by neoconservative observers too. This is why we must treat the argument with some caution. For example, in their discussion of Roland Paulsen's book about empty labour, *The Economist* quickly overlooks the author's condemnation of neoliberal capitalism and instead triumphantly confirms the managerial suspicion that workers are really a lazy lot: 'policymakers bemoan the epidemic of overwork. But as [Paulsen] explains ... innumerable studies suggest that the average worker devotes between one-and-a-half and three hours a day loafing'.[23] The reviewer concludes that most employees are skiving off far too much and we should quit complaining about labour intensification. A similar sentiment can be detected in Bolchover's account of the living dead:

> we are living in an era of workplace stress ... the increasing competitiveness of the modern economy has rendered people slaves to their workplaces ... but the truth for many millions is different. They go into a large office somewhere in the world every week day, they go to their desk at the same time, they leave the same time. And in between they do pretty much nothing. Zilch. The big Zero.[24]

Bolchover was recently asked in a radio interview why this is a problem. Sure, the modern office might be a veritable dead sea of activity, but at least people have jobs, spend money – so who cares? His response effortlessly slipped into an apologia for the capitalist work ethic. Yes, he said, it's very nice for the workers but the shareholders who pay their wages wouldn't be too happy about all this slacking off.[25] In a similar fashion, it is easy to imagine some sadistic technocrat coming across the 'bullshit jobs' argument, nodding with approval as she or he sizes up the next round of jobs to be axed from the National Health Service. Demythologising work clearly requires a degree of circumspection in order to avoid these implicit points of sympathy with right-wing nonsense. The critique of ceremonial labour – and it certainly deserves a good deal of criticism – can silently posit a highly misleading 'zero-hours contract' vision of what properly productive jobs look like. And in doing so the ideology of work strengthens its hold over us once again.

Post-utility society

Why do we work? The obvious answer is 'to live'. But it's not our actual job – giving a lecture, selling a car, nursing a patient or flying a passenger jet – that directly secures our life conditions. For sure, as we have already demonstrated, most occupations in the West have drifted far away from the baseline of biological survival, which is partly down to the massive division of labour that has arisen in the post-industrial era. But this disconnect between labour and subsistence is also related to the main medium in which inhabitants of any capitalist society must communicate. Our specific job grants us access to manmade vouchers we call *money*. We then redeem these so we can then purchase life. How many vouchers we obtain and what we have to do to get them is the political question par excellence in our society and its highly skewed class relations. But it's this fissure and complex mediation between labour (as an organic/social necessity) versus work (as a cultural artefact) that has been behind employment taking on a life of its own, spiralling out of control, absorbing everything else.

Of course, none of this is to say that there are not real jobs where people do real things with concrete outcomes. Cleaners, scientists, airline pilots, surgeons, publishers, farmers and factory workers around the world clearly attest to this. And let's face it, things need to get done. But when framed within a purely self-referential economic paradigm (growth for growth's sake, profit for profit's sake, etc.) work is decoupled from the original purpose of labour, which ought to be about securing our collective needs so that we can do other things, like relaxing, art, inventing, thinking or whatever. Instead, jobs have been separated from the life of the community and transformed into crude political artefacts, even jobs that really matter such as brain surgeons and midwives. They remain eminently useful ... but sadly that is no longer the point. Ironically, it is only in this *secondary* role (disconnected from the universal principle of survival) that work is able to colonise all of society, becoming the be-all and end-all of modern existence as such. Now anchorless and severed from nature, work assumes the role of a weird manmade universal, and painfully so.

Why has work morphed into this mass ceremonial function under neoliberal capitalism? No doubt 'useless labour' is probably a feature of any social system, capitalist or otherwise. A degree of slack or spare capacity is inevitable in most human organisations given the lag between structure and need (or what economists call 'stickiness'), which hardly ever finds perfect symmetry. But only with the advent of neoliberal capitalism does this ritualised excess appear to be killing homo economicus off in such a determined fashion. When addressing the link between work and excess it is tempting to blame grand narrative causes, such as the runaway immoderations of modernity (e.g., too much bureaucracy) or humanity's collective insanity (e.g., a work ethic gone mad). But the source is much more modest and closer to home. Work today is simply an ideology, designed to lock in a particular class relationship and naturalise the private ownership of the means of production. It does this by falsely evoking the ruse of physiognomic necessity: if we work in order to *live*, then only a fool would argue against the need to build society around jobs.

The unemployment industry

At this juncture, it is essential to consider the role of the state if we are to fully understand the strange and immense theatre of labour that is preoccupying societies around the world today. Take the perspective of someone employed under exploitative and precarious conditions in the City of London right now. With the rising tide of unemployment threatening job security, we can easily see how this enormous display function might provide a shelter to people especially vulnerable to neoliberal rationalisation. For example, I recently had a conversation with a woman who has struggled to find employment in the media industry. She told me that her current part-time job paradoxically allows her (and many others in a similar position) to escape *real work*, which she defined as the gruelling ordeal of justifying oneself before the punitive gaze of an unforgiving state apparatus.

To me the sentiment seemed counter-intuitive since work is supposed to be the epicentre of class exploitation and control in capitalist societies, not a space of escape. But I started to see her point. Many jobs are indefensible under crisis capitalism – often pointless, commonly soul destroying and sometimes dangerous to the social good. However, for the 99.9 per cent who do not own the means of production, jobs provide *cover* or an alibi to evade the egregious harassment of the neoliberal state complex, job centres, domestic chaos caused by poverty and the capitalist marketplace more generally. According to microeconomists, work organisations are a frustrating 'exception' to the marketplace because the *potential* to work – and thus its pricing signal – is completely removed from the market system once employed. Hence, their mission to crack open and expose this so-called organisational 'black box' to market forces via contracting, zero-hours contracts, self-employment and so forth. In this context our job might be superfluous and sometimes unpleasant but it provides a useful cover story to keep the authorities at bay.

This weird 'job as alibi' attitude is particularly evident among young interns, whose free labour within the present economy is nothing but a scandal. When I ask them about what they get out of working for a magazine company or media firm the answer is fairly straightforward. Useful industry experience? No, they mostly do photocopying. Networking opportunities? No, they're told to keep away from important clients. A path to a full-time job with the firm? No, most expect to be let go after six months to make room for the next intern. So what? *Protection*. Mainly from the state and an ugly labour market. Sure, they are broke, living with their parents or worse. But the placement at least buys some time before they enter the government-run (and increasingly privatised) misery called the *unemployment industry*, an important faux economy in its own right given how it keeps so many technocrats employed in empty jobs. In short, interns are left alone, perhaps the trademark desire of the twenty-first century workforce. The problem is no one in this environment is left alone for very long.

Marx at KFC

It would be curious if *The Economist* review mentioned above was right all along, that bullshit jobs, pointless bureaucracy and empty labour turned out to be a secret kind of work refusal movement designed to undermine capitalist rationality. This would resonate with a dodgy idea that G.W.F. Hegel developed in *The Science of Logic* when he argued,

> we must get over the distorted idea that the system has to be represented as if thoroughly false and as if the true system stood to the false as only opposed to it. By contrast, effective refutation must infiltrate the opponent's strong hold and meet him on his own ground. There is no point of attacking him outside his own territory and claiming jurisdiction where there is not.[26]

In other words, one must accept the terms of power in order to counteract it. The protestor ought to genuinely enter the territory of his or her own domination, perhaps making themselves at home for a bit, before fighting the system that keeps them down. What a joke this seems today. But even more so when we return to the gritty world of work and employment. Using 'a job' to escape the despotism of the unemployment office and a hostile marketplace is not too rebellious given how the neoliberal state is *in favour* of such behaviour. In fact, it actively encourages it. This is why it threatens (and sometimes taunts) the working multitude with the prospect of joining the reserve army of the jobless, perhaps our very own version of the gulag.

I remember my final visit to the unemployment office in Dunedin, New Zealand. This was in 1991, after I'd left high school and was trying to figure out what to do. The dole kicked in automatically back then and being from a working-class background my prospects weren't wonderful. Right-wing governments had been in power since 1984 and inequality was growing fast. So a steady income was important, no matter how meagre. But I knew something bad was about to happen when the unemployment office called me in for a 'client-update' meeting. It was scheduled for 8.30 am Monday. A no-show would immediately end my only source of income. That's why I took a battered copy of *Surveys from Exile* that my mother had given me a year earlier.[27] Thomas Kuhn's book on scientific revolutions was in the same wrapped present, but that wouldn't provide the kind of protection I needed for the coming encounter.

While carefully reading for an hour or so in the waiting room I was rudely interrupted by an angry, white, middle-aged man with bad teeth and a snarling smile. He marched me to a small grey cubicle that overlooked a vast floor of bureaucrats. Some had tattoos, even looked cool. But all were diligently processing unemployment forms. 'Where do you want to work, boy!!!', the man violently spat at me. 'Nowhere', I politely replied. Ah, rebellious youth … if only I was still so brave. A large blood vessel appeared on the man's temple and his face turned purple. 'What??!!!', he barked. 'KFC', I quickly responded. The squat bureaucrat suddenly backed off and stared at the floor. 'Good', he muttered and walked away. I remember slowly raising my eyes over his desk and stared at all the other technocrats. My mood suddenly lightened when I recognised some old high school friends who were buried in paperwork at their desks. They didn't respond when I waved to them. Then I decided to leave too.

Negative surplus value

The incident ought to have been forgotten. But it stuck with me. Work. Why on earth did it make people so angry? And why did there have to be so much danger attached to not having it? What exactly did I see that day? All employment agencies understand the importance of *danger*. It's not quite the same as fear but the two psychological states certainly intersect in the imagined communities forged during the 1990s as unbridled market liberalism was consolidated. That's why today's economic social architecture is so closely aligned with the near suicidal 'culture of danger' that Michel Foucault guessed was at the heart of the movement.[28] That has become the ultimate ethos of employment agencies today and their zealous attachment to the performance of work. So why is the capitalist state so amenable to this pointless ritualisation of work if much of it has little economic worth?

In addressing this question we really go to the heart of understanding the theatre of labour and its complex interrelationships with governance, capital and the workforce. One of the key roles of the neoliberal governmental apparatus today is to provide support, financial incentives and tax breaks to industry in order to keep people employed, even when they're unnecessary or a cost to the firm. A deal is made. Capitalist industry will employ people above and beyond the requirements of production if the state pays for the luxury. Hence, the vast subsidies to businesses via housing benefits, food stamps and all of the other forms of indirect corporate welfare we see in wreckage economies presently.

It is clear that capitalism simply no longer requires all these jobs. Indeed, following the financial crisis around 7 million people were left unemployed as a direct result.[29] Joblessness in the global economy grew massively too. According to 2011 estimates, the global reserve army stood at 2.4 billion people, compared to 1.4 billion actively employed.[30] Macroeconomic management in Western economies obviously use unemployment to regulate wages and inflation, appeasing the business class without knocking the wider confidence of the general public. But in terms of the equally prevalent trend of *overemployment* it is evident that the state is bribing industry to create jobs that really don't matter.

Hence, the major shift in the way governmental officials represent work, seeking to hide the true extent of unemployment by manipulating the figures. For example, reducing the 'workforce participation rate' or increasing the 'economically inactive' percentage (literally shifting people from one box to another) can give a very misleading picture of the actual number of jobs in an economy. Most worryingly, the very meaning of a job changes from a discernible *input* (where we collectively decide how and where our efforts are directed) to a characterless *output*, jobs that are nothing more than a forgettable number on a spreadsheet. We see this change in perspective when politicians and business leaders celebrate a (minor) drop in unemployment or a rise in self-employment. The *number* of jobs is all that matters, not their quality or social purpose. This is why so many of them being produced are so lousy, as we noted in previous chapters. Conditions are so poor that even robots wouldn't want to do them. Approaching employment as a quantifiable figure diverts attention away from the travesty that has befallen work today following years of deskilling, eroding pay and conditions, unfair part-time contracts, blind managerialism and so forth. Numbers intrinsically hide the reality, even when they are bad or unfavourable numbers. That's what they are for. No wonder why so many people find their job utterly meaningless.[31]

Militarising the soul

Overwork – the material and mechanical repetition of the industrious mind and body – is usually associated with the infamous work ethic. That is, the moral valorisation of intense effort. Max Weber's insights about capitalism in his essay on the subject was wonderfully ironic in how it presented a spiritual basis to what we until then believed was purely concrete.[32] Is it this, the Protestant-based work ethic, that is behind the unusual attachment to labour that we see defining ultra-capitalist societies so resolutely today? It depends on how we conceptualise it. From the inception of industrial capitalism the traditional work ethic was sold to us as a quasi-religious chance for salvation, an escape from the iniquities of human indolence. In pointless work we find freedom from the wayward proclivities of the undisciplined body. The idea was important because deeply private commercial activity could finally be allied with the otherwise collective doctrine of redemption. In this respect, *bios* (i.e., being for life as such) and toil (i.e., being against the living body) intersect to form a logical equilibrium under the auspices of factory production. The two poles of self-expression and denial could at last coexist in this strange no-man's-land of human effort, central to any society built around ultra-regimented employment practices. The pundits of economic liberalism could once and for all proclaim that suffering really does purify our souls.

In Western economies this novel conjunction discovers its golden median in times of war, of course, transforming the work ethic into something peculiar. The two world wars were *internally* oriented socio-economic systems as much as external geopolitical ones. Amidst large-scale and even apocalyptic conflict, the performative surfeit of labour literally shelters the social body and its organic faculties. In that milieu, work is seen to preserve life and therefore assumes a significant role within the militarised ensemble of institutional forms that is still evident. I use the word surfeit here for an important reason. The old biological validation of the labour process (we must work to survive) now implies an excess, seeing in work not only ontological survival but existential persistence as well (we work to prevail and win). Henceforth, employment takes on qualities that reflect how society must be defended *as a whole*. This is why labour comes to prefigure all other spheres such as childhood, education, religion and so forth. Industrialised mass slaughter in the first part of the twentieth century strangely gave the work ethic a turbo boost, and helped manifest the 'culture of danger' that continues to define neoliberal economic policy today and its never-ending war against terror. But an important change occurs here. The work ethic mutates into something entirely different, much darker, compared to previous eras. It used to help fill in or suture over the emptiness of human vulnerability (an attack) and help a community imagine itself in positive terms. Now, however, salvation and redemption comes to those who submit to work not because it makes them whole again but allows people to see past themselves, to retroactively perceive *the void* they always were, while simultaneously keeping that nothingness at bay through hard labour. This foregrounding of the disposable nothingness we already were is an inadvertent consequence of blending the ethos of war with the everyday convention of work.

The organic excuse for employment (physical survival), in this sense, almost becomes a distraction from this other existential register and its secret martial law. Max Weber's analysis of the Protestant ethic and its focus on a 'calling' inevitably misses this blend of faith and demise. For us today, work is no longer a vehicle for divine redemption. And it certainly does not save us. It merely forms the space in which existence can be judged by an immense absence or the void concerning the worthlessness of one's sacrifice. It puts the individual on the spot and summons a defence ... even though the death sentence has long since been handed down. Ultra-rationalised labour allows one to enter the gaze of justification in this manner. The judgement has already (and perhaps always) been passed, but is only announced once the human body has been declared post-factum an expendable asset to the cause. Here the aggressiveness of the law (mainly through state sanctions) organises labour to form a *workforce*. That the word has heavy martial connotations is no coincidence. Moreover, we can still see the effects of this death impulse today when people act in such an extreme manner in relation to their jobs, casting it in 'life and death', all or nothing terms. This we might term the moral militarisation of the soul.

Arbeit macht frei

This morose dimension of the neoliberal work ethic, derived from a war climate, is most evident when we see homo economicus struggling to reconcile the life preserving qualities of labour (being for life) and the echo of expiration (being against life) that it now so clearly represents. The connection is not new. Some very well-known institutions have intentionally exploited the secret synergies between work and existential negation. For example, it was this symbiosis that the Nazis used to remind their intended victims as they entered the death camps during one of the darkest chapters of the twentieth century. *Arbeit macht frei* ('work sets you free') shouldn't really make sense in this climate of mass murder. Perhaps the Nazis positioned the slogan at the entrance of an unjust death in order to taunt prisoners or dupe them into thinking that a gentler fate awaited them. This might be true. But we also know that there was a serious philosophical idea being expressed here too, an attempt to link work with the notion of authentic self-release. This makes it even worse than sadistic toying or dissemblance because the tone of *sincerity* gives the message a much more diabolical tone. It is tempting to wonder whether these administrators of death genuinely believed in some mystical interconnection between work and death, like some ancient pagan festival gone awry. As one commentator argues in relation to the decision by camp commandant Rudolf Höss to use '*Arbeit macht frei*' at the gates of Auschwitz:

> He seems not to have intended it as a mockery, nor even to have intended it literally, as a false promise that those who worked to exhaustion would eventually be released, but rather as a kind of mystical declaration that self-sacrifice in the form of endless labour does in itself bring a kind of spiritual freedom.[33]

This candour, however, is not so straightforward. The death principle underlying this vision of work frames it as both faithfully part of the divine order of things *and* understood to be arbitrary and purely manmade. Necessary but also (somewhat perversely) the result of chance and caprice. This is no paradox, since the two poles (an inevitable death through overwork that is yet totally avoidable) feed off and reinforce each other. Only when someone's victimhood is understood as manufactured can the higher destiny of the sacrifice be enjoyed by the sadist. This truly takes the *Arbeit macht frei* motif into the realm of horror, which of course, no simple psychology could ever grasp. Only in this atmosphere could it be pointed out that the Nazis perfected an attitude of deliberative evil whereby 'murders are committed like schoolboy pranks'.[34]

Cash collapse

There is something of this horror show in the culture of work today, which has infected the social unconscious so pervasively. The 'being for life' component of the traditional work ethic has not only been turned upon itself (a negation, being against life) but *past* itself, seeing strength and justification in its impending non-presence. In this respect, it is no coincidence that some accuse the neoliberal polity for being fascist.[35] The emphasis on sovereign purity, authoritarian brawn and an 'all of nothing' economic credo has bled into the fabric of the social body. For sure, the camps are back in Europe. It's not difficult to understand why some philosophers see in 'the camp' an ideal metaphor for understanding what society feels like for so many today.[36] Camps of the modern kind are designed to contain and concentrate work. They are a prolonged terminus. If we blend this nihilistic penchant for the void that our camp society inspires with the money-fication of the ensuing misery, we get something we might call *cashism* or the fascism of money.

This development is not particularly new. Back in 1944 US vice president Henry Wallace referred to this as 'American Fascism' in an article for the *New York Times*.[37] He wrote, 'A fascist is one whose lust for money or power is combined with such an intensity of intolerance toward those of other races, parties, classes, religions, cultures, regions or nations as to make him ruthless in his use of deceit or violence to attain his ends.'[38] We can see these traits everywhere today in Western capitalist economies. Money becomes a very useful precipitator or connector to more regressive political viewpoints that ought to have little or no place in a civilised society, of course. Once again the neoliberal economists and policy pundits get it completely wrong. They thought that building a society around money – and finance in particular – would strip extreme politics out of the social order since unlike demagoguery, money is meant to be somehow neutral. A technocratic exercise organised by dispassionate experts. Central banks in the USA and UK were especially susceptible to the conceit.[39] How wrong can you be? As philosophers of the Frankfurt School understood back in the heyday of European fascism, an overcharged economic discourse was crucial to the advancement of the fascist mentality.

Once again we're not that far away from the sick meaning underlying *Arbeit macht frei*. The 'dollar chasing animal' is still meant to look as if it's affirming *bios* (or life). But he is constantly pulled towards the unlit star of *thanatos*, the dark spectacle of an individual's own absence and release. Being held to account against an impossible ideal sees *bios* collapse into the negation it never was, the retroactivity we mentioned above. This allows it to use the language of self-preservation (e.g., working hard to support a family) to open up a new space that flirts with the limits of existence. The modern office finds pride in such extremism. For example, here's a leaked message from a manager at Barclay's Global Power and Utilities Group, presented to new summer interns in 2015, students who counted themselves very lucky to have landed a placement with a major financial institution. Note the expectant sacrifice conveyed in the memo and the near ecclesiastical phraseology. It is clear that the recipients are supposed to interpret office life as an all or nothing situation:

I wanted to introduce you to the 10 Power Commandments ... For nine weeks you will live and die by these ... We expect you to be the last ones to leave every night, no matter what ... I recommend bringing a pillow to the office. It makes sleeping under your desk a lot more comfortable ... the internship really is a nine-week commitment at the desk ... an intern asked our staffer for a weekend off for a family reunion – he was told he could go. He was also asked to hand in his BlackBerry and pack up his desk ... Play time is over and it's time to buckle up.[40]

One can imagine a boot camp for enlisted soldiers being readied for war receiving similarly worded decrees. While economic man has probably always represented an existence that negates its own viability, making the association with death inevitable, it's only in this post-2008 capitalist restoration period that we see the idea displayed so openly. Work is the perfect vehicle for conveying the 'culture of danger' that is so central in the neoliberal age, making it difficult to see what about you is not related to your job. This is how the work ethic functions today. Occupational roles are detached from their basis in productive utility and work becomes the wandering reference point for everything else. Not a concrete activity but an abstract and diffuse prism through which all of life is myopically evaluated and managed. Overwork is an obvious outcome. So is the way political questions are now so violently reduced to the topic of employment, which almost always yields deeply conservative conclusions. Should we welcome refugees and asylum seekers? No, they'll steal our jobs. How can we tackle gender inequality? More female CEOs. What is the leading cause of depression and suicide? Joblessness. Want to make America great again? More work. What is the objective of your government? Get Britain working. And the list goes on.

Less than zero ... a general theory of wages

Economists are amusing in this way. They're similar to the medieval mystics who fully understood that, for example, a solar eclipse was caused by the laws of nature (the objective truth), but were still convinced it signalled an omen for the state of man.[41] The same goes for dry economic formulae and labour market models. The patent truth (they have little basis in the real world) never disconfirms the economist's belief in the veracity of the model. The mind-set is strangely immunised to its own mendacity. The fiction of pure capitalism continues to inform their worldview, born from the overly abstract nature of the theorizing involved, which is entirely at odds with how wreckage economies now work in reality: poverty, cartels, governmental collusion with the corporate elite and so forth. In the meantime, homo economicus impossibilis struggles between the unreal fantasy that now structures the world (e.g., labour market policy) and the *unreal reality* that emerges when economic theology tries to make its madness real. Perhaps this is the proper meaning of what Mark Fisher calls capitalist realism: not some unadulterated business logic that steals reality but rather the imposition of an insanely unreal universe that everyone except the ultra-rich must confront and navigate.

The ongoing death of homo economics is everywhere in microeconomics today. When it focuses on the individual utility-maximiser (the microeconomist's term for you and me), the mantra of *Arbeit macht frei* is implicitly assumed, but as a subtext that symbolises a myriad of movements towards *nothingness*. Hence, the obsession with the numerical representation of zero in the present era: zero tolerance, zero interest rates, zero-hours contracts, zero marginal cost, etc. Neoliberal economics takes the capitalist work ethic to its logical conclusion in this respect, attempting to reduce the drag of labour to zero. This occurs despite (or because of) the modern firm's increasing reliance on workers to deliver qualities that are beyond the reach of the firm (e.g., emotional labour, self-managed know-how, etc.). Here the old paradox of capitalism is expressed anew. The resource that employers need the most – labour power – is now despised more than anything else. We see this mentality being expressed especially during industrial unrest. When workers announce a planned strike senior management become schizophrenic. They are openly furious (how dare workers do this to our company and committed customers) but at the same time totally adamant that there will be few disruptions, all will be normal ... as if workers are of little consequence to the business. When Virgin Atlantic pilots voted for industrial action short of a strike over the busy 2016 Christmas period management said they were both 'appalled' and convinced that 'our flying programme to remain unaffected during this period and want to reassure our customers that all flights are operating as normal'.[42] Labour is considered a zero, but a dangerous one that must be minimised.

The pressure of the old work ethic is still evident in this 'zerofication' of the workforce. Toil helps keep the otherwise intransigent body preoccupied. However, that requires a degree of stewardship and even paternalism on the side of the employer, something they're no longer willing to supply. It must be remembered that capitalist's motto today is *get something for nothing*. So the new work ethic aims to transform the autonomy enjoyed by labour power (those attributes it holds that employers need but cannot evoke using traditional management techniques) into a more negative experience of freedom. Capital itself seeks to become independent of labour (rather than the other way around) yet have it always ready 'on tap' and at its beck and call. New employment methods seem to have resolved this contradiction. Workers are both autonomous (or nominally free) *and* totally dependent on their employer. This is why the reproductive costs surrounding the act of labour today (including the cost of wages) is observed by the neoliberal enterprise through the lens of pure negation, be that zero or even *less than zero* if at all possible (think here of the introduction of 'negative interest' rates in the UK). The work ethic of the wreckage economics era simply aims to normalise the other side of the motto, the importance of *getting nothing for something.*

We can see this rationality in action when the labour market is approached as an equilibrated supply and demand problem. For many years the neoconservative argument against the minimum wage has been clear. It distorts the natural balance between wages per hour on offer (supply) and the willingness to purchase that labour (demand). State intervention through minimum wage legislation results in excess supply (or unemployment) because it inflates the price of labour above and beyond what a company is willing to pay. But what if the free market advocates actually got their way and the price of labour was supplied and purchased only at the so-called equilibrated rate. How much is a firm willing to pay for labour? Preferably nothing, of course, if it could get away with it. But if that wish was granted we would no longer be living in a capitalist society. Or any other type of society for that matter. This tells us what happens when these microeconomic models are taken seriously. The supply (upward) and demand (sloping) curves distort into an indecipherable mess without the minimum wage intervention because absolute zero becomes the baseline for the wagers per hour curve, which we all know is impossible in both theory and practice.

If this is the case, then, microeconomic modelling only makes sense if it gets what it despises – state intervention! The only place we can observe this demented supply/demand curve in the labour market – apart from slavery – is in the burgeoning internship sector where millions of employees work for nothing. This is how capitalist employers would like to see the entire workforce functioning. Because governments are not willing to risk the political instability of a zero-wage economy, employers find other ways to approximate the impossible supply/demand equilibrium they desire. Zero-hours contracts and self-employment are often used to bypass minimum wage laws. Or firms may reluctantly agree to pay the minimum wage but insist the state fits the bill for all the other costs associated with training, housing, childcare, transport and so forth. Governments need a lucrative tax base to cover these subsidies. Because corporations can easily avoid tax the state typically pursues an aggressive worker-focused inland revenue policy, which is a common characteristic of neoliberal economies as we know.

Evil Santa

The reason why billionaire Mike Ashley – owner and CEO of Sports Direct – was embroiled in a scandal is because his business pushed the envelope when endeavouring to realise the zero-wage economy. In December 2015 it was revealed that Sports Direct warehouses were using an extremely punitive management method. What really caught the headlines were the security searches before and after each shift. Since the time taken to search an employee was unpaid, their hourly wage in effect dropped to £6.50 (£6.70 is the minimum wage). Workers were also docked 15 minutes pay if one minute late and were banned from wearing around 800 sports brands during work hours given the paranoia about worker theft. Employees could receive their wages on a prepaid card for an initial £10 charge and then a £10 per month management fee.[43]

But other issues also emerged from the investigation, revealing how the Sports Direct warehouse atmosphere was negating the very life-force of its staff. Employees were in constant fear of being fired and a loud speaker system ('tannoy') constantly issued directives regarding performance in a penal manner. The trade union Unite said an inordinate number of ambulance callouts had been made to the Sports Direct warehouse in Shirebrook, which employs thousands of people. The reasons ranged from sudden chest pains, pregnancy problems and miscarriage. One female employee even gave birth in the toilets, presumably too afraid or desperate to call in sick that day.[44] Many staff were not immediate Sports Direct employees but hired by an intermediary agency. Each agency had a unique way of welcoming new recruits to Sports Direct. One letter of introduction reads, 'Your performance onsite will be monitored and if you do not meet the expectations of Sports Direct then your assignment will be terminated.'[45] Another agency called Transline drove home a similar message: 'Transline reserves the right to end an assignment at any time without reason, notice or liability.'[46] When questioned about these horrendous conditions, Mike Ashley was unrepentant, especially regarding union involvement in the scandal: 'I can do a better job for Sports Direct employees than Unite … I'm not Father Christmas, I'm not saying I'll make the world wonderful.'[47]

In September 2016 Mike Ashley embarked on a damage control tour of his warehouses, followed by the media. At the Derbyshire facility he too had to endure the invasive security checks, including a metal detector. When he started to empty his pockets in front of the watchful news cameras a look of embarrassment crossed his face. He gingerly pulled out a massive wad of fifty pound notes, an oversight that even he seemed to acknowledge was pretty stupid given the circumstances: 'I've been to the casino', was all he could say to the silent crowd of reporters.[48]

The house always wins

Mike Ashley was in some ways correct. But his fortune was not made by chance like a throw of the dice at the roulette table. That's because the house of Zero-Wage Employment *always* wins. Agency work, as demonstrated by the Sports Direct case, perhaps epitomises the microeconomic dream of wage termination. Instead of regulating pay directly (theoretically protected by minimum wage legislation) it instead controls the hours of work performed. And, in particular, how those hours of productivity are measured/controlled, with special attention given to the nullification (from the firm's perspective) of employment-related costs any normal employer would have to otherwise cover. This is exactly what zero-hours contracts achieve, where people are guaranteed zero hours and wait 'on-demand' for work to come in. Just as Uber, Hermes, Blabla Car and Lyft drivers are only remunerated for the labour they actually do (i.e., the time from when they pick up the customer to when they disembark), so too are cleaners, teachers, customer service staff and nurses on similar contracts. Because the model saves employers so much money, it has extended deep into the employment sector. We're not only talking about people working part time in a bar. A report found that 53 per cent of those employed in one of Britain's most prestigious occupations, university lectureships, are on insecure contracts.[49]

The trend defies, of course, some basic principles about how paid employment functions. Employers are meant to pay for your *availability* regardless of whether you are working all the time since it would be impossible to work every minute of a nine-hour workday. Imagine if a bartender was only paid for the time she spent pouring drinks. From this perspective, everything else around the job – including restroom breaks – shouldn't be paid for. If we took this logic to the extreme, then the actual time it takes to pour a glass of beer could also be disaggregated from the surrounding (and unpaid) waste of time – that split second, quick glance out the window, for example, should be subtracted from the wage bill too, and everything else that isn't directly related to pouring that glass of beer.

In the end, this economic model is unfeasible since it artificially distils what counts as 'productive labour time' down to such a bare minimum that if workers only performed this minuscule task then nothing would get done. Proper labour consists of both (a) the task and (b) the essential, supportive background activity all jobs require (using the restroom). The two can't be separated in any practical sense. This is also why it is difficult to measure individual productivity – or the marginal product – with simple quantitative metrics in an organisation. Numerically tracking an individual's performance misses a great deal about their real productivity since it is so intertwined with qualitative, collective processes. Assisting someone with a high performance task might look negligible on its own, but is vital in the overall picture. This truism extends to the capitalist employment system as a whole. For example, I might have a break mid-morning on Monday so that I can perform better during the evening 3–7 pm shift, but I don't get paid for that rest on a zero-hour contract, etc.). This is exactly how Sports Direct appeared to function. By halting pay at 5 pm when Sports Direct workers were still inside the company conducting their duties (being searched), the firm is able to come closer to realising the zero-wage dream of the neoliberal enterprise.

Such a reduction of labour to a fulsome economic zero (so that only one side of the capitalist relation ever benefits) no doubt follows the precepts emblazoned in the macabre declaration of *Arbeit macht frei*. Here we can note how the new work ethic doesn't simply seek abstention from the body and its temptations but from *life itself*. However, this kind of restraint is expensive and deathward. It is also ongoing and unending, which is where we see wreckage economies become a kind of living nightmare for those who must bear the mantle of homo economicus ... no matter what. Sports Direct punished workers not only for being late or prolonged illness but also 'horseplay', 'long toilet breaks', 'time wasting' and 'excessive chatting'.[50] That is to say, being human. This is clearly an *anti-life* management code. Even the cherished moment of childbirth is ambushed. Perhaps this is the flesh and blood apogee of the microeconomic view of reality. An individual employed in the most oppressive conditions, underpaid and too afraid to even chat with a co-worker. There is a weird irony here. Free markets and strident individualism were meant to counter the old aristocratic privileges of the rentier class. But only with the aid of neoliberal orthodoxy can the likes of Mike Ashley and Sir Philip Green step outside of the twenty-first century and live like

Georgian-era plutocrats, superior even to the state. At a parliamentary commission, Green growled at the MP asking him questions following BHS' failure, 'stop staring at me, it's really disturbing' and demanded the offender be fired from the proceedings.[51] He and his cadre of like-minded robber barons don't have to kowtow to the warped ideology of economic man. Nor do any of the other fat cats of the global elite who are enjoying a New Gilded Age. No, that is for everyone else since homo economicus was always doomed to be a poor bastard bound for oblivion.

Speed kills

This obsession with the speedy reduction of labour to nothing informs how we understand work today, but in contradictory ways. On the one hand, the discourse of employment is more prominent now than ever. Work is everywhere. On the other, the narrative signalling its decline and even death is also widespread, which one suspects is also somehow connected to its hegemonic grip over our imagination.

Let's look at the first part of this seemingly irreconcilable dualism. It's argued (with considerable evidence) that jobs are becoming less important to Western capitalism for a whole host of reasons, mainly connected to the reorganisation of the employment sector following the demise of the Fordist system. Many jobs in the US, Europe and elsewhere have certainly shifted to the Global South, which are in turn increasingly automated. And as we pointed out earlier, modern human resource methods associated with self-management and cost minimisation are driven by the ultimate objective to reduce labour to zero, or even less, in both economic, political and existential terms. In many respects, this represents a concerted class mission rather than the inevitable outcome of efficient methods of production. As Brynjolfsson and McAfee argue in their much discussed *The Second Machine Age*, technological innovations have been specifically channelled towards envisaging a zero-labour presence, despite the social turmoil that will create.[52] What is disconcerting about their argument is the claim that both manual and cognitive jobs are now being rapidly automated, including knowledge work, journalism and a whole host of occupations that were once deemed impossible to mechanise. This latest wave of technological digitalization is distinct to earlier trends because it may have little effect on demand (both in elastic and inelastic terms) since prices don't necessarily drop or products become more desirable. The 'compensation effect' (whereby automation creates jobs elsewhere) doesn't necessarily apply here. Mechanising light bulb production, for example, didn't create more demand for them, even if they become cheaper. The 'compensation effect' argument assumes that increased spending on less expensive products (due to automation) would inevitably create the need for skills in other sectors. In light of the latest wave of inventions, however, we learn there might be absolutely no job growth or redeployment in alternative industries if the millions of van drivers currently employed in the US and UK were swiftly replaced by machines.

Ryan Avent's *The Wealth of Humans* and Robin Hanson's *The Age of Em* also demonstrate how technology will take what we have called the 'zero-labour' movement to its natural conclusion.[53] Automation will rapidly kill more and more jobs and never replace them.[54] However, the death of work due to robotics has not really occurred in such a straightforward manner, which brings us to the other side of the dualism. The zero-labour movement among capitalists appears to coexist with the propagation of endless jobs, mostly of the crappy kind. As mentioned earlier, if the business class had its way, the technological replacement of labour would be far more widespread now than it actually is. Rolling out self-driving cars recently road tested by Google, Biadu and other firms, artificial intelligence algorithms that pen journalistic newspaper reports and so forth could all be applied wholesale tomorrow. It's almost as if mechanisation is more about the mythic framing of work as something that is no better than a big, fat zero. Perhaps a kind of expectation management for a coming generation of workers. The state plays an important role here as well. It has stepped in and negotiated a deal with the business world to keep the myth of employment alive, precisely by *not* automating everything. This would explain the recent and dramatic drop in technological investment in the UK and elsewhere. Business agrees to the arrangement not because it is a fan of workers but due to its major stake in the status quo. Once again we notice that the capitalist state is far savvier than the business class with respect to the self-preservation of the capitalist universe. The neocons currently governing the polities in the West and Global South fully understand Marx's law of the falling rate of profit.[55] Without labour or its vast theatre of loss, we could no longer have capitalism, for basic and obvious economic reasons.[56]

This artificial overemployment is the real reason why growth and labour productivity have slumped in major economies around the world, most notably in northern Europe. Economists in the UK call this the 'productivity puzzle' because following the recession employment has risen, whereas productivity (measured as labour output per hour) has stagnated. For some years after the 2007–08 crisis, labour productivity stalled 17 per cent below the expected rate if we extrapolate from pre-crisis figures.[57] One explanation for this bizarre disconnect between employment (increasing) and productivity (decreasing) is low technological investment. The *same job* being conducted in a high-investment environment versus a low-investment one will yield very different output levels. That's because workers in a high-investment environment can do more with the hour of labour at their disposal. This unwillingness to invest is certainly linked to the greedy shareholder model of capitalism and the infamous 'stretch and extract' rationality we discussed in an earlier chapter. But low investment (including in automation) is perhaps also due to the obvious deal struck between the state and capital concerning the problem of unemployment. Technological advancement is delayed to ensure a surfeit of jobs in the economy. The Bank of England calls this 'spare capacity' because it believes that it's a calculated response by business in a period of uncertainty: 'the resilience of employment could reflect firms making the active decision to retain staff, despite weak demand, in expectation of a recovery in demand'.[58]

But is that the real motivation? Given all we have discussed so far about extreme neoliberalism, isn't it rather naive to believe that capitalist enterprises would generously relinquish the greedy, almost suicidal short-termism they've otherwise displayed and keep workers on just in case? It doesn't add up. Regardless, such overcapacity combined with the dramatic decline in real wages since the 2007–08 crisis (England has one of the worst EU figures in this respect)[59] and the rise of draconian employment systems (e.g., Sports Direct), then no wonder the general workforce has given up on trying to be more productive. If someone asked you to work harder with the hours available, and you hadn't received a pay increase in ten years, would you happily reply, sure!? More likely you would nod obligingly and then fake the extra effort as much as possible. This is the real reason why the economy is now riddled with jobs that are pointless. And the main architect of this labour overcapacity or 'hoarding' is the neoliberal state of course. Its aggressive taxation strategy is used to subsidise industry and help create the spectacle of employment, fuelling a self-perpetuating fiscal loop of uselessness. Moreover, it must be remembered that in countries with diabolical levels of inequality, what might be termed *technocratic useless* becomes evident in the employment sector. Thousands of otherwise pointless jobs are created with the singular purpose of *displaying* power and authority, hoping to discourage any rebellious breech of the hierarchical order of things. A 'standing army' of security personnel are now considered a must by the capitalist establishment, as any visit to New York or London will attest. This sizable workforce remains redundant and unproductive until activated by the threat of social upheaval.

Ghostly demarcations

Why does the capitalist state and corporate sector desire this contrived pretence of work above the cool economic realism of a zero-jobs world? Perhaps because it maintains a semblance of normalcy and stability. Order is preserved. Moreover, the old bourgeois fear about the devil making work for idle hands might also have some influence on the phenomenon, troubled only by the fact that it is precisely in the workplace that people find themselves truly bored or even worse, using their free time to cook up nefarious experiments, as we have recently witnessed with criminal activity in the banking sector. However, the cultural inevitability of work also plays an important ideological role apropos socio-economic inequality. When everyone is acting *as if* they are workers – including the unemployed who toil for nothing in fast-food restaurants, disabled people registering as self-employed rather than endure another humiliating cross-examination at the local job centre – it helps maintain the illusion that all those freedoms we forsake in the name of paid employment are unavoidable because it is directly linked to survival. In other words, if it seems like living cannot be undertaken without work being involved, then the link must remain totally unquestioned.

The charade is rendered even more convincing if a little bit of material insecurity and induced scarcity is added to the mix, a neat trick that neoliberal policymakers have perfected. It makes it seem like work and nature are closely bound. But they're clearly not, despite the return of Victorian-era maladies like rickets in contemporary London.[60] In a society like ours, we simply do not require this immense theatre of labour in order to live well. That's the elephant in the room and capitalism will go to great lengths to ignore or deny it with a complex array of smoke and mirrors.

The ideology of work in the second machine age (a time where work ought to have probably disappeared) also serves another purpose. The flows and social patterns it generates through the aforementioned systems of visibility or exhibition doubles as a very useful (and highly camouflaged) form of social control. Here I am not only referring to onsite controls at the workplace (surveillance, peer pressure, wage discipline, managerial supervision, etc.) but regulation at the societal level. It's telling that when police are searching for a fugitive, the first place they visit is their fixed address of residence. The second is their workplace. Employment signifies more than an economic category. It's also an integral part of social control that allows the authorities to easily predict where people are at any given moment.

In his classic essay on societies of control, Gilles Deleuze argues that whereas disciplinary societies (described by Michel Foucault) functioned through closed space/time systems – like a prison – societies of control depend upon the violation of borders that once defined the industrial age.[61] We certainly see this when the work and non-work boundary is blurred. It was once policed with Hitler-like vigilance by management. Today such boundary-policing protocols would be considered an impediment to production. Enclosures like prisons and schools only make sense as a template of control if each separate sphere of society observes very different registers. Now that there is only one universal register (the economy) or *rhythm*, the need for these divisions has waned. Look at personal debt. In order to function properly, it must be able to follow us literally everywhere. Similarly, labour needs to be displayed no matter where it is. Perhaps it is this point that explains the state's obsession with maintaining a largely unproductive theatre of labour because it has become a suitable meme for identifying individuals. Mobile and productive but always locatable.

Wasted indeed

It is easy to get carried away and lose historical perspective in so many arguments around the politics of work in neoliberal societies. In an ironic twist, the assertion of the new – as a stage of development that is distinct from past eras of economic activity – blinds us to the significant historical continuities between the past and present. The very term 'neoliberalism' has this problem. As an oft-evoked prefix used to identify all that is wrong with economy and society today, it unwittingly lends itself to a 'new times' rhetoric, a weakness that pervades critical inquiry too. As a consequence, the apologists of this brutal economic model can at least stake a claim on its novelty and contemporaneousness, despite its various limitations and glitches. This illusion of being up-to-date carries important political implications. For example, it helps the ruling culture consign truly progressive futures to the realm of outmoded, obsolete and unwanted ideas. Almost any alternative is wrongly deemed backward, not the present situation that is literally crumbling in front of us, a useful conceit given the neo-feudal characteristics beginning to emerge in the current empire. In relation to work, exactly how new are any of the trends we have discussed in this chapter?

In a number of ways, the questions raised concerning the dual processes of technological unemployment and excessive work that characterise dialogue on this topic today share similarities to debates that have been ongoing for some time. Just as homo economicus has been critically questioned from its inception for being unreasonable, so has the (over)work ethic, its encroachment into everyday life and its apparent lack of content. So we must be careful how best to place this new age of 'crisis capitalism' in proper historical context. The past haunts us today more than we think. That's why the claim we live in new, uncharted times can obscure some basic features of capitalism that have always been 'extreme' from the beginning, fuelling the delusion that a more moderate and family-friendly variant might still be conceivable in this ultra-high-tech, future-orientated present.

Here are some examples of what I mean. The recent contention that we're now working more than ever certainly feels true. As noted in the opening sections of this chapter, the long-hours culture in mainstream enterprises is so pronounced that it is killing homo economicus off at an unprecedented rate. And this is where work/life balance programmes become deeply problematic in my opinion, designed to functionalise work-centricity rather than moderate or mitigate it. The claim may sound counter-intuitive. What do I mean? Many work/life balance initiatives – such as those funded by the UK government (tellingly classified as a flexi-work issue) – are profoundly misleading because they make it look as if workers can obtain a normal relationship between their lives and paid employment, implying that a serene *life of work* might be achieved. The deception is actually *heightened* by exceptional cases of burnout and scandals concerning over the top exploitation (e.g., Sports Direct). Because they're portrayed as horrible aberrations from an otherwise unremarkable norm, the hell that everyone else experiences as 'daily life' can falsely lay claim to be the highest standard of normalcy. The promulgation of work/life balance programmes supports the myth that there can be a well-adjusted, uncontroversial mode of exploitation. Not too much time at work, nor so little that employers are deprived of revenue. This brings us to an important point. Capitalist work systems are not defined by a numerical threshold, a kind of red line that only when crossed can we reasonably speak about exploitation. No, this is a *qualitative* relationship. For that reason, the capitalist mode of production by its very nature has always entailed overwork, no matter how much time is spent toiling in the post-modern office. This point is made very well by Kirsty Ross in relation to the anthropological investigations of Pierre Clastres:

> primitive societies do not, in our sense, work, even if their activities are highly constrained and regulated ... the work model is an invention of the state in that people will only work or produce more than their needs require them when forced to. What we disparagingly called 'subsistence economies', societies where one works to satisfy one's needs and not to produce a surplus, are to be seen, according to Clastres, as operating according to a refusal of a useless excess of *activity*. Work, then, appears only with the constitution of a surplus; work begins, properly speaking, as overwork.[62]

I think this remark is critical. Now we can easily see how pointless labour can strangely complement its punishing overabundance. Managing the convergence is one of the key purposes of the state. But these management systems have evolved over time too. It used to do so by faking a veneer of democratic universality. Everyone knew it was dishonest, of course. Self-preservation transcends all sectarian power struggles? No. But at least the establishment felt the charade was somehow necessary. Today things are very different. We're now dealing with an openly *capitalist state* or what the philosopher Alain Badiou calls 'capitalo-parliamentarianism' that is unapologetically dictatorial when prioritising the interests of GlaxoSmithKline, KFC and Sir Robert McAlpine over you and me.[63] Authoritarianism is its primary form of expression. Regardless, when we seek to see what is new or different about neoliberal capitalism it is of course still important to focus on the number of working hours we put in. But there's a danger that this detracts from abiding qualities (work *as* surplus) that have been present since the commencement of capitalism. The complaint of overwork, therefore, is not new. It's built into the very structure of capitalist employment relations. Any talk of some lost 'balance' simply mystifies this.

Speculation without a future

The real problem with the fable of balance, however, is the way it reinforces the fantasy of individual choice and freedom. This is one of the most seductive tendencies in the cultural logic of the present economic order. If the pressure to work (as an always excessive practice) is only understood in numerical terms, in which a healthy rebalance can be imagined, then personal agency inevitably comes to the fore of any regulatory or policy response. On the capitalist side, employers ought to take active steps to curb the long-hours culture that is harming employees. And on the worker's side, she ought to better juggle her occupational responsibilities and family duties. But there's a problem with this choice-led rendition of the issue. As argued above, *work begins*, properly speaking, *as overwork*.

Hence, the paradox that frames the very structure of paid employment today, be it part of the struggling precariat or the established salariat. The obligation to work is only binding if freely entered into. Of course, we have no choice in reality. But that is a situation of our own freewill, which is largely how neoliberal capitalism gets away with the travesties it currently represents. This double-bind is similar to the one faced by Lt. Col. Bill Cage, the protagonist in the sci-fi film *The Edge of Tomorrow*. When the inexperienced Cage is swiftly killed in action he finds himself reliving the day over and over again. He gets better at dodging the fatal bullets and progresses further only to be killed by a new misfortune. The repetition enhances his sense of agency over events that are completely preordained. Similarly, the same paradox explains why many find it so difficult to escape the culture of employment today, often blaming predetermined forces that lie beyond their control yet manifest through distinct decisions that could have been otherwise. This is how the ruse of work functions. What for millennia was correctly framed as servitude is today crowned as the apogee of free choice. Bill Clinton's old catchphrase, 'empowering people to take over their own lives' genuinely captures this awful moment in which a deeply bleak economic fate is lived as self-determination.

Nobody wants to hear that their 'here and now', immediate experience is one that has been endlessly repeated over generations; that the present feeling of visceral urgency or 'nowness' that defines our existence in all its existential uniqueness has happened all before. And no doubt will again. Having said that, it's striking how many questions of the day are symbolically expunged of their historical continuity and resonance. Here's another example we have already touched upon. The widespread belief that machines more generally and now computer technology will replace jobs at a rate never before seen feels like something novel. But like overwork, this has been a critical talking point for years and is not that new. In the 1930s, for example, technological development was predicted to replace most kinds of employment by the end of the twentieth century. Keynes' 1930 essay 'Economic Possibilities For Our Grand-children' made a very convincing case for the end of work on these and other grounds.[64] We can note the same concern in the 1950s when US firms like IBM invented amazing new business machines such as the Universal Automatic Computer.[65]

The discussion about the future of jobs and whether automation means an expansion of leisure or a life of hardship was as redolent back then as it is today. Indeed, it's interesting to examine the remarkable similarities between claims made in the 1930s, such as those by Social Credit advocates C.H. Douglas, and more contemporary books with titles like *The End of Work* (1995), *Robots Will Steal Your Job* (2012), *The Rise of the Robots* (2015) and so forth.[66] And of course the wonderful Bob Black had a massive presence on this front too in the 1980s.[67] In fact, it appears that the end of work thesis has accompanied each major shift in the way it has been reorganised. From early industrialism, Fordism, post-Fordism and today, the era of wreckage economics. Perhaps the critical discussion about the capitalist *underutilisation* of labour and its concurrent *maximisation* is somehow internal to the dominant ideological system itself; not in a simple call and response, dialectical fashion (since there is little functional equilibrium here) but as a conversation that is perpetually failing since its lexico-graphical structure cannot contain both poles. Total employment and excessive hours put in at the office on the one hand, and utter uselessness on the other. A kind of 'employed redundancy'. The two trends look opposed, but actually belong to the same method of economic misalignment. Perhaps capitalism can only function in this way. Demanding both labour's fullness and absence, often at the same time. And this perpetual misalignment is central to the historical development of employment regimes in most economies over the last hundred years. Let's call it *class struggle*.

5

Microeconomics
(*really is*) for Dummies

A well-known European budget airline recently made headlines when it was reported that almost 70 per cent of its pilots were self-employed. In countries like the UK and USA, the number of people classifying themselves as self-employed is rapidly growing.[1] Politicians and neoclassical economists generally celebrate the trend. For the first time in the history of capitalism, workers can now reap the full benefits of their own labour. People no longer toil for someone else, but are their own bosses, deciding alone when and how to do their jobs. Individuals are able to enhance their own 'human capital' and enjoy the revenues it accrues. What some commentators call 'free agents' and the 'creative class' are no longer alienated from the means of production like past generations.[2] Instead, they own their skill-set and call the shots on how they are used.[3] We are told, in fact, that this boost in occupational autonomy represents a major leap forward in workplace freedoms, perhaps heralding a new era of 'frictionless capitalism' and an end to industrial discontent.[4]

But it was not due to these glowing endorsements of self-employment that the story met with widespread public interest. No, these pilots were in revolt. From their perspective, this was no positive development but an exploitative extension of economic rationalisation. Now deemed self-employed, the pilots alone must bear the costs of uniforms, stopover hotels, identity cards and other expenses. They signed an exclusivity clause, promising not to fly with any other airline. Nor were they eligible for medical insurance or company pensions like normal employees. It was all beginning to look like a pretty bad deal.

The pilots protested that the system ultimately meant they were forced to fly since they would not be paid otherwise, even if unwell or fatigued.[5] So they collectively drafted a 'safety petition', arguing that the status of self-employment and the use of 'zero-hours contracts' (where workers are paid only for the hours they put in but guaranteed none in the advent of low demand) jeopardises passenger safety. The response from airline management was blunt: 'any pilot who participates in this so-called safety petition will be guilty of gross misconduct and will be liable for dismissal'. While the public are now familiar with the so-called precarious class or 'precariat', viewing highly trained professionals in the same light seemed strange and rather disconcerting.

You're on your own!

Autonomy. What liberating connotations it has when applied to the jobs we do. How could anyone be against it? However, it is amazing how a word and concept can be so thoroughly co-opted by the business world and redeployed in such divisive ways in society. This has certainly been the case with 'job autonomy', once the watchword for labour democracy and a rallying cry for more discretion and freedom over the way a job is carried out. But today it increasingly stands for something very different. Employment is being fundamentally *individualised* so that the costs of labour that firms once covered are pushed onto the employee with the help of labour-on-demand business models, self-employment, portfolio careers and zero-hours contracts. So pervasive are these shifts that some claim work is being 'Uberised', named after the company that has transformed the taxi industry along similar lines.[6] This has led to a massive increase in economic insecurity and disempowerment. Less choice rather than more self-determination. Indeed, it is difficult today to imagine the workers' movement ever campaigned under the banner of autonomy. For all it really means now is, 'you're on your own'.

There are many forces behind this ongoing individualisation of the labour process, including the growing power of big business, the decline of unions and even the genuine desire for freedom among the workers. I want to argue that one significant ideological precipitator can be found in a variant of neoclassical economics called *human capital theory*. The idea goes back to Adam Smith when he discussed how 'useful abilities and talents' are acquired by company workers. In the late 1950s and early 1960s a small group of economists began to formalise their own version of human capital theory. Jacob Mincer, Theodore Schultz, Gary Becker and later on, Robert E. Lucas applied the principles of neoclassical economics to individual behaviour, proposing that people shouldn't be considered citizens, students, patients or employees, for example. Instead they're *human capital*, a social classification that transcends all others. Human capital(ists) are competitive individualists, preoccupied with investing and enhancing in their own economic value. From this point of view, *life itself* is a personal and permanent commercial project that requires business ambition to generate future income and avoid losses.

Along with its academic proponents, human capital is today described by business, governments and even the United Nations as an unalloyed good. For if the concept implies investing in people, leading to more educated, heathier and wealthier employees and economies, then how could anyone be against it? The past 20 years has seen this once arcane theory come to fundamentally reshape the meaning of work and jobs in Western societies. It paved the way for related concepts that have become popular too, such as cultural capital, social capital and intellectual capital. But it is human capital theory in particular, I suggest, that really has a dark side. From the 1990s onwards the theory has been central for enabling the individualisation of the workforce, including the rise of zero-hours contracts and precarious employment arrangements. This has resulted in the rise of what I term the *ultra-responsible autonomy* among jobs, whereby responsibility for all the costs and benefits associated with being an economic actor are solely his or hers. This approach to organising work is based upon an extreme version of self-interested individualism, one that is largely unrealistic and unsustainable in practice. For this reason, human capital theory might be something of a hoax. Employees don't necessarily become wealthier, smarter or enjoy more self-determination by following its precepts. I aim to demonstrate a significant link between the tenets of human capital theory and the proliferation of economic insecurity, low-skilled work and personal debt that pervades many societies today.

This is clearly bad for individual employees. But I plan to go one step further in the analysis and evaluate the effects on organisations and the wider economy. In societies that have embraced human capital theory we can observe how many commercial activities that it is supposed to enhance (e.g., skills investment, innovation, productivity, etc.) are actually hindered by it. The UK, for example, has seen within the space of a few years a relatively skilled (but unionised) workforce converted into an army of isolated agency workers and Deliveroo bicyclists delivering pizzas in the neglected suburbs of London. That's why low productivity jobs have noticeably boomed.[7] With respect to education and training in particular, human capital theory has played its part in 'dumbing down' organisations and economies where its influence is evident, not upskill them. And this brings us to a key issue. Is resistance to capitalism still possible after such a devastating process of individualisation has taken place? Are there still ways in which employees might wrest the concept of autonomy back in favour of workplace democracy and economic sustainability?

Prison life

To fully appreciate how the notion of job autonomy was so successfully bastardised under neoliberal capitalism, we must first put the process in historical context. By doing so we can clearly observe the steady atomisation of the employee, which reaches its zenith in firms like Deliveroo, Uber and many others. The rise of industrial capitalism saw the birth of a very different way of working. Business owners needed to officially demarcate the time/space of work since control in the factory, and later the administrative bureaucracy, was crucial to the productive process. During the Feudal era, including the early mercantile and putting-out regime, work and life necessarily overlapped considerably. Replacing 'natural time' with 'clock-time' (as well as the spread of clocks) was an important precursor to changing this arrangement.

The separation of work and life was not easy, however, attracting a good deal of antipathy from the newly formed working classes. As the labour historian E.P. Thompson points out in the case of England, workers were accustomed to directing the labour process themselves, usually out of necessity more than anything else. Now they found themselves in an austere, regulated space for 17 hours a day, with little say over how a job was performed.[8] The ensuing battle between workers and employers over job autonomy deeply shaped management thought.[9] It was assumed that only scientifically trained managers ought to design the labour process, with

Fredrick Winslow Taylor being the most famous commentator to take this stance.[10] But in the factories of North America he was shocked by the degree of control and knowledge average workers had over their jobs. For him, this meant they had the upper hand. And that independence, he suspected, would be used for 'irresponsible' purposes; namely, *against* the interests of the company and *for* the interests of workers and their representatives, what might be labelled 'irresponsible autonomy':

> In nineteen out of twenty industrial establishments the workers believe it to be directly against their interests to give their employers their best initiative ... they deliberately work as slowly as they dare while at the same time try to make those over them believe that they are working fast.[11]

Taylor's mission was clear. Worker control on the shopfloor had to be stamped out. This was achieved in a number of ways, including the introduction of piece rate incentive systems that 'individualise each workman'.[12]

The tyranny of togetherness

The severe dysfunctions of Taylorism were known for some time, with the Hawthorne Experiments, the neo-Human relations movement and more humane management approaches decrying the lack of involvement among the workforce. Under Taylorism employees had been ordered not to think and simply do as they were told. But when given discretion over their roles, a happier and more creative climate emerged. This impacted on the bottom line and meant less strikes. Under the intellectual direction of Douglas McGregor and Rensis Likert inter alia, employers were encouraged to foster 'responsible autonomy' in the workplace.[13] Given the broad economic objectives of a department or division, teams and groups were allowed a degree of freedom over meeting their targets.[14] Rewards reflected this shift too, since only the best teams ought to be recognised for their initiative, commitment and resourcefulness.

Responsible autonomy reorganised the collective spirit, but unlike its 'irresponsible' predecessor, it was enacted in the name of the company's best interests rather than class or union priorities. The idea perhaps reached its pinnacle with the rise of corporate cultures in the 1980s and 1990s, based on Japanese motivation techniques and company pride.[15] The rationale was simple: teams will strive for excellence, do what's best for the firm and stay late to get the job done if they fell in love with the company.[16] An array of indoctrination techniques was used to foster this emotional bond between employees and employers. No wonder some compared them to the brainwashing methods used by cults.[17]

While the management of corporate cultures is still popular, I suggest another significant transformation has occurred over the last 20 years in Western management thought. The change was, in part at least, prompted by the dysfunctions that 'strong' corporate cultures caused and firm-level attempts to overcome them. For example, studies revealed that many employees were secretly cynical about the idea of loving their firm, with one researcher reporting how employees called the company newsletter 'Goebbels Gazette'.[18] The situation was not helped by the wave of layoffs in the late 1980s. The so-called 'IBM family', for example, turned out to be not so nurturing after all.[19] Moreover, the sheer cost of building and maintaining a corporate culture was yet another disincentive for employers.[20]

Other permutations were afoot that probably also curtailed the corporate culture fad. The massive emphasis on shared identification meant some employees were more concerned with fitting in and looking the part.[21] Innovation, entrepreneurship and productive risk-taking are stifled under such conditions. Changing demographics in the workforce too saw an appetite for authenticity and personal difference rather than pretending to approximate a cardboard cut-out version of the 'corporate (wo)man'. For a new generation of workers and managers, one's individuality outside the office mattered.[22] Moreover, its authentic expression in the workplace might be beneficial to morale and productivity since workers could be themselves and excel in their own way.

Autonomy for losers

The decline of the corporate culture movement also needs to be placed in historical context to fully grasp the implications. From the late 1990s onwards, work has been extensively reorganised in mainly Anglo-Saxon countries but also elsewhere. This has included the decline of unions and increasingly restrictive laws around industrial action; the deregulation of the labour market and the end of secure, lifelong jobs; the emergence of the so-called 'gig economy' and casual or freelance work; the polarisation between high- and low-skilled occupations and so forth.[23]

'Flexibility' is perhaps the most common term to describe employment today. The average worker no longer defines themselves in relation to shared class interests, nor collective iden- tification with a long-term employer. As Boudreau and Ramstad (2007) point out, a human capital approach takes us far beyond corporate clans and its emphasis on unity since workers behave in a much more individualistic manner, almost as a mini-corporation in their own right, viewing themselves as peripatetic agents in a competitive marketplace.[24] Given how market rationalisation has transformed employment law and regulation, perhaps it is the *individual contract*, rather than class or company culture, which matters the most to the new worker.

Multiple drivers have been identified behind these shifts in countries like the USA, UK, New Zealand and increasingly continental Europe and Scandinavia, including the consolida- tion of corporate power, neoliberal state policy, the offshoring of relatively well-paid manufacturing jobs to the Global South and the evolving, intrinsic requirements of work in the service and IT sector. However, I argue that the growing individualising of employment has been significantly enabled by an important intellectual movement associated with neoclassical economics, human capital theory, which has had a major influence on policymakers, governments and other powerful decision-makers. As mentioned earlier, the notion was formally developed by Jacob Mincer, Theodore Schultz and Gary Becker among others in the early 1960s, suggesting that individuals (i.e., their stock of skills, knowledge, education and even personal attributes) should also be conceptualised as capital along with equipment and so forth. According to Gary Becker, we often assume that capital only refers to things like Apple stock, plant and banks accounts. However,

such tangible forms of capital are not the only type of capital. Schooling, a computer training course, expenditures on medical care, and lectures on the virtues of punctuality and honesty are also capital. That is because they raise earnings, improve health, or add to a person's good habits over much of his lifetime. Therefore, economists regard expenditures on education, training, medical care, and so on as investments in human capital. They are called human capital because people cannot be separated from their knowledge, skills, health, or values in the way they can be separated from their financial and physical assets.[25]

Exactly who pays for the expenditure is central to the analysis that follows. And the idea that someone cannot be separated from this type of capital will be important too. The notion of human capital might sound relatively benign (if somewhat materialistic) at first. But it has a very negative side. I propose that it helped reimagine employees as competitive, self-interested agents that are somehow *external to the firm*, rather than an internal core resource that requires company investment, training and stewardship. And this has had some very detrimental consequences.

Diseconomies of loneliness

One of the first economists to theorise human capital warned his audience at the American Economic Association meeting in 1960 that treating living human beings as 'property or marketable assets' might seem distasteful to the average person.[26] The trick is to emphasise the importance of owning one's individual prospects, the freedom granting powers of self-investment and its impact on wider prosperity. Gary Becker extended the argument in his discussion of employee training, dividing human capital into two types.[27] *Specific* human capital are skills highly particular to a job and non-transferable to other firms. Whereas *general* human capital are abilities that can be used in different organisations or/and industries and are unbound to any particular site of production. Becker then asks an important question. When human capital is transferable (or general) as it increasingly is, who should pay for its development? Probably not employers since that kind of investment might one day literally walk out the door or be poached by a rival. In competitive markets, 'firms would provide general training only if they did not have to pay any of the costs ... hence the costs as well as the return from general training would be borne by trainees, not by firms'.[28]

Schultz' address to the American Economic Association reluctantly comes to similar conclusions about education. Once a student is reconfigured as human capital, it stands to reason that the initial investment ought to be made by them alone since they are the primary beneficiaries. One can easily detect Schultz hesitate on this point since he's evidently a fan of public education, understanding its importance for national economic wellbeing. The prevarication ends, however, when a colleague asks for clarification: 'Should the returns from public investment in human capital accrue to the individuals whom it is made?'[29] He wants to say yes because state investment in a collective (yet privately articulated) utility such as tertiary education, for example, can stimulate the wider economy as public goods often do. But he falters under the weight of the question, perhaps detecting in it a taste of things to come:

> The policy issues implicit in this question run deep and are full of perplexities pertaining to both resource allocation and to welfare. Physical capital that is formed by public investment is not transferred as a rule to particular individuals as a gift. It would

greatly simplify the allocative processes if public investment in human capital were placed on the same footing.[30]

The reply is ambivalent and includes two possible conclusions: (1) returns on human capital derived from public investment (e.g., taxes) ought to remain in public hands or (2) returns on human capital derived from public investment (e.g., taxes) cannot be a 'gift' if organised along the same principles as any other private enterprise, in which the beneficiary naturally bears some or all of the investment costs.

The first option is state communism and logically anathema to the very idea of human capital since it can only be owned by the individual who embodies it. As we have learnt, human capital and its living carrier can never be separated. The implication is clear. Nobody else can own my human capital because that would be slavery, which conclusively rules out it being linked to 'welfare' programmes run by the state.

So only the second option remains tenable. Schultz cannot have what he really wants. His cake (i.e., skill acquisition as a private, individual responsibility) and eat it too (public investment in everyone's skills). We learn in a footnote who the colleague was that prompted Schultz to ask whether human capital is a private or public good; no other than Milton Friedman, a vociferous supporter for privatisation in the Thatcher and Reagan years whose influence is still being felt today. From now on the underlying message of human capital theory is simple: there is no such thing as a free lunch.

Friedman had found the ideological lure he was looking for because an individual's human capital (including earnings and liabilities) can be owned by nobody else. More importantly, human capital theory provides the ultimate neoclassical retort to the Marxist slogan that workers should seize the means of production. If each person is already *their own* means of production, then the intractable conflict at the heart of the capitalist labour process must logically dissolve. As it turns out, according to Schultz, all workers are in fact consummate capitalists: 'labourers have become capitalists not from the diffusion of the ownership of corporation stocks, as folk law would have it, but from the acquisition of knowledge and skill that have economic value'.[31]

The stalker

Given the basic premise of human capital theory forged in the early 1960s, we can easily observe how it smoothed the way for *ultra-responsible autonomy*: where each individual human capitalist becomes entirely responsible for his or her economic fate. By the 1990s human capital theory had found a wide audience, especially in the business world.[32] Viewing employees as individual mini-enterprises was soon all the rage. Kunda and Ailon-Souday note how HRM practitioners largely abandoned reference to clans, family and culture, all of which connote collectivist values.[33] Instead, they adopted a market rationalist perspective when considering the firm's relationship to its employees and vice versa. With concepts like the boundaryless and portfolio career moving to centre stage, Kunda and Ailon-Souday note how the metaphor of love and marriage suddenly seemed old-fashioned when describing contemporary organisations. By the beginning of the twenty-first century, short-term affairs and one-night stands better captured the climate, especially as the ideals of economic self-reliance and independence supplanted expectations of a long-term relationship with an employer.

Following Peter Drucker's pontifications about the coming 'employee society' the next most read proselytiser of this approach was Tom Peters and his notion of 'liberation management'.[34] Retracting his 1980s obsession with strong organisational cultures, he now claimed that the workplace ought to be defined by personal difference and entrepreneurial risk-taking. The pursuit of individual self-interest creates way more shareholder value than any slavish adherence to a collective identity. This is why, according to Peters, it is best to treat employees as if they were their own micro-enterprises. Organisational members are encouraged to discover 'The Brand Called You'.[35] This intangible asset can be leveraged and capitalised upon at the crucial moment for those who understand both the external and internal job market.

This is certainly telling of a sea change in popular books about organisations, management and business. But how exactly does ultra-responsible autonomy play out in practice? It can do so in several ways, I suggest. Freelancing, self-employment and agency work associated with on-demand contracts are obvious examples we have already discussed. But organisations might manage their permanent workforce along the same lines too. For example, Ressler and Thompson note the rise of what they call 'Results Only Work Environments' (or ROWE) in a number of US industries.[36] Rather than focus on productive inputs, as much management wisdom prescribes in relation to monitoring, training and motivation, ROWE firms are only concerned with outcomes. Once again the employee is somehow external to the organisation, which is used to good effect.

Academia partially follows this flexi-work model. My employer is largely unconcerned when, where and how I prepare for a Tuesday afternoon lecture, be it in the middle of the night or the weekend. Indeed, it would be counter-productive to insist I clock in at 9 am on Monday morning and be at my desk present and accounted for. As long as I arrive to the lecture hall and do a satisfactory job (which, of course, is measured rather rigorously!) my employer is happy. Unlike managers of yesteryear, Ressler and Thompson suggest, businesses don't worry that ROWE workers are going to shirk their duties if nobody is watching them all day: 'It's not about giving people more time with the kids. ROWE is not about having more time off ... you might even work more'.[37]

It is with the individualistic contract-based business model that we see human capital theory really come into its own. As mentioned earlier, such contractualisation exemplifies the narrow manner in which human capital theory interprets self-interest. People are now monadic and self-contained enterprises rather than members of a wider group. For example, in Western economies there has been a boom in self-employment over the last ten years, with a staggering 14.6 million people registered in the USA in 2015.[38] In the UK, the self-employed workforce has grown by 45 per cent since 2001, standing at almost 5 million workers.[39] Additionally, it is estimated that in 2014 about 1.8 million 'on call' or 'zero-hours' contracts existed, a figure that probably underestimates the true extent of their presence in the hotel/restaurant, education and healthcare industries.[40] The so-called 'gig economy', whereby contractors perpetually move from job to job like journeymen or a musician, is said to capture the future of work in OECD economies.[41] But one thing is clear in this new environment. Whereas homo economicus was thought to be a person who fervently pursued commerce, today the direction of exchange is revered. Now he or she is quietly stalked by a predatory and hostile economy.

Bad gig

Neoliberal ideology overwhelmingly supports these shifts in how work is organised, proclaiming the benefits for employers, workers and consumers alike. Echoing the tenets of human capital theory, this is all about empowering people. We now thankfully live in a 'Free Agent Nation' where choice and preference are considered basic occupational attributes. Unlike our parents and grandparents who had no option but to conform to mass patterns of employment in and out of the office, actors today can tailor work around their lifestyle. This sentiment is best exemplified by Semco CEO Ricardo Semler:

> imagine a company where workers set their own hours; where there are no offices ... [where] you have the freedom to get your job done on your own terms and to blend your work life and personal life ... smart bosses will eventually realise that you might be most productive if you work on Sunday afternoon, play golf on Monday morning ...[42]

In many ways, this economic individualism probably still echoes the appeal for autonomy that has informed so much employee dissatisfaction from the early industrial period onwards. Discretion over how, where and when a job is performed remains attractive to many today. Yet, as I have demonstrated, the basis upon which that independence is defined has been systematically desocialised over time; from industry or even economy-level *class interests*, to a narrower set of *company interests* and then finally to *individual self-interest*.

This isn't to say that self-interest was not present in the earlier forms of autonomy. Of course it was, but filtered through the prism of what was deemed worthy for one's referent class and/or company. It is more difficult to imagine synergies moving in the opposed direction, in which individual self-interest draws on lasting cultural bonds to the firm, let alone class solidarity, when enacting autonomy today. And while human capital may have a normative appreciation of society beyond itself – a strong marketplace, for example – this is very different to group identification, as Lane notes in her fascinating study of itinerant, semi-employed and unemployed IT workers in the USA.[43] Something is irrevocably lost when self-interest is redefined as ultra-responsible autonomy. People described others like them in terms of a network (which required investment and nurturing) rather than solidarity. Moreover, even those workers who felt themselves unfairly dismissed by their employers expressed understanding and sympathy for the company. These individuals truly understood themselves as a 'company of one' with no lasting or sacrificial bonds of fraternity outside of the immediate family.

Do these trends really yield the splendid benefits that human capital economists, management gurus and government officials so often imagine? I argue that ultra-responsible autonomy in the workplace has a nasty side, one that economically and politically disadvantages workers, and eventually hurts industry more generally. For many entering this new era of employment, financial insecurity, declining wages and *less* job autonomy are expected. In other words, the individualism promoted here creates vulnerabilities to the forces of concentrated economic power, particularly in economies that lionise privatisation, limit state public spending and expose almost every facet of life to the marketplace. In this way, the politics of work is now closely interwoven with other social justice concerns related to 'life' more generally like affordable housing, the cost of living crisis, personal debt and access to education. Let's survey some of these negative outcomes in more detail.

Intimacies of ruin

Employment relationships inspired by human capital theory are lucrative to individual workers if their skill is scarce and demand is high. In the majority of cases, however, contract-based independence generally has a downward pressure on income because of competition and the asymmetrical power relationship that develops between firms and workers.[44] Why so? As dictated by the principles of neoclassical economics, when a person is reconceptualised as human capital, they become an external agent with their own set of interests. A mini-corporation. It's only a small step to then conclude that they ought to be liable for meeting the financial overheads of that economic interest. The pilot example mentioned earlier is a good case in point. Individualised liabilities include not only fringe benefits like medical insurance, training and pensions, but also basic equipment to get the job done: uniforms, ID cards, transport and other essentials that would render the labour process impossible if absent.

Wages are also depreciated by the sporadic and unpredictable nature of such employment compared to standard jobs. Fluctuations in labour demand, coupled with a one-sided power relationship that sees employers alone decide whether you will work and be paid today inevitably lowers income expectations. This is often backed up by state legislation. For example, at the time of writing basic employment law, including the national minimum wage, does not apply to self-employed or independent contractors in the UK. Neither are they entitled to other benefits that normally apply. A government website lists these as:

Statutory Sick Pay.

Statutory maternity, paternity, adoption and shared parental leave.

Minimum notice periods if their employment will be ending, eg if an employer is dismissing them.

Protection against unfair dismissal.

The right to request flexible working.

Time off for emergencies.

Statutory Redundancy Pay.[45]

A report in England revealed the economic fate of many who are classified as self-employed. Most notably, the likelihood of ending up as the next uber-rich Richard Branson is rather low: 'Self-employed people on average have experienced a 22 per cent fall in real pay since 2008–09, with average earnings of £207 a week, less than half that of employees, with no sick pay or holiday pay, and no employer to contribute towards their pension'.[46] According to another study, the burgeoning class of self-employed workers in England is paid in 2016 less than a typical employee received in 1994.[47]

We can see why this is the case in a recent account of a Hermes courier driver in Huddersfield, UK.[48] First of all was the training. The driver spent two days shadowing another contractor, which he wasn't paid for since, as Gary Becker proposed, that would be economically irrational to the firm. Once the driver was on the payroll, he calculated his income to be about £4 per hour before expenses. And after figuring these expenses into the equation the bleak reality became clear:

> The Hermes model offloads all the risk on to the 'independent' courier, but the potential reward is absolutely limited. You are responsible for the packages, any problems with the system, your car, paying for your holiday time, covering any sickness. I learned that the postman in one of the villages recently had an operation

on his hand as a result of an injury at work. His job was pretty much the same as mine, but he was a Royal Mail employee and had just had five weeks off on sick pay. Hermes couriers don't get any sick pay. The postmen often help out the couriers because they feel sorry for them. They know the Hermes guys get a raw deal.[49]

Given the unfolding trends in wreckage economies of the West, it is easy to imagine Royal Mail management accountants reading this excerpt very carefully, thinking about how they too can transform their workforce into independent contractors. Moreover, with dropping wages and increasing economic insecurity, no wonder the pressure to work – no matter what – is more apparent under systems of ultra-responsible autonomy. And this can require marathon-like feats of stamina.

Wi-Fi for masochists

Melissa Gregg's study of freelancers in Australia highlights the long hours of work involved in order to make ends meet.[50] The trouble with human capital theory is that the ideal enterprising individual categorically ignores the traditional boundaries that were once erected between work and non-work. For they are now 'permanent enterprises', a phrase coined by Michel Foucault in his lectures on neoliberalism, since life itself becomes an all-encompassing economic venture.[51] Human capitalists never 'check out' in this respect. And if that means working all night to meet a deadline then so be it. Overwork and burnout are soon foreseeable.

In addition to overwork, another important consequence arises when employment is organised in this way; namely, *unpaid work*. Gregg found that when economy and life become one (the ultimate datum of human capital theory), people find themselves working on their own time, say on Sunday night in order to prepare for a meeting on Monday morning. Work colonises everything else since life as such (Gary Becker even includes our choice of romantic partner) is nothing more than a commercial venture. In the context of her study, Gregg observed flexi-workers personally paying for what ought to have been a company expense, such as postage and software, in order to meet deadlines.[52] We might term this tendency 'free work capitalism'. It affects not only freelancers but also many in stable jobs too as mobile technology makes it difficult to tell when the work day is truly over. Indeed, the use of handheld devices almost perfectly expresses this development. Since money never sleeps, neither should human capital. Under mounting pressure to perform well people end up working longer hours than formally remunerated for. It is not surprising that a 2016 study by the Chartered Management Institute in the UK found that many employees technically cancel out their entire annual statutory holidays given the after-hours work they do.[53] Burnout, hyper-tension and low productivity are an inevitable consequence, according to the study.

And therein lies another important facet of ultra-responsible autonomy. What employers consider cheap labour is actually very expensive for everybody else to maintain. For instance, a company would find it almost impossible to hire a restaurant worker on minimum (or below) wage without the state covering the shortfall with tax credits, housing benefits and so forth. This amounts to a generous public subsidy to corporations who are not willing to pay a basic living wage. In 2012–13, the UK taxpayer gifted the corporate sector £93 billion or about £3500 from each household in direct and indirect subsidies.[54] The figures are important. Low-wage work and its ultra-responsible autonomous management systems not only exploit workers directly but also extract wealth from the public purse. Corporate welfare such as this undermines the very self-reliance and flexibility flaunted in popular arguments that advocate individual contracts. Now workers are super-dependent on both their employer and an increasingly disciplinary government apparatus. And of course, the story wouldn't be complete without mentioning the banking industry. Only under these socio-economic conditions could credit card debt get so out of hand among the working poor (and increasingly the middle class) as they struggle to maintain a semi-decent standard of living.

The gift of debt

The radical individualisation of work described above is inter-connected with other disconcerting trends that can easily be traced back to human capital theory. The early economic thought in this area was preoccupied with training and education as a key self-investment opportunity. Recall how Gary Becker and Theodore Schultz argued that any benefit derived from *public* investment in human capital cannot be owned by a *private* person. This is no gift or welfare programme. The corollary being that for human capital to hold any water as a concept he or she must ultimately be responsible for the investment outlay. That is because they're inseparable from their own 'value' and nobody else can take ownership of it.

At the firm level, as Becker averred, it's irrational for an employer to cover training costs because in a competitive labour market turnover is expected.[55] At the state level, Friedman popularised a similar attitude. Why should hard working taxpayers 'gift' to a complete stranger the resources required to accumulate their human capital given that only the said stranger benefits from the investment?[56] In the end, this means training and skill acquisition is largely the individual employee's responsibility. The implications are clear. If someone seeks to enjoy the relative advantages of being employed as a skilled employee, then tertiary education and or/ training is essential. This is no public provision, however, since only the individual in question profits in terms of future earnings. To see the rationale in practice, just look at the language used in the 1997 Dearing report that effectively ended free tertiary education in the UK. It has human capital theory written all over it:

> The level of investment needed in a learning society is such that we see a need for those who benefit from education and training after the age of 18 to bear a greater share of the costs. As a result, we expect students of all ages will be increasingly discriminating investors in higher education, looking for quality, convenience, and relevance to their needs at a cost they consider affordable

and justified by the probable return on their investment of time and money.[57]

The terminology represents a major paradigm change in how the resourcing of tertiary education is understood, transforming what was once considered a 'public good' into a private investment. Unless they're already wealthy, most people won't have immediate access to the funds required for tuition fees. So personal debt becomes a solution. There is thus a clear connection between the reschematisation of people as human capital and the tremendous rise of student indebtedness. Exacerbated by aggressive fiscal policy and a predatory finance industry, student debt has become enormous in many OECD economies.[58] In the USA it stood at $1.2 trillion in 2014, with over 7 million debtors in default. In the UK the figure is around £2 billion and steadily growing. A report in the UK found that the average 18-year-old entering university today will be making loan repayments well into their old age.[59] Moreover, a recently study by the Intergenerational Foundation found that the 'graduate premium' (i.e., the average pay increase a graduate enjoys following a university education) is all but cancelled out by student debt.[60] A spokesperson for the report concluded that 'the current system is fuelling a self-perpetuating debt-generating machine which short-changes young people'.[61]

Architectures of abandonment

A number of dysfunctions beset a society that finances the acquisition of knowledge and skills using unsafe levels of credit. Many members of what Howker and Malik term the 'jilted generation' are simply unwilling to take on such a lifelong liability, especially in economically deprived neighbourhoods where the dream of a well-paid graduate job remains simply that, a dream.[62]

When David Bowie died in 2016 an astute commentator wondered if such groundbreaking talent could ever emerge in present-day London given how the working-class Bowie enjoyed free art college and so forth. With almost daily reports about the dreadful anxiety experienced by student debtors,[63] it is no wonder that a study by Callender and Jackson found that perhaps whole generations are trying to keep the debt collector at bay by avoiding higher education altogether.[64] Was another Bowie among them? Who knows? But sadly we wouldn't ask the same question regarding another Donald Trump who would have no problem paying the fees.

That's the point. Skill and innovation are structurally compromised under these conditions of inequality because the potential pool of talent is so drastically shrunk. Only a small group of individuals from wealthy families end up with jobs that require expertise and attract high incomes. For everyone else, a self-reinforcing, downward spiral emerges. The sequence goes like this. Low-skilled job creation is inevitable in light of substandard labour market capabilities.[65] This discourages capital investment and labour productivity subsequently falls. It's easy to understand why an employer would not be overly enthusiastic about investing in new machinery or an IT system if there is no labour force to make the most of it.[66] In the meantime, evolving at the other end of the labour market is a serious skills deficit. Restricted training opportunities mean there are not enough qualified people to fill the available vacancies.[67] Anti-immigration policies clearly exacerbate that problem. And so on. To summarise, economic growth seems to *contract* in economies that endorse human capital theory. The old prediction that post-industrial societies would produce an immense, upward 'skills revolution' almost seems comical today in light of the evidence.[68]

Such chronic underinvestment in training and education (or its individual privatisation) perhaps reflects the vast withdrawal of public maintenance and capital infrastructure expenditure more generally following the rise of wreckage economics. In the USA, for example, some have argued that America is literally falling apart. As one report states, 'our roads and bridges are crumbling, our airports are out of date and the vast majority of our seaports are in danger of becoming obsolete. All the result of decades of neglect.'[69] From my own experience, I was amazed how inner-city Atlanta and Los Angeles looked like neglected, rundown slums. The UK isn't far behind. Similarly, private firms too have significantly stalled on capital investment in their own enterprises. This has had some surprising outcomes. Take the growing ugliness of office space in the UK, for example, which is probably a consequence of underspending. When times are tough, sprucing up the decor, renovating the heating or IT system can easily slip down the list of priorities. The most depressing office environment I have seen was in a large London bank. Having passed through so many levels of security that Fort Knox would have been envious, I finally reached the nerve centre of the organisation. Open plan. Rows upon rows of forlorn faces. A dull, putrid green colour scheme that was perhaps briefly fashionable in 1986. But only briefly. It was rumoured that some staff opposite each other had never spoken to each other. Studying the suicide-grey workstations, I could kind of understand why. Peter Gibbon's sad lament in the film *Office Space* summed it up: 'we don't have a lot of time on this earth. We weren't meant to spend it this way!'

Capital underinvestment is perhaps one of the reasons why a recent survey of 12,000 employees across twelve countries found that British offices are easily the ugliest and coldest.[70] According to this research, 30 per cent of British respondents found their work environment very impersonal; 13 per cent said their workspace was plain ugly, which is double the global average; 45 per cent were unhappy with the temperature. Too cold. It was the lack of choice and autonomy over their work environments that really caused concern among British respondents. When a grown adult has no control over their most basic physiological needs, including temperature, light and posture, they soon begin to suffer. It's not just the corporate hierarchy that can feel undemocratic but the geographical space itself. The quality of our workspace might seem a trivial thing, one of those indulgent 'first world problems' that doesn't really matter in the larger scheme of things. However, the research says otherwise. Cooler temperatures can trigger a matching mood of 'social coldness', making us feel lonely and isolated, even in a room full of people.[71] Another study suspects that ugly workspaces might be linked to mood disorders and suicide.[72] This is serious given how much time we spend in the workplace.

Depression and suicidal thoughts are at least an emotional reaction to such surroundings. But for many others even that would be a luxury. Without any sense of moving ahead or betterment, which is a consequence of low investment in training and development, *boredom* is added to the mix of employee experiences in the contemporary workplace. What was once heralded as an exciting and dynamic post-industrial age, driven by creativity and imagination, has actually turned out to be deadly mind-numbing for many. Stasis and a sense of languishing in a world frozen in time has become endemic in industries that don't provide career development. It is little surprise that productivity has bottomed-out in OECD economies when everyone is so bored. A recent report on 'bore out' (the 'burnout' equivalent for the unengaged) gave an account of a 47-year-old insurance worker in the UK.[73] Steve Coster said, 'It was just so boring. I felt ill knowing I had to go back on Monday morning. Every aspect of it was the same. The commute every day is the same, the people are the same, the lunch is the same. You turn up every morning and sit there.'

Couple the lack of investment in training with the overcapacity trend we mentioned in the previous chapter (whereby people spend hours being idle in the office), Steve had to find ever more novel ways to relieve the boredom: 'I used to go and sit in the toilet cubicles. I would always be the most eager person to get up and make the tea. I would hide behind my screen and surround myself with files so I looked busy, but I wasn't doing anything.'[74] According to one study, this is a growing trend with serious consequences. Surveying a sample of 7000 UK public sector employees over a 24-year period, bored workers are far more likely to die earlier than those who found their jobs interesting and fulfilling.[75]

You've got hate mail

Ugly offices. No career developments. Deadly boredom. Low pay and insecurity. Human capital theory really has a lot to answer for!

And this means that large groups of people being subjected to these trends are deeply unhappy. Hence, the most surprising outcome of the ultra-responsible autonomy revolution. The dramatic expansion of management. I argue that so-called 'free agents' are actually more micro-managed, monitored and directly supervised now than ever. This observation is missed by celebrants and critics alike, who emphasise self-management and self-regulation, albeit insecure and stressful. Even seasoned critics of new capitalism like Andre Gorz wrongly assume that old-fashioned organisational hierarchies disappear with the advent of individualised, market-based employment practices.[76] But here is the rub. Employees are certainly *on their own* when it comes to absorbing the risks and costs of economic insecurity. But this doesn't mean they are *left alone*. Just the opposite. Authoritarianism is now a definitive aspect of this approach to labour relations.

Perhaps it is here that the promise of freedom made in the name of human capital is truly betrayed. In an extensive study of organisational-level employment practices, researchers recently found that deregulated labour markets tend to attract 'thicker' and more ridged management structures: 'organisations employing high shares of flexible workers have higher shares of managers in their personnel. We argue that flexibility in labour markets (i.e., easier firing and higher labour turnover) damages trust, loyalty and commitment. This requires more *management and control*.'[77] The managerial function – especially its policing facet – returns with vengeance given the unhappiness that ultra-responsible autonomy fosters, a trend foreseen back in the mid-1990s by more perspicuous economists like David Gordon.[78] He suggested there was a kind of sociological 'law' when it comes to hierarchies and bosses. Under conditions of inequality, they can easily take on a life of their own and automatically proliferate. Because insecure workers feel hard done by and fight back, we see the spread of bosses precisely in those industries we would expect to see less. They're hired to keep a lid on the seething dissatisfaction caused by zero-hours contracts and Uberised jobs. Then companies end up needing more supervisors to check on the supervisors.

Blend this management distrust with technological surveillance and then some really alarming work environments emerge, even in relatively skilled and secure occupations. For example, in January 2016 journalists at a well-known London newspaper were suddenly ordered to wear heat and motion sensors that monitored if they were at their desks.[79] The initiative was unannounced. Employees simply found the devices at their desks on Monday morning. They had to Google the brand name to identify what they were. An edict was afterwards issued by senior management. The sensors must be worn at all times during work hours. For many it didn't make sense. Journalism doesn't operate this way. It flourishes when workers can rove from their desk, not be needlessly tied to it. And it'd be doubly difficult to do the job while being micro-managed – one on one – by some little-Hitler on a secret computer in the back office. But perhaps getting the job done well wasn't the point. In any case, all of this seems very far away from the ROWE organisations that were predicted to be the norm by 2017.

Office trolling for beginners

Another case is very germane for highlighting this counter-intuitive trend towards over-management in an era of ultra-responsible autonomy and competitive human capital. Namely, the 2015 exposé of white-collar employment at Amazon revealed by *New York Times* journalists Kantor and Streitfeld in an undercover report.[80] We are frequently led to believe that the IT sector thrives on flexibility, a caring management style and creativity because of the goods and services being produced. We know how bad the Amazon warehouses are, but surely the madness of micro-management would not apply to its white-collar staff too? The *New York Times* report found a fairly brutal situation. Much of the attention was on the highly individualised 'rank and yank' performance review where employees are regularly reviewed, stack ranked, and the worst performers fired. Kantor and Streitfeld's exposé described a data-led performance management style that documented almost every action – including how long it took to reply to an email.

There was also the Anytime Feedback Tool, where workers could leave anonymous comments about each other's performance to the boss. A former employee complained it could be used to sabotage co-workers and exact revenge. It 'promises to turn the annual performance review into a daily event', the report said.

Amazon CEO Jeff Bezos responded angrily to the *New York Times* report. In a memo to staff, he accused the paper of grossly misrepresenting the firm: 'The article doesn't describe the Amazon I know or the caring Amazonians I work with every day.' Much of the media hoopla pointed out the unusualness of these types of controls in a professional firm. But is the Amazon management philosophy really an unusual outlier in the corporate world? It's worth looking at the reader responses to the story. Apart from the predictable outrage ('After reading this article, I want to vomit') and notes of approval ('America needs more companies like Amazon') the comments section teems with 'my firm does that too' nuggets of insight. For example: 'I am an engineer at the biggest semiconductor company in the world. I have worked here for 17 years. I can only say the work environment described in this article is very similar to where I am working.' The vision of Amazon's office culture set up in the *New York Times* article really is no deviation from the classic precepts of managerial capitalism. If the *New York Times* allegations were true, Amazon has simply taken a fairly traditional managerial creed – numerically record every human employee action in the workplace so that it can be completely controlled – and enlisted 'big data' to invent an inescapable surveillance machine.

This is interesting since in the case of Amazon, we see the management paranoia of the old 'irresponsible autonomy' era blend with the 'ultra-responsible autonomy' ethos. In some ways, the worst of both worlds is the worker's fate today, giving contemporary management approaches (even in the info-tech world) something of a draconian feel about them. We can recall that for control-obsessed Frederick Winslow Taylor the first principle of management was very simple. He wanted to scien-tifically measure every part of the job so that he understood it far better than the employee actually doing it. For this he used a stopwatch. Then he ranked each worker's output individually and rewarded them accordingly. Taylor was driven by a deep worry. If employees hid their behaviour from managers, especially in group settings, they would end up controlling the production process rather than supervisors. It is fairly clear that this legacy of distrust is still prevalent in today's modern offices. However, the reason workers despised this so-called 'scientific management' style was not because they wanted to stage a revolution or take over the means of production. No, it's just very difficult to do the job well under such conditions. We become more concerned about what the metrics say, compulsively comparing ourselves to others, usually in a state of anxiety. And let's not even mention cooperation. In other words, getting the job done well becomes a secondary issue.

It might be argued that using hyper-individualised big data to control workplace behaviour truly enters another arena with Amazon's Anytime Feedback Tool. But similar systems have been common in offices for some time, most notably the '360 degree' appraisal method where employees are evaluated by their supervisor and anonymously by their co-workers and subordinates. It's been around since World War II. The trouble is that anonymous assessments hardly ever promote objectivity. Especially when the comments capture spur of the moment gripes. It's similar to the 'disinhibitor effect' among internet users. All kinds of devious and ugly thoughts end up being expressed, many of which may not actually be genuinely endorsed when the evaluator is confronted face-to-face. This is why seasoned business advisors are so wary of anonymous peer appraisals. The opportunity for what might be called 'office trolling' is ample when everyone is cast as competitive human capitalists. Things can get nasty at this point.

Almost every business guru now pontificates about the virtues of 'completing the feedback circle' as swiftly as possible. This is the circuit between performance (what we do) evaluation (by a customer, boss, peers) and feedback (the packaged information returned to the individual so that their behaviour can be corrected). The faster the feedback, the better. Electronically derived data makes it possible, perhaps for the first time, to close this circle instantaneously. A process of constant performance review. But do abstract numbers really give us a complete picture about how well an individual is performing in, say, a meeting? Or a team's effectiveness given it can consist of different individuals with diverse roles? Many would say not. What once used to be conducted with stopwatches has now been taken to the nth degree with computers. Perhaps this is why so many managers today – in the public and private sectors – suffer from a crippling 'spreadsheet mentality'. Screeds of numbers are mistakenly treated like some sacred truth about what makes employees tick. Frederick Taylor would have loved 'big data' and the Anytime Feedback Tool. In his time, however, Taylor's ideas sparked widespread riots. Will the data-led management fad exemplified by Amazon do the same?

'Great wrist action'

The important point is that we see the circle of neoliberal managerialism closed in this power structure. Ultra-responsible autonomy (or human capital personified) meets intrusive, big data metrics and the results are not pretty. Workers are now 'on their own' in terms of owning their own fortunes in an ever volatile economy. As I have demonstrated in relation to human capital theory, this simply transfers the costs of work – including tools, transport and the time to organise – onto the worker themselves. However, the famous indeterminacy of the labour process (i.e., the gap between the command to work and its realisation in practice, a space where resistance can flourish) is no longer feared by the corporation, regardless of the distrust it still has towards employees. Why so? Well, this new kind of employee 'freedom' can be exploited and utilised, propelled by economic insecurity and anxiety. The return and amplification of methods that were prevalent under regimes characterised by 'irresponsible autonomy' (so meticulously outlined by Taylor) are designed to micro-regulate workers' 'freedom' in a manner that is frequently punitive and exceedingly harsh. With a large labour pool available and wage stagnation, a certain degree of perverse competition is entered into the mix, making these employment conditions resemble something out of *Hunger Games*.

But matters are more worrying than this, since today's workplaces display characteristics that even Taylor couldn't have imagined. Alongside the dire precarity (being on your own) and heightened managerial control (harassed every minute of the day) is a rapid *deformalisation* of the employment relationship. The old official employer/employee relationship has been recast in more personal terms. Sounds nice, doesn't it? Well, not exactly. Now what matters is not simply your formal skills and abilities but how well you're able to curry favour with the boss. Does he like me? It really oughtn't to have any bearing, but now it's everything. This shift was inevitable given how contracts are now temporary, typically exempt from rules that protect full-time workers, following the human capital emphasis on personal qualities. I suggest that this deformalisation of work is really linked to increased dependence as the balance of power turned heavily in favour of employers (and customers). When a worker is desperately reliant on a job, competing with others for the best shifts, and managers fully grasp this situation, the less powerful party will feel the need to ingratiate him or herself. This has been a prime complaint for many working in the on-demand economy. A recent anonymous account of agency work in a bar is telling.[81] The young woman tells the reader that the paperwork (filling shift-rotas, etc.) and security measures at the start of the shift took 45 minutes, which were unpaid. Then there is the uncertainty. Another worker turned up to the agency and was told he wasn't needed that day. But at the actual bar, however, it was how employees and managers interacted that really shocked the writer:

A bar manager took to calling one of the girls 'treacle'. The 19-year-old student was told she had 'great wrist action' as she mixed a G&T. She visibly squirmed when he asked her to 'stop flirting with him', but she felt powerless. The overweight, balding 40-year-old was her temporary manager; if she started filing complaints, she was unlikely to be given a valuable 12-hour shift again. We agency staff were continually reminded how lucky we were to be working there.[82]

When this deformalisation of employment blends with traditional power relationships it clearly presents an opportunity for some rather primitive gender politics. An anonymous female contractor at Facebook's Trending team tells a similar story.[83] Her job was to find links for user's Trending Box on the website. Mentioning her co-workers, she said there was an 'extraordinary amount of talent on the team, but poor management, coupled with intimidation, favouritism and sexism, has resulted in a deeply uncomfortable work environment. Employees I worked with were angry, depressed and left voiceless – especially women.' Californian pop-management writers have been proclaiming for some time the benefits that can be gained if firms deformalise their staid bureaucratic structures. The point is to render the office more human again. However, when authority and high dependency is involved too, a culture of informality can often bring out the nasty, capricious side of people. That's pertinent when it comes to more sensitive issues like promotion or misconduct procedures. As opposed to the trendy 'be more human' doctrine sweeping the employment sector, a bit of bureaucracy can sometimes be useful to ensure more unprejudiced outcomes. The same applies to food safety and fire regulations. Steve Hilton, the one-time Tory guru who apparently wandered No. 10 Downing Street barefooted, seems to have missed this point when writing his anti-bureaucracy tract *More Human*.[84]

Making desperation pay ... the sharing economy

It was only inevitable that the so-called 'sharing economy' would develop out of these socio-economic conditions. Technology, desperation and the continuing individualisation of culture has seen this industry dramatically expand in the USA, UK and elsewhere. Governments now officially speak about its importance and contribution to a nation's economic wellbeing. The sharing economy has a list of alternative titles that make it look as if we are entering into a new age of utopian collectivism where amateurish goodwill reigns supreme: the peer economy, networked economy, on-demand economy, collaborative economy, gig economy and so forth. But once again we see a typical feature of wreckage economics behind the trend. Business platforms such as Airbnb ride on the informal economy, opportunistically exploiting the insecurity that has become a norm under crisis capitalism. The once laudable commons-based system of peer production has been commercialised by big business using old school middle-man or rentier tactics, thereby generating profits *without production*. They say that it's about saving 'waste' (idle cars could be taxies, empty bedrooms could be holiday accommodation, etc.). But it's really a method of exploiting the societal devastation that has unfolded following the recession. For example, house and car sharing might be seen as a useful way to make some cash given how these resources might have otherwise been lying dormant. According to the fans of the sharing economy, this kind of exchange is based on trust and mutual respect. And drawing on 'matching theory', firms say they're just providing a platform to help sellers identify buyers more efficiently.[85] However, a journalist for the *New York Magazine* investigated the nature of these customer-to-customer relationships, and found an atmosphere quite different to the hype:

> In almost every case, what compels people to open up their homes and cars to complete strangers is money, not trust ... Tools that help people trust in the kindness of strangers might be pushing hesitant sharing-economy participants over the threshold to adoption. But what's getting them to the threshold in the first place is a damaged economy, and harmful public policy that has forced millions of people to look to odd jobs for sustenance.[86]

The same can be said for business-to-customer setups. Uber, Deliveroo, TaskRabbit and similar firms function through a three-stage process: seek an impoverished sector of society, capture their time and resource (with minimal investment costs) and then present that resource to a customer for a surcharge. This is why some have suggested that the sharing economy is more about *access*. But access to what? Life itself, of course – which is where human capital theory really arrives at its logical conclusion. To tap life itself in a 24/7 economy that is endlessly fed by people who are willing to sell their time, space and labour for a fee (the firm 'Whats Your Price' uses the correct terminology in this respect). But it is important to further ask exactly whose lives are being captured in this manner. Generally, it is those who have been most negatively affected by the recent polarisation of wealth distribution as neoliberal capitalism crashes and burns. It is only for this reason that we could possibly fathom a firm like Uber to ever see the light of day. These workers will serve as on-demand drivers for one-off customers for as long as they can sit behind the wheel. An Uber employee recently described what it was like:

> Everyone looks like they're doing fine, but they're really working 80–100 hour weeks and even then, constantly feel like they're behind. Working for Uber is a sprint, with marathon hours ... At Uber, you work nights, weekends, and holidays. Some teams split it up so you get some real time off during the week/weekend, but that's rare.[87]

And as with their Amazon white-collar counterparts mentioned earlier, big data means that these workers are on their own but never left alone since they are ranked by customers and constantly tracked by the software.

According to Steve Hill, a tireless critic of Uberisation, we are witnessing the coming of the '1099 economy' in the USA because these workers file a 1099-MISC form. It classifies them as independent contractors for tax purposes.[88] Businesses with 'perma-tempt' employees in the 1099 economy can cut labour costs by 30 per cent. Based upon Hill's own experience as a 'perma-lancer', he explains why any (economically) rational business will find these new arrangements attractive because

> it is not responsible for a 1099 worker's health benefits, retirement, unemployment or injured workers compensation,

lunch breaks, overtime, disability, paid sick, holiday or vacation leave and more. In addition, contract workers are paid only for the specific number of hours they spend providing labour, which increasingly is being reduced to shorter and shorter 'micro-gigs'.[89]

The socio-economic logic of the Uberised economy is clear. It's not only a process of exploiting workers directly but also eroding workers' rights indirectly and more pervasively. Normal taxi drivers, for example, feel under pressure to compete with unlicensed Uber drivers, and lower their costs. The same knock-on effect resonates through the entire economy. This is an important point. The 1099 worker is not only bad for themselves and the standard workers they compete with but the workforce more generally as more industries and sectors gravitate towards zero-hours contracts and the ultimate objective of the human capital theorists, a life entirely dedicated to commercial activity, day and night ... be they a Deliveroo cyclist or a desperate student who signs up to the 'Whats Your Price' dating sight to find a 'Sugar Daddy' who will pay their tuition fees.

White van nation

There are other adverse side-effects rippling through society when it turns to Uber as a guiding economic metaphor. In the UK, for example, most of us have encountered the classic white van man at some point. He helps us move flat, fits our new kitchen, yells at us when we drive too slowly or force him to brake by running across the road. We don't mind his rough edges because he's so much cheaper than his smoother rivals. Well, this is the stereotypical and rather snobbish image of the white van man. But it seems that he (or sometimes she) is getting too widespread to be pigeonholed as an idiosyncratic amateur. A 2016 report by the Society of Motor Manufacturers and Traders has revealed that there are now more than 4 million commercial vans in Britain.[90] In 2016 van traffic across Britain rose by 6 per cent. Together, those millions of vehicles covered 47 billion miles. Almost six out of ten of them are actually white, by the way. Silver and blue are the next most popular colours. The report puts much of the increase down to online shopping, and many of us will greet the rise of white van man with optimism and delight.

However, there is a much bleaker side to this trend. The service and knowledge economy is often touted a cleaner and more environmentally friendly way of organising our society. Bill Gates once heralded this as the era of 'frictionless capitalism', a spotless, shiny and pollution-free world.[91] But now we are realising that web-based business models associated with Uberisation can have concrete and very dirty consequences. The dramatic increase in traffic is taking a toll on our air quality. In London, for example, air pollutants have been linked to a wave of untimely deaths.[92] The deluge of more and more white vans on our streets catering for our online shopping obsession is the gritty underbelly of so-called frictionless capitalism.

The rise of the White Van Nation also tells us a lot about the kind of work that has been encouraged and normalised with the rise of the gig economy. One in seven workers in this country – 4.8 million in all – are now their own bosses, and many of the drivers delivering flowers for supermarkets or mattresses for department stores will be self-employed contractors, which indicates the spread of the Uber principle deep into the employment sector. As mentioned earlier, this means a significant drop in real wages compared to permanent employees. And, willingly or not, many nominally self-employed workers find themselves working full time for a single client, without any of the benefits of regular employment. White van man can spend 40 or more hours a week delivering parcels for the same supermarket or telecom company, without any right to sick pay or pension provisions. It's time, then, to update the cliché of the white van man which used to be a famous facet of working-class culture. Instead of a self-reliant and contented plumber or electrician, that Ford Transit or Citroen Relay is probably being driven by a tired and exploited zero-hours worker. And while its shiny bodywork may suggest a clean, frictionless capitalism, the reality is a dirty and polluted country gasping for air.

Inhuman capital?

Let's briefly summarise the argument before proposing some solutions. I have aimed to demonstrate how human capital theory provides a kind of ideological alibi for the radical individualisation of jobs and the workforce. Developed by neoclassical economists such as Gary Becker, Theodore Schultz and Milton Friedman, human capital theory fundamentally atomises people across all of society, placing the costs of economic activity onto the employee, student, caregiver and so forth. When it comes to work, the normalisation of mass self-employment, on-demand business models, freelancing and the Uberisation of the workforce effortlessly follows from the idea that people are ultimately responsible for their own economic fate. Human capital theory is widely celebrated as a framework for explaining how organisations and societies can build skill, innovation and economic security. I have argued, however, that it can result in the opposite. Instead of being freer and wealthier, human capitalists are just as likely to be mired in debt, insecure and dominated by authoritarian management systems. Of course, not everything wrong with contemporary employment should be blamed on human capital theory. But given how it is continuously discussed in such positive terms, I have tried to reveal the negative side of human capital theory, especially the employment practices that have been so patently inspired by it, some of which border on the inhuman.

Is it possible to resist or even reverse these socio-economic trends? Given how profitable ultra-responsible autonomy is to big business it's not surprising that they will often resort to drastic measures to eradicate opposition. For example, when the mayor of Copenhagen banned his staff from using Ryanair in 2015 because of poor pay and work conditions, a major fracas arose as the company fought back, labelling him the 'high fare mayor'.[93] According to Social Democrat MP Peter Hummelgaard, 'Ryanair has been screwing workers since 1985' and emphasised the point by tweeting an image of Ryanair CEO –Michael O'Leary – seemingly performing a rather sordid sex act with one of his planes. Other Ryanair employees spoke out.

An ex-pilot for the firm who now is vice president of the Flight Personnel Union said that 'Ryanair's style is management by fear. There is a widespread disdain for employees, you are not treated with trust or respect as an individual – irrespective of whether you are a pilot or cabin crew. I cannot comprehend that you can be treated like that.'[94]

The Danish union said Ryanair workers ought to be covered by a collective contract, regardless of whether these workers were part of the union, which they weren't. The company's response? Ryanair simply abandoned the route to Billund airport. CEO Michael O'Leary stated his position bluntly: 'If we sign a collective agreement with the Danish unions, we will then be asked to sign 15 French collective agreements, 55 Spanish collective agreements and a lot of Italian collective agreements. We are not going to do that.'[95] This angry anti-union stance is now commonplace in the UK. For example, in 2016 it was revealed that major construction firms illegally blacklisted workers who were union members, denying them jobs.[96] Forty major firms, including Balfour Beatty and Sir Robert McAlpine, secretly collected and shared information about thousands of workers. This reveals the lengths some businesses will go to banish unions from the brave new world of work. As far as this theory of economic behaviour is concerned, living human capital certainly doesn't belong to a union.

De-Uberising class consciousness

An important first step is to demonstrate how ultra-responsible autonomy isn't a more effective and efficient form of economic rationality. On many levels it is *economically irrational* once we step back and look at its wider effects. Zero-hours contracts, Uberisation and low-skilled jobs are tiringly expensive to the state and individual workers alike, damaging labour productivity and economic growth. Employee wellbeing undeniably declines because of poorer pay, onerous management structures and lack of investment in training. Neoliberal discourse attempts to cloak these dysfunctions by emphasising individual choice and responsibility once again. If you're a loser in the new world of work it must somehow be your fault. Human capital theory perfects this maxim.

The most obvious conclusion from my analysis is that workers today have been grossly disempowered by these employment relationships. This has allowed the genuine yearning for employee autonomy to be hijacked and transformed into an instrument of proletarianisation. Rebalancing the employer/employee relationship is the only way the situation might be rectified. This means employee collectivisation, breaking the spell of human capital theory and its impoverishing ethos of individualism. But is this realistically possible? In many ways it is already happening, with labour collectives around the world opposing the human capital hoax. For example, London Uber drivers took their case to the UK Employment Tribunal in October 2016. They claimed they were employees (rather than self-employed) and thus eligible to be paid the minimum wage. The court agreed.[97] From the 'alt-labour' movement in the USA, to employee cooperatives in Europe (such as the inter-European CECOP network) and the rise of employee activism.[98] Even Uberised workforces, which epitomise the worst excesses of radical individualisation, have recently united to fight against their ghastly treatment.[99] For sure, recall how the disgruntled pilots mentioned at the beginning of this chapter formed a concerted response to their de facto employer.

The return to solidarity does not necessarily have to be in the name of class interests, which has significantly diminished as an 'imagined community' in recent years. Perhaps championing the broader idea of universal workers' rights is a more effective strategy, potentially reaching a richer audience than any appeal to increasingly fragile class loyalties. Regardless, a more balanced employment relationship is indispensable if self-determination is to be successfully renegotiated to create fairer life chances. No doubt this may have a positive impact on the economy more generally (in terms of engagement, productivity, less cumbersome management, higher wages that drive growth, etc.). Only on these grounds can the desire for a socially responsible independence be practically achieved. The point needs emphasising, which also highlights the flimsy foundations upon which human capital theory is built. One cannot truly express individuality, self-reliance and choice when desperately dependent on an unequal power relationship. Wider societal backup and support is necessary.

Governmental policy must play a decisive role in promoting a more just organisation of work. Many Western nation-states have been openly hostile to the collective empowerment of workers. When the workforce has meaningful input into their occupations, however, disengagement will no longer be the overriding experience. Democratising the workplace requires legal support and incentives, which the state can readily deliver (for example, the New Zealand government recently outlawed zero-hours contracts after pressure from labour unions).[100] Other measures are also possible. A universal living wage would effectively neutralise the existential fear that has led so many to settle for so little in contemporary organisations.[101] Detractors wrongly argue that society cannot afford such spending and inflation would run rampant. However, given the genuine independence that a universal living wage permits, which would be a kind of formalisation of the gulf that already exists between income and jobs, economic utility and work, the bill is typically *less* compared to the cost of funding a vast bureaucratic infrastructure to manage the unemployed and working poor.[102] Inflation doesn't rise because no new money is printed, only more fairly redistributed. And the presumption that businesses must *automatically* shift the expense of fairer wages onto the consumer (via the hiked prices of goods and services) was always dubious economic reasoning.[103] Of course, a universal living wage is open to manipulation by neoliberal capitalists as well, becoming an excuse to deepen individual responsibility.[104] After all, Milton Friedman was a big fan of one variant of the idea (i.e., 'negative income tax') because for him it also meant abolishing food stamps and seeing the poor embrace the logic of the open market. So if the idea is to be endorsed, it ought to be only done so alongside a broader set of counter-capitalist initiatives that aim to reinvent property relations rather than become yet another excuse for extending hopeless consumerism and the private tyranny of exchange value.

An important basis of occupational empowerment is skill. However, as I have tried to explain in this chapter, major organisational and economic dysfunctions emerge when skill is treated simply as a private good. It instead ought to be framed as a public one: embodied in specific individuals, work groups and organisations, but if enhanced will substantially contribute to broader prosperity in an egalitarian economy. We can already see this ethos fermenting in counter-business initiatives related to the creative commons and cooperatives. These organisations grow precisely by sharing know-how rather than privatising and hoarding it. While the much vaunted notion of the 'sharing economy' has partially fallen prey to corporate interests,[105] it has helped spark debates about how value might be generated outside the datum of private property and competitive individualism.[106]

Once knowledge and skill are deemed a public concern, we must inevitably abandon human capital theory because it is congenitally wedded to the axiom of private, individual ownership. Robert E. Lucas' interesting attempt to square the circle in the human capital paradigm only concluded that there must be some external and unobservable force that adds value beyond the individual human capitalist, a mysterious 'factor X' that prevents 'cities flying apart'.[107] Isn't this telling of the wilful blindness of neoclassical economic theory? A presumably intelligent Nobel Prize laureate feels more comfortable using the term 'factor X' than the public sphere or public goods.

Written-off forever

De-privatising the skills pool would mean radically rethinking the provision of higher education and training, not to deny the individual (as right-wing ideology would have it) but allow him or her to shine. In particular, reversing the massive dependence on student debt that has disfigured many Western economies today is crucial if the skills base is to be rejuvenated and true innovation cultivated. The debt refusal movement is gaining traction in this regard and holds hope for conceptualising education outside the human capital agenda. We have seen some positive movement on this front as well. For example, Simon Crowther gained notoriety in March 2016 when he sent a letter to his local Minister of Parliament complaining that there was something deeply flawed with the student loans system. He simultaneously posted the letter online and received a good deal of media attention. His initial debt was a modest sum, but it had somehow ballooned into £41,976 by 2016 and was paying £180 a month in interest payments. As Crowther's letter of protest points out, he and fellow students,

> feel we have been cheated by a government who encouraged many of us to undertake higher education, despite trebling the cost of attending university. I was still in sixth form at school when I agreed to the student loan. I had no experience of loans, credit cards or mortgages. Like all the other thousands of students in the UK, we trusted the government that the interest rate would remain low – at around 0%–0.5%.[108]

The government had increased the interest rate on the loan. When Crowther had first signed the dotted line this was around 0 per cent to 0.5 per cent. Now he was paying 3.9 per cent. Crowther said, 'I can't see how I will pay it off. The monthly repayments seem geared up just to pay off the interest.'[109] This might seem like an extreme case, but it resonated with the wider public. When Crowther posted his letter to Facebook it was immediately shared thousands of times. It had hit a nerve. Given the misleading information and ill-informed borrowers, there is even talk that student loan debtors might have a legal case similar to the mis-selling of Payment Protection Insurance that has rocked the banking sector over the last few years. The UK government's most recent response to this slow motion crisis is to announce the sale of the student loans book (as securities) to private investors, an example of wreckage economics par excellence.[110]

Given the indenture-like nightmare that personal debt entails, the debt refusal movement is an important first step towards a fairer socio-economic system.[111] Similarly, governments must seriously consider debt relief if we are to dismantle the harmful economic edifice that has been built around ultra-responsible autonomy. I argue this in the name of social equality. But it could also be defended in terms of innovation, productivity and a properly functioning knowledge economy. Moreover, it'd be fairly easy to calculate the wider socio-economic value that a trained doctor, for example, adds to our society (not themselves) due to the education they've received: the many instructors employed to train them, the broad catchment of patients who can now continue to contribute (as workers, mothers, etc.) because of the healthcare they receive, the higher income collected from a skilled versus unskilled worker and all the rest. By the time they're ten years into their careers most university graduates have already paid their dues. A massive student debt on top of that is patently short-sighted and ultimately a recipe for economic backwardness.

In conclusion, human capital theory is just one manifestation of a set of comprehensive neoclassical economic ideas that accentuate self-interested individualism as the only way to envisage the organisation of work and society. However, when set upon the backdrop of wider socio-economic inequalities and uneven power relationships, this excessive individualism recasts workers as complete owners of their economic failure. This is why it's misleading to say that human capital theory is about investing in people. It may also represent a form of *divestment*. Given the important link between neoclassical human capital theory, individual responsibility, personal debt and a massive skills/education deficit, it is no exaggeration to suggest that neoclassical economics *really is* for dummies. This economic doctrine has actually dumbed-down societies, stunted any meritocratic distribution of skilled know-how, and perhaps most evidently, shot itself in the foot since business firms also soon suffer as a result. While this system might easily produce another Donald Trump if uncorrected – a man who declared in his 2016 US presidential election campaign, 'I love the poorly educated!' – it's pretty clear that we won't be seeing another David Bowie anytime soon.

6

The Quiet Earth

In 2010 JetBlue airline assistant Steven Slater was at the end of his shift. Flight 1052 had landed in New York City and was taxing to the terminal. What transpired during those few minutes was later the subject of much speculation. According to Slater's version of events, a cantankerous passenger persistently ignored the request to remain seated and went for her overhead luggage during the taxiing process. As Slater rushed to reseat the non-compliant passenger, the bag fell and hit him in the face. He was distraught and asked for an apology. But the passenger instead decided to add insult to injury and called him 'a motherfucker'.[1] According to other passengers who witnessed the furore, as well as the Port Authority Police investigation following the incident, Slater's story might be a little inaccurate.[2] The media tried to seek the overeager woman who had allegedly annoyed Slater so much. They guessed it might have been a 21-year-old student called Hilary Baribeau, who had somehow popped on the radar. But she denied the allegation when they tracked her down: 'I saw the male steward get up and say, "please sit down and wait", and then the female stewardess, said "Please wait, please wait until the light has turned off."'[3]

Slater's lawyer provided another version of the scuffle. Two female passengers at the beginning of the flight had a heated disagreement about the overhead locker space and this escalated when Flight 1052 landed. Steven Slater was caught in the middle and injured during the melee.[4] Whatever the initial flashpoint was, Slater's subsequent actions were well documented.[5] He stormed to the PA system and started to scream at passengers, unleashing a barrage of expletives: 'to the passenger who just called me a motherfucker, fuck you. I've been in this business 28 years, and that's it, I'm done.' The drama then only intensified. He activated the inflatable emergency chute, grabbed two cans of Blue Moon beer and slid down to freedom (this was caught on CCTV). He made his getaway over the tarmac, weaving between planes to the parking lot. Slater then drove home to Queens.

The police eventually apprehended the flight attendant that same day and charged him with criminal mischief and reckless endangerment. According to one Federal Aviation Authority official, 'Clearly, you're not supposed to pop the slides unless there's an emergency in the aircraft. We're continuing to investigate circumstances as well as any violations that may have occurred.'[6] Slater failed to post the $2500 bail at his arraignment and was detained at a South Bronx prison situated on a floating barge. Claiming that he was suffering from mental illness and other mitigating conditions, Slater apologised for his behaviour. He was eventually sentenced to a year probation and order to pay JetBlue $10,000 to cover the cost of deploying the escape chute.

Cracking up

Steven Slater's actions hit a chord with the American public. He was front page news. The US service culture was to blame. It had resulted in people like Slater becoming dehumanised, mere slaves who had to put up with all sorts of horrible behaviour because the customer is always right. Only days after the event, while Slater was facing felony charges, a groundswell of sympathy and adulation emerged in defence of his actions. Facebook pages such as 'Free Steven Slater' and 'I hate the motherfucker who called Steven Slater a motherfucker' became popular.[7] According to a *Huffington Post* survey, 45 per cent of its readers stated that 'Steven Slater is my hero'.[8]

But it was the idea of someone employed in the service industry dealing with humiliation every day, year after year, and then finally 'snapping' that really sounded a note for both fans and detractors of Steven Slater. It appeared that millions of working people recognised their own predicament in his dramatic meltdown. Even staunch business advocates could understand why people like Slater sometimes flew off the handle. A writer for the *Wall Street Journal* opined, 'once we were a great industrial nation. Now we are a service economy. Which means we are forced to interact with each other, every day, in person and by phone and email. And it's making us all a little mad.'[9] *Forbes* magazine ran an advice piece for managers who didn't want to see another Steven Slater blow-up in their workplace. What if he had a gun? In an article titled 'How to head off the Steven Slater in your organisation', for example, readers were told that this is no joking manner.[10] Employees who can't take it anymore can cause real and lasting damage to a business. As far as *Forbes* was concerned, none of this was Slater's fault since he had fallen victim to a common neurological imbalance when the human brain confronts unbearable stress:

Neuroscientists tell us that under pressure we are far more susceptible to emotional hijacks in which the amygdala, the primitive emotional center of the brain, overrides our logical thought processes, and the flight-or-fight response kicks in. The result, more often than not, is neither pretty nor productive. In some cases we fight back, becoming aggressive. In other cases we run away. Slater did both, first hurling expletives and then absconding down the chute.[11]

The commentaries inspired by the Slater incident started to get bizarre. For example, according to business health and safety experts looking into the case from a risk management perspective, 'nobody ever just snaps'.[12] There's always prior warning signs and red flags that ought to be identified before the final curtain drops. Here are some that managers should be on the lookout for in their team:

> **Indirect threats**. John is mad at Jim so he goes to Tom and says, 'If Jim does not knock it off, I'll be waiting for him in the parking lot.' … [t]he person is seeking attention and the situation can be defused at this level – if it is reported.
>
> **Loud outbursts**. Again, this behavior is intended to generate attention.
>
> **Direct threats**. Instead of griping to Tom, John confronts Jim directly.
>
> **Mood and behavior changes**. These include uncharacteristic tardiness, absences, poor hygiene, and drug or alcohol use.
>
> **Withdrawal signs**. For example: An employee taking down photos and packing up his desk even though he is still employed.[13]

Of course, what is not said in this report is that these signs of trouble only matter if displayed by *subordinates*, those lower down in the hierarchy. We all know that most employees have seen their bosses 'absent', engage in 'loud outbursts' and issue 'direct threats'. But that doesn't appear to count as a problem here. Violence is only allowed to flow downwards but never upwards. That is no doubt the golden rule of most hierarchies. Regardless, in the customer service hell that Slater inhabited, his superiors also included the customer, his passengers. And this dynamic – control from above and below – has been impressively accentuated in the era of crisis capitalism, where enduring authoritarianism, even in the most banal interactions, has become a fact of day-to-day life.

Getting even

Whatever the neurological basis or missed warning signs, this type of abrupt 'no' to an *all-inclusive* form of capitalism is telling of the way our modern socio-economic paradigm is perceived today. When we hear terms like 'cognitive capitalism', 'immaterial labour' and 'semio-capitalism' often being used to describe the current organisation of production, it is tempting to think that it is somehow more abstract and less concrete compared to the dirty industrial variety. But as I have demonstrated throughout this book, in many ways the opposite is the case. Because our work and economic lives have become the only way of being in the world – with the help of human capital theory and emotional labour as previously discussed – the productive process becomes weirdly *extra*-concrete. It feels as if the economy, with all of its fluctuating and erratic ups and downs, is both more than us (since we have little control over it and are spectators to the ongoing crisis) and also *part of us*; namely, our personalities, bodies and relationships, especially when things go wrong because negativity gives the meme of worker better 'stickiness'. Unlike past generations of employees in Western economies who could simply walk away at 5 pm and mentally check out, many in the Western mode of capitalism today feel completely surrounded because the economic abstraction of labour has become deeply implicated in daily routines. And once again, what we might call the *infection* of labour is attracted to trauma and self-harm to feed its internal fire. We drink excessively, indulge in useless sex and search for ways to escape. But that only prolongs the process in which a 'conclusion' seems tantalising near but always just out of reach. For those individuals who have completely 'had it', to quote Steven Slater, a violent and drastic existential 'snap' seems like the only plausible way out of this eternal drift.

For sure, this abrupt and finalising 'break' with the capitalist routine appears to be one of the main ways that people resist and refuse neoliberal pan-capitalism today. Refusal itself – the way we voice our grievances and push back against the institutional forces of the wreckage economy – has suddenly become urgently intimate given how homo economicus, or what is presently left of him or her, has infiltrated personal and social life on almost every level. Under these conditions everything feels so extreme and non-ending and requires something drastic to break the spell.

But what do we actually mean by the term resistance? When people resist they have usually come to a simple realisation: I/we cannot go on like this and therefore must act. This is an important point because those who resist often feel they have little choice. They simply must, which renders it less 'tactical' in the Foucauldian sense (since there is little freewheeling opportunism involved) nor determinist in some Marxist perspectives (because there is theoretically still a choice not to resist) but more proto-existential, particularly in light of the conditions we have mentioned above. That sense of 'it cannot go on like this' is generally driven by three motives. People resist activities that might *economically* undermine their interests (e.g., a pay cut). Individuals/groups resist practices that are *politically* threatening, which is often linked to social identity (e.g., if I am a member of a workers' union who calls a strike over a particular issue, I maintain a united front even if not directly affected by the issue in any economic sense). And resistance might occur if a practice or circumstance is deemed *ethically* unacceptable (e.g., a whistle-blower who reveals dubious corporate behaviour even when those practices do not economically or politically threaten the individual). In many cases, including gender and race discrimination, people will resist for a combination of these reasons. Economic inequality may interlink with questions of identity (or political considerations), and ethical issues (i.e., hurt, indignity to others or oneself, etc.) may cross-hatch with all of the aforementioned.

Defriended

Conventional forms of collective protest have not disappeared regardless of what is currently being said about the rise of this dangerous brand of *pan-capitalism* that appears to be able to absorb everything – including revolt. And no doubt class is still the central fulcrum for resisting capitalism successfully since it is the only emancipatory category that also seeks to abolish itself when it confronts the source of economic servitude, not just perpetuate its own self-identity, which is why a number of non-class protest movements can happily subsist alongside capitalist hierarchies.

However, something strange has happened to resistance when it is being expressed by people like Steven Slater who suddenly 'crack up' and lash out. The moment of 'not being able to go on' takes on overly personal qualities that seek a severe and often ferocious moment of withdrawal from the roles we have become and our immediate circumstances. Whereas the schema of resistance outlined above can take on collective or social qualities, the individualisation of homo economicus (as ultra-responsible human capital, for example) has seen the rise of a commensurate I-centred expression of his or her discontent. Often this is transposed into self-hate, since what one really despises about the economy is not just outside their person – the student loan, the corporation, an unforgiving state, a nasty manager – but also something inside, especially since we often feel but a living appendage to that symptom of hate in these biopolitical times. With homo economicus in ruins all around and especially *in* us, apparently now built to fail, we can understand why totally unsustainable rituals of self-harm or self-medication have become but the flipside of economic man once fully realised. Unsurprisingly, this part of the 'dollar chasing animal' is seldom mentioned in the economic textbooks. Nevertheless, it underlies the outward bursts of revolt that shattered the veneer of normalcy for Steven Slater, the Empire State Building shooter, Jeffrey T. Johnson and so many others.

How far an individual gesture of revolt is willing to go is generally proportionate to how much the economic environment is perceived to be inescapable. At first this seems like a paradox. If we are trapped in an all-encompassing ideology that feels unstoppable, then resignation or a numbing quietude should be the most predictable response. In many cases this is certainly true. But for the contemporary worker a slightly different attitude has evolved because they have insight into their own futility. A sort of readymade 'outside' is part and parcel of the totalisation process. It allows people to express a certain self-awareness, a torturous one at that.

Maybe this is somehow linked to the amygdala part of the brain mentioned above, functioning more as a dialectic between freedom and alienation than any quantitative threshold that we pass across before all hell breaks loose. Matters get more complex because the hypothetical external point from which we attempt to gather perspective on what is happening to us is pure *nothingness* given the vacuous nature of human capital and the type of person we have been forced to become. Regardless, the dialectic of capitalist realism (i.e., an inevitable and ontological force) and a teasing outside (i.e., nothingness) mostly keeps people in place, no matter how forlorn their worlds become.

You won't quit

This might account for why so many find it difficult to quit their jobs or frequently resort to incomprehensible acts when they do. Instead of going nuts and hurting oneself or others in a gratuitous manner, why not simply walk away? It turns out that things are not so simple. When you enter 'How to quit …?' into the google search engine, the number of results on how to quit your job are only exceeded by 'How to quit smoking' and 'How to quit smoking weed'. Sending that special email to the boss to 'go fuck yourself', to paraphrase Steven Slater, ought to be easy. But once again, as with many facets of the pan-capitalist socioscape, a dialectical relationship is operating in which a negative sense of entrapment actually bolsters and feeds a positive vision of an outside that is the polar opposite to the present. This vision is often false, of course, like a shimmering light of bliss up ahead in the distance that turns out to be nothing more than a garish hotel in the Californian desert. In any case, this encourages the perception that an extreme incident or breach needs to occur in order to reach that lush world of freedom.

A veritable escape industry (including web-blogs, business pundits, consultants, left-wing newspaper commentators, etc.) has mushroomed overnight to offer its services to tired middle-managers who want to throw it all in, move to Provence, France and start their own cheese business, but don't quite know how to break the news to their spouse and banker manager. Philip Larkin nicely captured the futility that often accompanies exit-fantasies like these in his ode to the despondent office worker, *Toads*:

> Ah, were I courageous enough,
> To shout *Stuff your pension*!
> But I know, all too well, that's the stuff
> That dreams are made on[14]

Larkin's lament concerning the impossible act of quitting still holds true. But this acknowledgement of helplessness has assumed another, more harrowing dimension. The sense of total ideological capture doesn't just create despondency. It also inadvertently ups the ante. In order to break out of this factory of nothingness that has no walls and feels infinite, we must do something really desperate. Foucault called neoliberalism a 'culture of danger' for this reason.[15] To base a society solely upon the image of competition and enterprise means convincing its citizens that life itself is a kind of life and death struggle, with only winners and losers left at the end.

For these reasons, I believe, power no longer seeks to garner our consent by telling us fanciful lies about how great and wonderful society is. In fact, the opposite seems to be the case. It has given up on the 'good life' rhetoric. We are bombarded on a daily basis with dire warnings about how bad things will be if we don't put up with our zero-hours contract, dilapidated pension scheme and vindictive boss. Our natural instinct is to recoil and flee. Yet again, one of the main reasons we don't is because of an odd variant of the battered spouse syndrome, whereby economic man becomes more dependent on and even *attracted* to institutions that inflict pain. This we might call the obscene side of austerity.

Floating prison in the Bronx

Homo economicus extremis is both singularly *attached* to an economic agenda that flirts with extinction (or what I have labelled homo economicus extinctus in other parts of this book), a sort of mad over-identification, but also *ultra-detached* from its ability to act anything like an economic agent in the textbooks, a perverse mis-identification with the ideal. The admixture of the two inevitably results in worrying behaviour, deeds without moderation that seem to come out of nowhere. Steven Slater presents an image of a new type of disempowerment and alienation. Deleuze persuasively argued (after Spinoza) that schizo-capitalism creates unhappy people because it alienates them from their ability to act and do beautiful things.[16] This is one of the key outcomes of power more generally. Either overtly or covertly, it controls us by separating us from our potential. We ought to be happy because of the good job, kids in the suburbs and a retirement plan waiting for us. All of the boxes of civilisation are ticked. But it is all experienced as a major subtraction at the heart of our lives. As if something immensely beautiful is missing and systematically being denied us. This is why a darkening emptiness often accompanies the institutional arrangements that are ostensibly meant to rescue us from the gutter.

What is this void, draped in the garb of safety and satisfaction, that slowly robs us of our spirit on a daily basis? The missed opportunity of living all those lush potentials afforded to us as human beings whenever we come together. Over a period of time these possible futures that are otherwise essential to the social body and individual wellbeing have been systematically removed from our field of action. As with a caged tiger that hopelessly paces back and forwards hour on end (most notably including those born into captivity), the alienated agent of economic mis-practice instinctively recognises in its bars a life beyond the cubical-life and its prolix emails. Hence the tragic countenance of the white-collar office slave.

In a short and concise essay on this topic, Agamben argues that there is a more serious and depressing form of power than the one described by Deleuze.[17] And I think it underpins the uncalculated outbursts that frequently characterise homo economicus extremis in decline more specifically. According to Agamben, power doesn't just separate us from our potential or what we could do, as Deleuze would have it: for 'there is another more insidious operation of power that does not immediately affect what humans can do – their potentiality – but rather their '"impotentiality", that is what they cannot do, or better, can not do'.[18] For Agamben this alienation from our capacity to say no mainly refers to the all-American 'can do anything' attitude where people bullshit their way through job interviews and dupe unwitting clients. However, it also might apply to the deceptive double-bind that we see operating in relation to homo economicus; she sees no alternative to the course of action being followed, one that she ought to be able to halt or plead unable to fulfil. When someone is unable to do nothing, is separated from what they can not do (rather than cannot do), then it's easy to see why he or she might conclude that only some kind of cataclysmic line of escape will do, a massive cut into the very fabric of reality. Or in the case of the usually calm, pleasant and genial Steven Slater, calling passengers 'motherfuckers', deploying the escape chute and sliding out of this unbearable world with a few cans of larger.

From this perspective, we can see how being separated from our concrete inability (rather than our ability) to continue bringing an intolerable mode of being into existence can trigger a sequence of events that ultimately ends in carnage. As Agamben puts it, this type of disempowerment is in play when a person becomes 'blind not to their capacities but their incapacities'.[19] Such as the incapacity to 'go on like this' experienced by the over-economised, 24/7 employee in the age of extreme capitalism. Gradually becoming wearier and needlessly harassed, months and years can listlessly pass by unaccounted for. The sadness regarding what might have been (our potential) is nowhere near as bad as the realisation that one has betrayed one's incapacity and created a certain reality that really shouldn't be. *Can't be.* That forgone incapacity fuels a gravitational field that ties us closer to a way of life that one is unable to endure ... but does until it's too late. Not only can I not quit but I can't even redeem by inability to go on. Therefore, I must go on, which is painful, so I fuck around on *Pokémon Go* all day instead.

This must surely represent a more disturbing form of economic tyranny. Someone who sees what *is possible* but cannot enact these various futures is certainly lamentable. They remain profoundly incomplete. But think about someone who sees what *is impossible* but is still forced to act out those incapacities in full: cute-talking a vile customer, writing another email, signing a student loan contract, ingratiating oneself to a misogynistic boss and so forth. After years of that these individuals must be downright unstable. This is where my formula for resistance – I/we cannot go on like this and therefore must act – probably mutates into a form of delirium when it comes to homo economicus extremis, since the impulse is filtered through a prism of individual deprivation destined for implosion. His or her own intrinsic impossibilities – what they can not do – finally catapults them out from the shadows of daily life and into a sort of TV-show oblivion, often concluding on a floating prison in the South Bronx.

Steven Slater is no doubt a hero of sorts. But we might not say the same of those many others who picked up a gun instead and walked into the local school. There has to be another way to direct this kind of irate psycho-political impasse if we are to undermine pan-capitalism successfully. One problem is that hyper-individualised instances of protest are purely vertical. Its line runs from the hierarchy, through the enraged person and finally to earth like a lightning bolt. People are cut in half by it. To be a productive force, resistance has to instead be given more horizontal qualities in which rage is couched within a fellowship of others facing the same insufferable situation. That is the only path upon which relief can be gained; collectivism proper which also insulates, protects and is thus doubly menacing to power and its divisive class hierarchy.

Manhunt

It is important to note that Steven Slater like others who find themselves hemmed in to an unworkable way of life act out their grievances in a way that involves some kind of tactical *retreat*. This too represents a particular articulation of empowerment, since disappearing is always liberating. But the gesture of retreat also activates a particular framing of the situation as far as power is concerned, as well as a new form of subjectivity for the now-fugitive. After he vented and the police were called, Slater naturally went *on the run*, just as so many before him have. The desire to retaliate, exit and disappear that has become an important fixture of counter-capitalist activism today is understandable given the claustrophobic universe we are told to call home. This prison-house of faux-universality, as we noted earlier, naturally prompts a reckless impulse to swiftly throw in the towel, pull-the-pin and depart the game altogether rather than remain and fight for a stake. But this creates a different type of medium through which one engages with power; just as Steven Slater discovered after his heroic rejection of being an airline service mule. When you go on the run, the law will follow.

In his book on the topic, *Manhunts*, Gregoire Chamayou presents a brilliant philosophical history of going on the run.[20] For when the state authorities pursue a suspect or outlaw, the relationship between the chased and chaser is very different to other forms of domination. In particular, the dynamic changes the subjectivity of both parties in important ways. The state is no longer concerned with the bandit who might have connections to the peasant masses or stand for social justice issues. Nor is the pursuit about territory, such as the millennial siege cities of the Middle Ages. The reasons why are complex. To begin with there is the individualisation that inevitably takes place. The hunted does not connote any broader sociological category but are now a unique person, literally stripped of their sociality by the indefatigable will of the state and police. As an aside, obviously the Western philosophical plea to treat everyone as a standalone person is now seeing some very authoritarian chickens come home to roost. But none of this matters, of course, if the runaway reaches a welcoming territory outside of the jurisdiction of the pursuers, as the Amerindians ex-slaves did when they reached the Maroons.

In this respect, the manhunt process has much wider implications once the capitalist state apparatus matures and embraces the broad range of war-like surveillance technologies currently available. Part of the governance structure of wreckage capitalism is about fostering an everyday environment that offers absolutely no friendly support to the fugitive. This may include threats against neighbourhoods which are tempted to harbour the escapee. But a general environment of excruciating exposure and transparency, including spies, surveillance, media broadcasts and so forth, is invaluable to the authorities in this regard too. Indeed, it's not a coincidence that Chamayou's follow-up book focused on the philosophy of drones.

Chamayou's observations are very germane when fascinating pamphlets like *How to Disappear in America* are defining the exit movement in the present era of capitalist expansion (the anonymous author includes tips such as carry little cash, change hair colour, destroy all photographs, know that guns and jewellery are quick pawns for quick money, and if you're thinking about taking your children with you, DON'T!).[21] Tracts like this coupled with urban heroes such as Steven Slater give substance to the desire to cut n' run in the popular imagination. But this requires us to rethink the new truths of the manhunt as it is practised in the dying wilderness of post-industrial society. In particular, when the power/resistor couplet changes into a hunter/hunted dyad, a certain transition in subjectivity occurs that presents a number of challenges for the now hunted/resistor. According to Chamayou, the intersubjective economy between the two poles can become mutually reinforcing and self-perpetuating, and produce paradoxes for those wishing to avoid the oppressive psychological weight of predation. In particular,

> The first difficulty has to do with the identification of prey as being essentially victims. I have tried to show how this kind of political identification bore within itself a dilemma, the dilemma of the victim, in which the subjects find themselves confronted by a false choice between the recognition of their status as victims at the price of negating their power to act and the recognition of their power to act at the price of negating the guilt of their tormentors. This antinomy constitutes a powerful political trap.[22]

For those who rely upon *retreat* to resist wreckage economics and will thus also activate the state as a predatory entity, certain tactics can be used to avoid the trap described above. The trick is to breakout of the cycle of mutual self-reinforcement, especially where the prey is ultra-defined by the force that hunts it. The real problem occurs when the victim internalises the gaze of the hunter and thus is unable to rethink its political affiliations or strategies beyond the confines of the hunt. Even the trapper is trapped in this respect.

The psychology of economic prey

In order to understand how this mutual reinforcement might be overcome, it is perhaps useful to broaden the scope of the present discussion. The hunter/hunted dualism is not only applicable to those who literally go on the run from the law like Steven Slater and hope for the best. With economic precarity, debt and an intrusive governmental apparatus constantly harassing homo economicus, stalking him or her by commercializing their every move, life itself comes to approximate the experience of the hunted. And the experience is totalising, as with any mode of predation since one must always be on the lookout. In this respect, it seems that being hunted implies a number of things. The predator's rules have been violated and this legitimates the chase, of course. The hunted person or group has some semblance of mobility and movement. This might look like a strength for the victim, but when they are being pursued this mobility is converted into transience. This therefore predefines them as the weaker party since power enjoys geographical stasis, controlling the map or territory. Thus, the environment in which the 'game' is played out is generally rigged in favour of the hunter with the help of CCTV, roadblocks and maiming potential sympathisers, sometimes in advance.

The hunted always understands the value of hiding, of course. But in the context of crisis capitalism, it is tempting to suggest that hiding itself is part and parcel of the game fostered by extreme neo-liberalism. Indeed, isn't the 'culture of danger' that ensues, whereby wilful invisibility is a rational reaction by those seeking to avoid a vindictive gaze of the state, a key feature of our present ideological climate? The student debtor who flees their home country to evade crippling repayments is hunted by governmental agencies, using various methods of detection (e.g., shared databases) to track down its prey. Those who owe tax are pursued in the same manner. Indeed, for some, the entire socio-economic system can feel like a predator in which withdrawing into the shades and staying out of sight is the only way forward, especially for people who have little power to fight back.

Drawing on the previous argument concerning the sadistic qualities of wreckage economics, it is important to note the 'sport' with which the hunter or predator treats their prey. This is particularly the case if the victim is *already trapped* just as the hunt commences. The victim might be highly dependent on an environment that has been prefabricated by the hunter (e.g., an auto-loan defaulter who still requires their car to work, etc.). Or the end result of capture might already be a forgone conclusion and the process simply extended to present a false image of open-endedness, indeterminacy and thus fairness. This is the case with state benefit recipients in the UK who have their benefits reduced and thus must defy the rules in order to get by. A touch of paranoia was recently added to the hunt when government posters appeared in bus stops stating, 'Benefit Thieves … Do You Know Who Is Following You? Undercover Fraud Investigators Operating in this Area'. However, it is clear that when escape is the only practical alternative and the authorities are in pursuit, a new set of political coordinates are necessary if the hunted is to avoid reproducing a narrative that sees them never winning.

Chamayou evaluates a number of possibilities in this respect. For example, one course of action that is much romanticised but often ill-fated is trying to turn the tables on power. Here the prey internalises the predator's view of themselves and thus attempts to spark fear in the hunter and reduce *them* to a frightened animal on the run. In other words, the hunted becomes the hunter. But there is a problem:

A reversal then occurs in which the former prey becomes a hunter in turn. But at the same time an *aporia* appears, that of the simple reversion or nondialectical reversal of the relationship of predation, in which the positions are simply inverted, whereas the fundamental relationship remains intact. That is the tragic irony of the prey who escapes only by becoming what it sought to escape from.[23]

The thematic of the predator becoming the prey might suit bad Arnold Schwarzenegger films from the 1980s, but can be practically difficult to pull off without once again ending up in a floating prison barge in the South Bronx (or worse). And it does not really disrupt the dangerous synergies between hunter and hunted. Indeed, if these roles are so unstable that they can be reversed, then there is no guarantee that they might revert back to the original dyad once the fight is over. What is more, when the hunted – the poor, debtor and so forth – internalise the gaze of the hunter, the original predator (the state) is often able to displace the now new hunter's aggression onto other prey. Isn't this how populist politics functions with respect to xenophobia? We saw this occur among the dispossessed working classes during the 2016 UK referendum on whether to remain in the European Union.

So there is only one way in which this game can be decoded and disrupted, whereby the hunted successfully escape their burdensome identity as prey. And that is by seeking protection or sanctuary:

> The study of predatory relationships among humans and their political history raises in a central way the problem of protection. If withdrawing the protection of the law produces prey, it also gives us, by contrast, an essential clue to what should be the vocation of a universal political community, its telos: providing collective protection against interhuman predatory relationships.[24]

Hence, the importance of social refuge, collective or communal forms of life that deindividualise the prey and transform their predicament into a moment of solidarity. More importantly, this allows the escapee to divest themselves of the predator's language, which otherwise seems to always lead to the same bad ending, that prison barge again.

Reality shriekback

Putting aside the issue of the escape/hunter dualism for a moment, the involuntary sequence of first 'snapping' (or 'cracking up') and then 'retreating' is useful for describing how resistance manifests today for another reason. In many ways, our acts of withdrawal are simply mimicking what is happening in the natural ecosystem around us, mirroring the wider event of a pan-global *recessional resistance* within nature itself. For like the human multitude that has passed its breaking point and has no other reasonable options, the natural environment is simply closing down and fleeing. In order to see how this might be the case, we need to return to the meaning of resistance in the present capitalist juncture. As I have already mentioned, the term 'resistance' often refers to people fighting back in some way and saying no. This, of course, carries rather romantic connotations, with resistance automatically positioned on the side of life and self-preservation.

However, we can also observe the prevalence of a less idealistic method of saying no. For those caught up in the never-ending factory of economic anxiety, everyday life feels like an underground war in which the only reflex that makes any rational sense is to either escape or hide. Self-control itself becomes a kind of resentful reminder of an uncaring reality. The overworked, over-fixated, over-paranoid and over-stressed normalcy that is daily life for many in the metropolis means that people only have limited opportunities for reasonably refusing to do what they otherwise 'can not' do. They face a deadlocked present.

And here we arrive at an important point. Under these conditions the act of resistance is somehow taken out of the hands of homo economicus. We are no longer speaking of deliberative choices and decisions because the body itself steps in and begins to fight back regardless of what we are thinking about; a fight not against the external enemy like the economic elite, payday lenders or the corporate hierarchy, but its own ability to go on. By 'snapping' the organism takes over the reins from the presupposed rational agent and momentarily closes down, seeking the inner protection of existential minimalism: pure anger, total madness, complete uncontrollability, catatonia and so forth. According to Conway and Siegelman's extended study into people 'snapping', Steven Slater-like episodes have become an American epidemic.[25] They investigated hundreds of cases where people suddenly went totally berserk, including businessmen, homemakers, students and professionals: 'symptoms included a gradual overloading and breaking down of their everyday reasoning and decision-making capacities … chaotic swings of emotion, from sudden euphoria to flaming outbursts of anger, to states of burnout and an overall numbing of emotional response'.[26]

For Conway and Siegelman snapping is undoubtedly an individual expression of a certain emotional and mental condition. However, it is generally involuntary. And moreover, snapping cannot be completely divorced from the environment in which it occurs. After that, however, Conway and Siegelman fail to really politicise the likes of Steven Slater or place them in a proper socio-economic climate (eg. neo-liberalism). For example, it is easy to expect major synergies and complex feedback loops between a hostile office culture and an otherwise ordinary person going ballistic and then mentally hibernating. And that office culture, as I have mentioned throughout this book, stems from a particular configuration of neo-capitalist power relations. In this respect, homo economicus begins to carefully track his broader surroundings, as economic theory says it should, but with a slight difference. Like the hunted creature who imitates its habitat to blend in, economic man too is merging with what the natural environment has become in the vice-like grip of global commerce: the dead and dried-up lake, a retracting high mountain glacier, the last species of a particular rainforest lizard and so forth.

It is no surprise, then, that the retreating environment in which the human organism finds itself becomes an intimate part of its way of dealing with modern capitalism. Our metabolism and physiology take on qualities that can be clearly identified in the dying ecosystem that encloses mankind. For the human body senses a crisis, copies its modulations and then also decides also to shut down and recede into its private inner nothingness. For isn't mimesis the basic code of life?

Mother Nature will win

We have suggested that economic recession and human withdrawal/retreat map onto each other. Indeed, I don't think it's an exaggeration to add the natural environment to the mass exodus we see everywhere in the human economy. Perhaps the trees, wildlife, glaciers and ocean species too are resisting in this manner as the present configuration of pan-capitalism hastens the complete ruination of earth's ecology. More precisely, nature is resisting *us* and expresses this in the same form as those humans who have 'had enough' and withdraw. The only problem is we cannot do without the protection nature provides. Let's survey just a small part of the mounting eco-recession that is growing before us. Once the natural environment countered human interference by presenting before it insurmountable trials: mountainous waves that wrecked ships, hurricanes that destroyed villages, the cold and the punishing sun. Today many of these ancient obstacles have been conquered. So now it has to give mankind the middle-finger in other ways now that technology has all but eliminated any impediment to our dominion over it. This is when it *recedes*.[27]

We can see this kind of retaliatory eco-exodus almost everywhere, and unfortunately for us, and to quote a scientist in the apocalyptic film *World War Z*, 'Mother Nature can be a real bitch.' In the winter of 2016 something unprecedented occurred in the dark Artic. A massive part of the ocean around the North Pole refused to freeze as per usual. According to an expert studying the disaster, 'I've never seen such a warm, crazy winter in the Artic ... the heat was relentless.'[28] A report released in January 2017 by the US National Oceanic and Atmospheric Administration revealed that global temperatures intensified to new levels three consecutive years in a row, a pattern that is unprecedented.[29] Similarly, in the UK we have seen successive months of record-breaking temperature due to the withdrawal of hospitable conditions and the rapid increase of air pollution. Nearly 9500 people die every year in London due to the high concentrations of nitrogen dioxide.[30] According to a study by Royal Botanical Gardens Kew, one in five plant species face extinction. With the rise of farming, palm oil plantations, deforestation for timber and the spread of roads, flora have done the only rational thing possible: *disappear*. This is a big problem for humans since we couldn't reproduce ourselves in their absence. As the director of science at Kew Gardens puts it, 'plants provide us with everything – food, fuel, medicines, timber and they are incredibly important for our climate regulation. Without plants we would not be here. We are facing some devastating realities if we do not take stock and re-examine our priorities and efforts.'[31] Ironically, arable land itself is disappearing too at an alarming rate due to soil fatigue and so too are many plants of the wrong kind (e.g. crops, etc.).[32]

If the normally habitable non-sentient ecosphere is retreating through melting permafrost, pesticide pollution and untenable CO_2 emissions, a similar process is underway among the animal kingdom too. According to the World Wildlife Fund, 58 per cent of global wildlife has disappeared since 1970.[33] That's one hundred times more than it ought to be and is only getting worse. Large fishing stocks around the world have suddenly collapsed due to over-fishing. In the North Sea and the East China Sea, for example, fisheries have not had the chance to replenish and have literally disappeared en masse. Daniel Pauly, a scientist who has done a great deal to demonstrate the negative impact we've had on our oceans, uses strong words to describe what has happened:

It is almost as though we use our military to fight the animals in the ocean. We are gradually winning this war to exterminate them. And to see this destruction happen, for nothing really – for no reason – that is a bit frustrating. Strangely enough, these effects are all reversible, all the animals that have disappeared would reappear, all the animals that were small would grow, all the relationships that you can't see any more would re-establish themselves, and the system would re-emerge.[34]

Other species are also resisting the human-centric war against the natural world. The level of extinctions due to the dying habitat has shocked some scientists. The last Black Western Rhino died out in 2011.[35] The Bramble Cay Melomys, the only mammal indigenous to the Great Barrier Reef, was eventually wiped out in 2016 by climate change.[36] And the list goes on and on.[37]

Totality for kids

It is clear that nature is now resisting our developmental presence on unprecedented levels as we enter the Anthropocene era.[38] Or as Jason Moore more accurately terms it, the *Capitalocene*, since this round of mass extinction (unlike previous ones in world history) is linked to a very specific, reversible manmade economic system.[39] In this context, however, some recommendations on the political Left seem strange and almost counter-productive. The 'accelerationist' perspective, for example, is a philosophy of political intervention that has recently gained popularity. Accelerationists suggest that capitalism is now so totalising that it can absorb almost any form of protest or opposition. In fact, it might even thrive on dissent. Thus, being *against* capitalism has become a futile exercise. Instead we ought to use its own untenable and destructive principles, speed them up, so that it too 'snaps' and disintegrates, leaving a clean horizon within which we can rebuild a more democratic polity. As Steven Shaviro, a leading commenter in the movement suggests in his book *No Speed Limit*,

the only way out is the way through. In order to overcome globalised neoliberal capitalism, we need to drain it to the dregs, push it to its most extreme point, follow it into its furthest and strangest consequences ... the hope is that, by exacerbating our current conditions of existence, we will finally be able to make them explode, and thereby move beyond them.[40]

In other words, our resistance should focus on pushing the system and ourselves to the limit, encouraging a whole multitude of Steven Slaters to 'explode' and then rebuild a better society from there. It is true that nothing has ever died of contradictions. But speeding up the destructive forces latent in the deathward gaze of neoliberal capitalism must surely be more representative of a death-wish than emancipatory thinking. After all, Donald J. Trump and Goldman Sachs would probably not discourage what the accelerationists have on offer.

While accelerationism sounds romantically brave (and optimistic) on the surface, we would do well to examine its misguided and somewhat nihilistic message more closely, especially as it tries to come good on the ideas of Nick Land and his notion of the Dark Enlightenment. First of all, accelerationism trades in a rather simplistic *threshold analytics* to make sense of social struggle. It implies that when power dominates the weak (and itself) there is an inbuilt threshold or tipping point that when crossed causes revolt. Continue to deepen capitalism, let all hell break lose as the system immiserates everyone, at some point an equal and opposite reaction will follow. Revolution. Of course, the study of resistance would be rather straightforward if it functioned in such a predictable and formulaic manner. But it doesn't, of course. Resistance is no system-effect of power that is triggered after domination crosses a limit. We often see very little opposition in situations that are otherwise so oppressive that violent revolt would be 100 per cent expected. For example, in Nazi-occupied France most did not resist and wilfully collaborated. On the other hand, resistance can occur in some of the most unexpected moments. Historians have long noted how major social revolutions hardy ever transpire when the oppressed reach rock bottom. Strangely, it is when socio-economic conditions actually begin to improve that revolt becomes a more feasible idea. If this is the case, there is a danger that the practitioners of accelerationism come to look exactly like the capitalists they seek to destroy. This is how critical theory can easily slip into a de facto right-wing, pseudo-capitalist position, albeit adorned with Che Guevara tattoos and a left-wing library.

If there is no threshold when it comes to human political struggle, the same cannot be said for nature. This is where an element of nihilism plainly enters into the accelerationist fantasy of seeing society (and us) burst. If extreme capitalism continues to escalate then, yes, we will probably see an explosive outburst of resistance. But not necessarily among *Homo sapiens*, for they can often put up with the worst kinds of bullshit thrown at them, which is a somewhat pathetic quality of the species unfortunately. No, it wouldn't be people rebelling in the accelerationist vision of politics, but nature; namely, by receding in the manner we have noted above. And that would inevitably necessitate the end of humanity. In his 1976 essay entitled *This World We Must Leave*, Jacques Camatte discusses the difficulty of overcoming capitalism in terms that seem remarkably prescient when it comes to the accelerationist argument.[41] If there is no external point to capitalism's own dire machinations, argues Camatte, we must question whether it is able to survive because there is no non-capitalist raw material around for it to feed off:

> having subjected humans to its own being, can capital survive? Is this not a progression into the absurd, but an impossible development? This is thus an end to capital, but also that of the species and thus nature ... put another way, one cannot and must not go to the end of this project.[42]

Pushing the totality of the capitalist mode of production to its inherent conclusion – as the accelerationists would have it – would unleash a new kind of bedlam on earth and probably the demise of life itself, of which the evidence is now before us as nature pushes back and disappears. And if nature implodes, then we must inevitably vanish with it.

This world we must leave

Hence, the sense of dark pessimism (if not nihilism) that we see in much recent theorising about the fate of the capitalist social system and human life as such. This is why the cultural theorist Mark Fisher used to call this facet of the neoliberal impasse 'nihil-liberalism'. According to the radical ecologist Derrick Jensen, for example, ending civilisation might be the only way of saving the natural world since humankind has long passed the point at which it could have rendered itself sustainable. Now there's no going back. Cities and their dependence on resources, especially the megacities ruled by corporations, are intrinsically hostile to the natural habitat because (a) resource dependencies inevitably generate terrible inter-societal wars that detract attention from and deepen (b) the tremendous carnage that occurs when plants, water and animals are transformed into mere factory objects to be processed. In reading Jensen's *Endgame*, as well as other authors in this ecocentric and apocalyptic genre, including John Michael Greer's *The Long Dissent* and Alan Weisman's *The World Without Us*, we can discern a palpable antipathy towards the human race. Earth would be better off without us.[43] Alan Weisman even joyfully speculates about how long it might take for nature to spring back if everyone in the world suddenly disappeared or in Weisman's words, imagine 'something has just happened that takes us away before we can wreak anymore havoc on the environment ... to what extent could it cover up our traces'.[44] Weisman appears to take particular delight in reeling off the many ways that mankind might suddenly be killed off, which is fair enough I guess.

Homo sapiens are now so dependent on a violent and exploitative way of life, its very existence degrades not only the ecosystem but also other human beings on a routine basis. There is little hope that globalised capitalism will change its ways by choice. This is notable when you listen to the power elite speak. Take for example Gina Rinehart, one of the richest women in the world. She inherited her father's Australian mining interests and has little time for the

myth of manmade climate change or the scientists who are raising
the alarm:

> Let's consider climate change ... even before human civilization,
> the world went though ice ages and periods of global warming.
> There will always be changes that affect our climate, even if we
> close down all the thermal-fire power stations, steel mills and
> other manufacturing operations, putting employees out of work
> and drastically changing our way of life. Furthermore, there will
> always be geothermal activity that spew out heat and ash and this
> activity does affect the climate.[45]

The denial of manmade climate change and the resulting
Anthropocene is perhaps unsurprising given the vested interests
involved. But it's easy to almost detect a sense of hatred for trees
and animals in the billionaire's words, a tone she directs towards
the poor too. Anyway, Pauly might be correct after all. Capitalism,
big business and the nation-state *is at war* with Mother Earth, so we
can see why Derrick Jensen, in particular, is so pessimistic about the
prospect of late capitalism's desire and capacity to change.[46] So along
with its own resistance – by disappearing – Jensen argues that we
too can help its cause by dismantling the large commercial centres
that hold the earth to ransom as it slowly dies.

While Jensen issues a convincing rallying call for people to
destroy civilisation whenever they can, it's the overall misanthropic
sensibility that is particularly interesting. We can note an avid
strain of human self-disdain that also resonates with the aforementioned accelerationist school as they encourage us to embrace the
deathward tendencies of extreme neoliberalism as a way out. Would
any credible revolt against neoliberal capitalism really endorse
speeding up the institutional logics of Gina Rinehart? For that would
surely result in the obliteration not only of society but ourselves.

James Holmes at the movies

In forensically mapping the present age of global capitalism as it
spirals out of control, critical theory has embraced the thematic

of death in a variety of ways. Most of which seem to end in less human beings, which is the ultimate expression of exit I guess. For example, some have scrutinised those individuals who sadly follow the schizophrenic logic of capitalism to the nth degree and end up as suicidal mass murderers. According to Franco 'Bifo' Berardi, for example, people like Seung-Hui Cho (killed 32 and himself), Eric Harris and Dylan Klebold, (killed 13 and themselves), James Holmes (killed 24), Anders Behring Breivik (killed 77) and Pekka-Erik Auvinen (killed 8 and himself) are *heroes*: 'I write about spectacular murderous suicides because these killers are the extreme manifestation of one of the main trends of our age. I see them as the heroes of an age of nihilism and spectacular stupidity: the age of financial capitalism.'[47]

Berardi spares the reader none of the gory details as he tries to demonstrate how the principles underlying the broader economic system are lived truly by these mass killers. Perhaps Seung-Hui Cho and James Holmes are not the type of modern-day rebels that the accelerationists had in mind, but Bifo insists that their moment of madness faithfully compliments the psychosis of semio-capitalism as it reaches a climax. They and their actions are a fulfilment of the secret capitalist message rather than an aberration and thus deserve respect for bringing out the ideal form only you and I approximate. He calls this murderous authenticity a *spasm*. In physiological terms, a spasm is an uncontrollable 'acceleration', 'intensification' and then 'exhaustion' of the nervous system's own propensities. It is not external to the organic structure but an amplification of it. As with a physiological spasm, when the lonely and bullied James Holmes finally lashed out, the event was not only a form of retribution to a deeply unfriendly market society. It was actually a more genuine and pure rendition of it, embodying all of the madness we'd find if neoliberal capitalism could be boiled down to its basic fundamentals.

And herein lies the problem with Bifo's analysis. The world conjured by *Heroes* is one that we ought to refuse to recognise because in saying it is so, the dark desire of the neoliberal phantasy itself comes to the fore. In order to reject the death-drive of the present period of economic development, such a fixation on cold-blooded killers is never enough because it partially reproduces the same madness it seeks to oppose. Sometimes silence is wiser. Bifo's book reminds me of a friend I used to know in my teens. A really kind guy. But he was afraid of violent street bullies, although he had never been beaten up. So he took some self-defence classes. He really got into it, showing us the different techniques he had learnt in the classes with an ex-gang member. If someone grabs you from behind, this is how you gouge their eye. The simple ballpoint pen can immobilise the average aggressor ... like this! Of course, as a result, my friend started to get into more and more fights. He saw the world in a very different light and the tail had begun to wag the dog. Even I was scared of the little bastard. As T.W. Adorno puts it, he who imagines disasters in some way desires them. This is why high pessimism certainly feels like the most authentic response to our broken world, but it clearly has to be handled with much care.

After civilisation

This underlying death obsession (that undoubtedly resonates with the dying natural and social landscape around us) can manifest in critical theories of capitalist society in other, more sophisticated ways. A good example is Michael Madsen's magnificent 2010 documentary, *Into Eternity: A Film For the Future*. The filmmaker investigates the construction of a deep geological depository for nuclear waste situated near the Olkiluoto power plant in Finland. Built several miles down into solid granite rock, the facility consists of a multilevelled, underground vault that will store dangerous radioactive waste. Once completed, it will have enough capacity to receive waste for about a hundred years. Then it will be backfilled and sealed. The problem is that nuclear waste is deadly for at least 100,000 years. So in order to protect the facility in the future, it will have to be well hidden and erased from official records in case it falls into the wrong hands.

Of course, we are only talking about Finland's nuclear waste. Around three hundred thousand tons of the stuff exist around the world, sitting in special tanks of water that require around the clock management and surveillance. The authorities don't know what else to do with it. The genius of *Into Eternity* lies in the way it is pitched as a letter to future civilisations, races who will walk the earth long after our society has destroyed itself and been forgotten. The film opens with the following narrative, a warning to anyone who might inadvertently discover the facility:

> I would say that you are now on a place where we have buried something from you, to protect you. And we have taken great pain to be sure you are protected. We also need you to know that this place should not be disturbed. You should stay away from this place and then you will be safe. I am now in this place where you should never come. We call it Onkalo – Onkalo means hiding place. Where I stand is not finished, although it began in the twentieth century when I was a child. It will be completed in the 22nd century long after my death. It must last 100,000 years. Nothing built by man has lasted even a 10th of the timespan. But we consider ourselves a very potent civilisation.[48]

The narrator continues, 'if we succeed, these will likely be the longest lasting remains of our civilisation, and if you in the future find it, what will it tell you about us?'[49] One of the more intriguing parts of the film is a discussion about what symbolism or language ought to be used to warn people away from the site many thousands of years from now. It is likely that wars will ravage the surface in coming millennia, as well as earthquakes and volcanoes, and the entrance of Onkalo might be accidentally exposed. Therefore, some kind of visual caution is needed. But how does one communicate such a thing? English, Mandarin and modern Finnish would have all certainly disappeared by then. Will signs reading 'DO NOT ENTER' and 'RISK OF DEATH' make any sense? Probably not. What kind of remote inner primitivism do we need to tap in order to discern the correct tone and lexicon when making contact with those who will come long after us?

Perhaps more relevant to us is the underlying image of a non-present that the narrative masterfully weaves in the imagination of the viewer. They gradually enter a world without them, perhaps long after modern civilisation has collapsed and all signs of you and I have disappeared forever. Our only lasting testament to future generations a highly toxic cavern of radioactive waste; and going one step further, the film implies our civilisation will undoubtedly be incommensurable with any possible future peoples, not simply because the sands of time naturally erode human continuity but *because of us*, as bringers of death over a period of aeons. They will ask themselves, what kind of people were these that they can still kill so long after they have vanished? We are encouraged to see that disconnected and standalone incommensurability in ourselves from a future age. This subtly places a gaping hole of nothingness at the centre of our present. *Into Eternity* is disturbing for this reason.

The narrator continues by asking the people of this imagined future whether the world's nuclear waste has accidentally made its way into the natural environment, perhaps after another vicious global war, causing large-scale death and devastation: 'did that happen? Are their forbidden zones with no life in your time?'[50] We are neither able to identify with our future selves (because an unknown species has replaced us) nor our present selves (since all we really add up to is deadly poison in the ground). In this manner, the ultimate exit-fantasy is accomplished because we are paradoxically able to be present *after* it occurs, witnessing our own passing and the coming funeral of civilisation itself, which is, of course, ultimately impossible.

No exit

The motif of exit and separation has significantly reshaped how we think about resisting the governance structures of wreckage economies in neoliberal societies. Proponents of exit present a very different scenario to how the accelerationists engage with protest.

The point is not to exacerbate the contradictions of capitalism, but collectively withdraw and escape them instead. We see this model of praxis in the works of Michael Hardt and Antonio Negri, especially their books *Empire* and *Commonwealth*.[51] They refine the idea of exodus, drawing on the obvious biblical connotations, but also the US black power movement and its separatist mandate for autonomy and self-governance. The idea is fairly straight forward. Most political activism has aimed to fight against an oppressor, either taking over its organisational base or cutting a better deal with it to achieve freedom. We might term this recognition politics because the point is to be seen and heard so one can engage with power. Resistors strive to be recognised as a legitimate voice so that certain grievances and claims can be made.

We might contrast this petition for recognition with the politics of exodus. Whereas the former involves acts that seek to be understood and *included* by power, exit politics follows a different type of political grammar. Here actors are sceptical about participating in dialogue with those whom they resist, since it often turns out to be merely a ruse for identifying troublemakers and silencing collective grievances, especially by way of consultation and other forms of *inclusive exclusion*. Exit politics does not want anything to do with the enemy or its sad institutional structures. As a North American militant group recently put it, 'One does not tidy up in a home falling off a cliff.'[52]

This type of separatism is refreshing since it correctly identifies the completely wrecked nature of power, so why even bother engaging with such a catastrophe in the first place? What political exit exactly entails in this regard was always a bit problematic, however. The idea, of course, is loosely based on the collective self-reliance and communal independence of the working class. Moreover, this isn't some faraway space of exteriority. Independence may actually already be partially formed given the way capitalism so heavily relies on an autonomous substratum of sociality among the 99%-ers in order to reproduce itself (e.g., self-organisation, knowledge sharing, amateurism, informal knowhow, self-help, etc.). But translating that latent potential into a wider social reality has proven difficult. The freeloading and parasitical clutches of the ruling class have consistently undermined the full and independent realisation of the common. For sure, look at what happened to Aaron Swartz, who we discussed in Chapter 1. He defied copyright law and was unforgivingly crucified as a result. The message has in fact been very clear over the last few years. There'll be absolutely *no* self-valorisation of the multitude's commonwealth and its 'invisible republic' if capitalism has anything to do with it.

When obstructed in this manner, the thematic of exit can easily morph into escapism. Indeed, if the wish for absence is filtered through the grid of ultra-scepticism it can easily lead to some extreme individual behaviour. Once again, because the surrounding economic stasis is deemed so impregnable, some sort of outlandish 'breakout' is seen to be the only possibility left. And no other occupation has been so successfully individualised in this manner than academia. For example, in 2010, Jonathan Gottschall was sitting in a cubicle, thinking his career was 'dead in the water'.[53] Moreover he was bored, frustrated, constantly hassled by petty demands and his life was not indistinguishable from the job he hated. Jonathan was in his late 30s, had a PhD, worked as an adjunct professor in English and was paid $16,000 a year. As he paced about his office and looked out the window, he suddenly noticed something he'd not seen before: a sign reading *Mark Sharder's Academy of Mixed Martial Arts*. In the shopfront display, two men inside a chain-linked metal cage were dancing, kicking, punching and falling over: 'they were so alive in their octagon while I was rotting in my cube'. It was then the idea suddenly came to him: 'That's how I'll do it ... That's how I'll get myself fired.'[54] He soon began training as a cage fighter at Mark Sharder's academy, gradually building up his skills. A few years later Jonathan found himself in a cage in a Las Vegas hotel, face-to-face with a young man he had never met before and who he was about to beat unconscious.

Jonathan's story represents a new genre of academic writing that has recently emerged called 'quit lit'.[55] A similar theme reoccurs in this literature. Most quitters report a deep investment in developing an academic career, train for decades and sacrifice large parts of their lives for it. They become successful and suddenly get dejected with the extreme demands placed upon them by retarded bureaucrats and students, excessive workloads, high levels of insecurity, increasingly meaningless work, and impossible performance targets set by bosses who have never taught and so on. Fighting back is no longer an option – these people just want out.

Plughole of the present

The problem is that quitting is not an option when life itself has become inextricably implicated with the hated totality one seeks to escape. For sure, the desire for withdrawal represents a kind of failure in itself. The dream of social independence dies and prompts a commensurate, yet inferior individual isolationism that seeks to acquire some existential compensation. What's more, the failure to detach the social common and realise its rich possibilities for freedom has unfortunately seen some commentators disappear down the plughole of nihilism. This has been especially so when the exit-drive is introverted and the solitary individual begins to flirt with his or her own nothingness. As the lone rebel confronts the giant goliath of late capitalism, it must surely seem impossible to overcome no matter how accurate their aim may be. As the horizon of hope slowly disappears it is either (a) internalised as a personal threshold that one must cross (e.g., escaping yourself in evermore dangerous ways) or (b) matures into a hardened shell of despondency, as we saw with Bifo and his heroes above.

It is sadly telling that one of the founders of Marxist autonomism, who influenced a rich cadre of writers including Hardt and Negri and Paolo Virno, has apparently succumbed to this black hole of individual escape. Mario Tronti's writing in the 1960s had a major impact on the anti-capitalist movement in Italy and beyond. He and others helped form the basis of autonomism, demonstrating with acuity that capital was dependent on the working class, not the other way around as previously thought. The implications of this viewpoint are still being worked through today. In any case, a deeply candid 2013 interview found the man in total despair, only kept going by his retreat into t'ai chi. Tronti was asked if he ever dreamed things would end so badly:

> **Tronti:** I always expect the best. Then come the knocks. Coming up against facts without an airbag can do you damage. I was a communist, Marxist, operaista. Some things end. Some things last. I have learnt and applied the lesson of political realism: you can't ignore the facts.
>
> **Interviewer:** Do you feel like you've been defeated, or you've failed?
>
> **Tronti:** I am defeated, not a victor. The victories are never final. But we have lost – not a battle – but the war of the twentieth century.
>
> **Interviewer:** And who has triumphed?
>
> **Tronti:** Capitalism. But without class struggle, without an adversary, it has lost its vitality. It has become something of a monstrosity.
>
> **Interviewer:** You don't expect anything else?
>
> **Tronti:** The future is stuck in the present. It's impossible to imagine anything that isn't just a continuation of the present state of things. This is the eternal present of which we've been speaking. I'm very happy to be obsolete.[56]

One has to give the man credit. At least he's honest. But there is something worrying about this interview. Tronti (as with Bifo) is convinced that capitalism has won. We need to face the facts. This discourse of despair is inevitable when the quest for exit is stripped of its collective moorings, particularly in the face of an all too totalising totality that feels insurmountable. As Hardt and Negri accurately state, exodus only makes sense as a socio-political category when a new territory of protection and sanctuary is formed. Otherwise, it plays very much into the hands of the Thatcher-Trump-Theresa tripartite to come. This *mis-individualisation* undermines the very refuge of sociality that people like Tronti ought to be attracted to. But for this unhappy consciousness even the ultimate sanctuary to this barrage of economic persecution – the social itself – is now bereft of any redeeming qualities. Hence, the withdrawal into t'ai chi, an activity that is also popular in California. Perhaps the most tragic facet of this mass privatisation of the withdrawal process is that the wonderful security of being together is denigrated and perhaps even exploited, just as that primary provider of shelter is today, the natural world. When the ecosystem flees, aghast at the atrocities being committed against it, so does the nihilist subject, who just wants to get out and evaporate into nothingness.

The super-individualisation of the exit-desire expressed by Jonathan Gotschall, Steven Slater and Mario Tronti usually turns to shit when enacted in real life. Even t'ai chi becomes a vacuous reminder of the intense possibilities that one can no longer realise, not even partially. The main reason everything goes bad is because the force of capitalism is often mistaken for *actual people* and sometimes humanity itself. Gotschall only sees academic administrators and students. Slater irate passengers and unsympathetic bosses. Tronti a compliant and defeated working class. But we now know that the totality of neoliberal capitalism gathers its power chiefly as a lifeless abstraction. The defeated escapist, on the other hand, mistakes this tormentor for real folk, be they co-workers, customers, children and perhaps even the overall tyranny of the human face. In other words, the 'nihil-liberalized individual' wrongly perceives universal oppression in everything, everyone and sometimes even themselves. In many ways this is understandable given how money hides its virtuality in the concrete, immediate human deed, which accounts for its 'real abstraction'.

As we discovered in the preceding discussion, when life and the economy blur into each other and abstract economic woes are lived as personal ones, some begin to see real human beings as part of the problem rather than the solution. This represents a sort of converse nihilism. The individual finds him or herself languishing not just in their own nothingness but in that of other human beings. This is then introjected back into the individual's cognitive map and is frequently expressed as a desire to depart mankind. Following a brief but twisted euphoria this persona quickly descends into psychosis, of course, since they can only see themselves in the complete absence of everyone else.

Misfutures of the past

This was the theme of one the most underrated sci-fi films ever, Geoff Murphy's mysterious *The Quiet Earth*, made in 1985.[57] Zac Hobson, played by the brilliant, late Bruno Lawrence, is a scientist based in New Zealand, working for Delenco, a multinational corporation that is developing a radical new energy source called Project Flashlight. The film opens with Zac asleep in bed as a new day dawns, still wearing an employee ID card around his neck. Then for a brief split second the sun blacks out, glows red, and then quickly returns to normal. When Zac awakes something is amiss. The clock has stopped at 6.12 am. The radio simply emits white noise. He tries to call someone on the phone. No answer. As Zac begins his daily commute to work he cannot believe what he sees. Nobody is around. The city is totally abandoned. Planes have dropped out of the sky. But where are the bodies? No one. Empty cars lie in the middle of the road, or have veered into the sidewalk, as if their drivers somehow instantly vanished. He begins to explore this bizarre people-less wonder-world. Part One of Zac's fantasy has been fulfilled. He turns on his voice recorder, and logs the first diary entry to nobody in particular:

Zac Hobson, July 5th. One: there has been a malfunction in Project Flashlight with devastating results. Two: it seems I am the only person left on Earth.

The protagonist begins to feel playful. He sleeps in the mansions he could never afford. The expensive wine flows. Posh champagne and raw egg cocktails. Caviar. Shopping malls are plundered of their luxurious treasures, free of the stifling guilt that such a bounty would otherwise invoke in someone like Zac. For there is nobody around to judge him. Thus, he is relieved of the duty to judge himself. No obligations or responsibilities. This double sense of freedom to act as one pleases and the simultaneous acknowledgement that the gaze of conscience is impotent under such unusual circumstances could only be captured by the studied, silent brutalism of Bruno Lawrence. Easily New Zealand's finest actor during this period and perhaps ever. But for Zac, there is a catch. In the back of his mind is a growing concern. It's the worldwide malfunction he terms 'the Effect'. Another might soon occur ... very soon. But that doesn't mean he can't have fun in the meantime. Society drained of people presents an entirely new way of being. He is literally able to do anything he likes. Pure and unalloyed liberty.

Soon the excitement subsides, however. And as the days drag on it is obvious that Zac is slowly losing his mind. He dresses in women's underwear, perhaps something he always wanted to try but never dared until now. Gazing into a mirror, he weeps in joy as he adorns a woman's silk slip. Now Zac begins to extend his newfound empire. Uncontrollably giggling to himself, he declares that he is President of the Quiet Earth. When God didn't appear after Zac demanded him in an abandoned church, the lingerie-clad President pointed his shotgun at the Crucified Jesus and asked again – 'if you don't come out I'll shoot the kid' – and blew him to pieces. He quietly whispers to himself, 'and now I am god'. Zac's mental health declines even further. In his new mansion on the hill, he creates life-size cardboard cut-out figures of Elizabeth II, Bob Marley (in full football regalia), Pope John Paul II, Elvis Presley and Adolf Hitler among others. He addresses them as their President, giving a short and rather compelling speech about the way power can corrupt. Zac is particularly irked by Hitler. He jeers at the dictator, 'look, I haven't got time to talk to you, I'm a very busy man! Besides, you've had your turn.'

Inherit the dust

Then something even more shocking happens in the film. Zac unexpectedly finds another survivor. Joanna is also alone and confused. They immediately embrace and Zac begins to feel a glimmer of hope. After becoming a romantic couple, they wonder if anyone else might be out there. And indeed there is. Zac finds a large man called Api, played by Maori actor Pete Smith. Zac has rediscovered the wonders of sociality in this new family. He is lifted from himself, which offers both a fundamental sense of relief and an abiding feeling of sanctuary that frees him from the immense weight of being.

Although very different people, the three survivors learn that they were all about to die when 'the Effect' occurred. Joanne was being electrocuted by a defective hairdryer, Api was drowning and Zac was committing suicide using pills. Then while Zac is away trying to devise a plan to prevent the next Effect, Api and Joanne fall in love and have sex. Joanne explains her understanding of friendship to Api and perhaps touches on the underlying truth of togetherness, albeit in blunt kiwi dialect:

> You know, the interesting thing about friendships is that they're not logical. You know how somebody will come up to you and they'll ask you why do you like so and so, and you'll give them all these interesting reasons why you do. But you've actually made them up after you've decided you like them. I reckon you decide that you like somebody in the two seconds that you meet them – you stick to it regardless. So, if you like them, you're gonna find good things in all the bad things they do, and if you don't, you're gonna find bad things in all the good things they do, ay?

This is obviously a retrospective theory of friendship. We like people and then invent a rationale for that connection. In this manner, Joanne expresses an interesting theory of time with respect to the social, as something that is always catching up with itself. But what does it mean to be together, in those backward-looking terms? It certainly isn't instrumental. Nor has it anything to do with furthering your career, like a networking event. One must conclude that it is its own destination, a final resolution. Being together consists of internalisation of the other as a reciprocal guarantee for one's own self-understanding, an *a priori* stance of attraction, perhaps what is calculated before the calculations begin.

This is the connectedness Zac had lost in the real world before the Effect struck. Even more unfortunate is what the quiet earth reveals to him in the glaring daylight of a New Zealand town. Zac, the suicidal nihilist, perhaps not dissimilar to one of Bifo's heroes, discovers that a habitat without faces is a crime to life. He must reach out in order to find himself again.

But here is the nub of the problem. This newfound sociality has betrayed him once again, just like it did back in his previous life, which made him want to die. This is when he calculates that another 'Effect' is imminent, and decides to blow up the Delenco complex with a truck of high explosives. As he nears the plant the truck accidently explodes with Zac still at the wheel. Now the second 'Effect' takes place. The sun briefly flickers and an intense red light spirals into infinity, cutting a singularity in this quiet universe. At the end of the film Zac awakes alone once again, this time on a beach watching hundreds of mushroom clouds far out to sea. The last scene shows our anti-hero holding the voice recorder unable to speak, staring in astonishment as a giant, ringed planet rises on the horizon. Now he's *really* alone.

The Quiet Earth

The film was ostensibly about the mass paranoia that matured towards the end of the Cold War. In 1984, New Zealand had banned nuclear powered/armed vessels from entering its waters and the Americans were angry. Ronald Reagan was president and he liked violence, as we know. At the same time, the newly elected 1984 Labour government was undertaking what would later be known as the 'New Zealand Experiment'.[58] The then Finance Minister Roger Douglas applied a strict, verbatim version of Thatcherism and neoclassical economics to the tiny country and watched what happened. Short-term pain for long-term gain was the motto. This included mass privatisation, abolishing trade unions (they folded surprisingly quickly) and spreading self-centred individualism into all facets of society. These changes too had a swift 'Effect' in the national culture as money rather than people was privileged above all else. Within the span of only two years, the country was viewed by neoliberal wonks around the world as a faraway, ultra-capitalist utopia. *The Quiet Earth* correctly predicts the outcome. And the country never really recovered. Just look at the outlandish child poverty figures, for example, an entire generation has truly been disappeared.

In this respect, Zac provides an accurate picture of the nihilistic fetish underlying homo economicus in its essence, the dream of forever separating the individual from his or her society. So-called economic man, after the torrent of caveats provided by behavioural economists and liberal philosophers, really is a distorted synthesis of the self-regulating marketplace and its human nobody-ness. But we can also see in Zac the fate of a certain type of exit politics when it is filtered through frustrated hopelessness; not homo economicus in full bloom but its radical opposite, the resisting 'hero'. The experience of being the only person left on earth who is able to do anything seems empowering at first. No cops or bosses. Women's underwear. But this freedom is lived in the first half hour of the movie as a vacillation between joy (or pure agency) and escalating terror since Zac requires others to see himself. In a disappeared world, one where the 'other' has been erased completely, it is the face of another that is first missed. When Zac finally does find the shelter of people, he is betrayed. The gift of being-unto-others – Zac instantly regains his sanity when he meets Joanna and Api – turns bad. Perhaps it is the fear of being double-crossed that inspires the nihilistic dream of nothingness, something we see in the privative narcissism and the ultra-individualism that passes for humanity today. When de-collectivised in this manner, the social is something to be repelled since even a single face symbolises a totality of despair. This is so even when people like Zac fully understand that ironically they are nothing without the face of someone else. This is why his first attempt at escape – suicide – actually results in what he really wanted all along, the disappearance of everyone else, not himself. Finally he is alone.

Of course, Zac finds out the hard way that under these conditions there can actually be no such thing as individuality. To be someone, subject-object relations are required since a unique self can only flourish in a supportive social environment. Otherwise the person becomes a weird type of madness, without shape, qualities or distinctiveness. In *The Perfect Crime*, Jean Baudrillard argues that this is why the modern individual probably no longer exists. The subject/object dynamic has been decompressed, rendered into a theatre of narcissism: 'since he has become truly indivisible, and has thus achieved his perfect- that is to say, delirious, self-referential – form, we cannot speak of the individual any longer, but only of the Selfsame and the hypostasis of the Selfsame'.[59] This really summarises what has happened to the once vibrant form of emancipatory politics that centred on the notion of exodus. Hopes of escape and exit have quietly moved from a clean theory of freedom to a universalised economy of being alone. And that increasingly results in an eternal stalemate, a world that reverberates its own abandonment deep into our future, as Zac Hobson and Steven Slater sadly understood. Is that dark and spinning biosphere now looking for new inhabitants to play the game of life? Perhaps somebody like me or you?

Conclusion:
A Marginal Model of Nothingness

Oscar Wilde once observed that the modern industrial personality is extreme precisely because it inhabits its self-imposed chamber of horrors with such calm and diffident normalcy. In particular, that strangest aberration of them all – money – has somehow transcended all other qualities like an ill begotten deity. It's no longer just *part* of our world. No, money *is* our world, which is crazy given how unreal and immaterial it actually is. As a result, Wilde quips, people now know the price of everything, but the value of nothing. A mute blindness sets in when money rules the world, eradicating all faculties of judgement concerning what goods, service or even life itself actually are. Of course, this represents a complete inversion of how humanity had hitherto approached social reality, one that turns all values upside down in the most diabolical jinx. Foul made fair, wrong right, base noble, coward valiant.[1] Hence, perhaps the ghostly qualities of currency. As a token or idol that we interminably pray to, it stands in for an absent mankind that has never learnt to live, a darkness that haunts every human exchange to its roots.

Oscar Wilde's insight hasn't dated at all and is particularly prescient for unpacking the economic mania that has so thoroughly colonised the present age. Maybe through it we might find a way out, forge tools to break free from the mass cash psychosis that we have been forced to call everyday life. So what exactly did Wilde mean? Price and its limitless abstraction from the concrete product or service ironically leaves the commodity holder with nothing to hold onto. Human values originate from what we consider to be the ultimate ends of what we do, allowing us to decide whether collectively behaving this or that way is best for everyone, including the natural environment. At some point, all individuals and societies must inevitably encounter this moral reckoning. It is the good part of being alive. What broader social objectives ought we commit to? What do present institutions truly stand for? Should they exist in their current format? Even if you have no answer to such questions, a significant sense of communal empowerment is derived from the ability to pose them in public. However, there is one catch. This is no exercise in beige pluralism, where all views are equal to others. No. There are *correct* answers to these questions. But are we worthy of them?

Phantom prices

In the richer countries of the West the significant provocation that these value-questions open up can no longer be avoided by recourse to biological survival that we so often hear from the power structure; as in, we're all struggling to secure our physiological self-preservation and these are the only organisational forms (e.g., capitalism) that can allow us to do that properly. Bad (and dangerous) economics has for too long been justified by the conceit of necessity, as if being stuck in an office all day sending pointless emails somehow coincides with hunting and gathering from a previous age. I say, leave my body out of it!

But there are other ways to undermine our wish to take stock and look at the big picture concerning what we are collectively doing. One is to transform performative means into ideological ends. That erases the horizon of thought almost immediately. Money, prices and the endless quantification of social behaviour ought to be considered mere *means* for getting things done, for accomplishing value-laden goals. But today they move centre stage and shine on their own accord, an object of desire in and of themselves. As a result, public debate about how we should live disappears. What once used to be the sedate countenance of the bureaucrat has now become the worldview of an entire civilisation. Life itself is simply about being endlessly concerned with solving technical problems, many of which have none (e.g., debt, etc.). For example, it's crucial for any civilised society to have a functioning and affordable nationwide public transport system (value). But the job of delivering it has been handed over to organisations who view that value-goal as secondary to making money (means). So much so that it utterly fails in its wider mission. The problem is that society as a whole is being run pretty much in the same way.

The reign of instrumental means (money rather than societal goals) and pragmatism is now deeply institutionalised. Just to be clear, none of my argument here is against pragmatism and its concrete pressures. Who doesn't think that the ability to unblock a drain, for example, is important? Or mathematical models in relation to pension schemes? But when pan-practicality becomes the centre of all things, the instrumentalism I'm speaking of inevitably enters into dangerous territory for two reasons.

First, because practical reason is now constantly being set against itself, usually by conditions not of our own making. For example, if I have insufficient funds and wish to enrol at university the practical thing to do is take out a student loan. As the years pass I am increasingly pressured to honour that student debt ... but how? I've long left university and am in my early 30s. I have a family and elderly relatives. For sure, this is the real travesty being visited upon younger generations at the moment. Responsibilities for them that later ought to be satisfying (e.g., caring for loved ones) are now deemed impossible in light of, say, that loan repayment plan or stagnating income. Henceforth, the good things in life are forever marred by the stain of some invisible sun that is being fuelled by bad economics.

And second, the simulacra of practicality proliferates as a cultural ideology that provides an alibi for activities that are much more sinister, deeds that are not practical to anyone you and I know. Without the emblem of usefulness, how else could technocracy justify the ongoing litany of horrors of the present phase of capitalism? We must work to earn our keep. Budget cuts are about society living within its means. Privatisation serves the utility preference of a customer far better than a public service. And so on. Of course, the irony is that this particular form of practicality is fairly impractical much of the time. Even anti-social and against the needs of large swathes of the population. But when it colonises our imaginations, as it was perhaps invented to do, the act of valuing fades into the fringes of nothingness, a non-entity that lies beyond the reach of even the sharpest and most perspicacious specialist, especially economists and policy advisors. When Sir Paul Collier recently argued we all ought to forget ideology (reading Marx is like consulting Harry Potter) and get down to sorting out *practical*, non-partisan *solutions*, what he really ends up supporting is a weird type of proto-nationalism.[2]

Economics does not exist

The singular focus on abstract means has reduced the study and practice of economics to a simple exercise of calculation. If it has any ethos, it'd be a sort of self-referential mysticism of numbers. In the mainstream economic discipline, including micro, macro, game and even new-wave behavioural economics, you will be hard-pressed to find any normative deliberation on exactly why our society is designed as such. For the modern economist, marginal utility, interest rates, capital gains, price signalling and a host of other means-oriented mechanisms are all that matter. This can lead to some serious lapses in judgement. After the 2008 global financial crisis, many asked why economists and business school experts missed the warning signs. A few years before the crisis, Nobel Prize laurette, Robert E. Lucas even said, the 'central problem of depression-prevention has been solved, for all practical purposes, and has in fact been solved for many decades'.[3] If these economic minds were so smart, then why couldn't they predict such a catastrophe?

The answer has to do with the dire lack of perspective that conspires against the mind when only concerned with means. The Romanian playwright Eugene Ionesco captures this wrongheadedness in his 1959 anti-fascist play *Rhinoceros*.[4] A herd of unruly rhinos (symbolising 1930s fascism) have unexpectedly roared through town, upsetting the tranquil calm of the market square. After the dust settles, the Grocer, Proprietor and the Old Gentleman begin to discuss what's just happened. They are interrupted by the Logician. He is the only one qualified to theorise the situation properly given his training. The Logician convinces the small crowd that the primary and most logical question is whether the rhinos had *one* horn or *two*? This consumes much discussion. Bérenger, the play's anti-hero, a thoughtful and dishevelled drunk, looks on in disbelief. He's the only one alarmed enough to ask the most appropriate question under such circumstances. Who cares how many horns they bloody have! People, there are rhinos taking over our town! Although nobody listens to him, Bérenger puts the calamity into perspective by calling it as such.

So what does economics do besides speculating about horns? One might be tempted to conduct a deconstructive reading of neoclassical economics in the style of Jacques Derrida to try and discern what precisely is the 'absent presence' quietly animating this vast machinery of means in the dark margins of its own impossibility. On the other hand, perhaps there's good reason why Derrida steered clear of economics as such. For its social centre is strictly void, a perceptive abyss that is bereft of wider political reflection. This variant of nothingness is frightening since it consists of interminable tautologies: 'the reason you do this is because you do this ... now let's model it'. From the rise of the Chicago School onwards, we are no longer permitted to ask why, for example, we have banks, prisons, markets, the cumbersome institution of work and so forth. Challenge any official about this and their gaze slowly drifts away into nothingness with a dumb 'huh?' expression. In a universe ruled only by means (especially prices and money) the unassuming margins that Derrida argued were so important for grasping a discourse (i.e., it's what is not said, continuously deferred that gives a text its deceptive positivity) are suddenly missing.

Obsessive marginality takes over at this point, with problems of less and more the only ones that really count. As a result, a gaping hole of *present* non-existence destroys the ethical texture of the semantic system. One suspects that Derrida might arrive at an equable conclusion. Economics does not exist. It can't account for itself even in the unspoken whispers we'd expect it to draw upon to make itself whole. Perhaps this marginal absence explains the latent mindlessness that characterises economics as a discipline. Not stupidity as such. Econometric theorists and practitioners, for example, are often very smart people. The trouble is that this intelligence is without value. Once again, in making this criticism I don't want anything to do with the populist right-wing attack against 'experts' that has recently become fashionable in the UK and USA (or what climate change sceptics like Myron Ebell

– Donald Trump's advisor on the environment – deride as the 'expertariat'). That's just an excuse for barring informed opinion from the sphere of democratic process. I'd rather listen to a doctor concerning the state of my health (or the healthcare system) than Michael Gove any day.[5] And much more besides. No, the issue here is the opposite. Doctors are hands-on professionals who deal with their subject matter at the coalface on a daily basis. They should be listened to. Mainstream economics on the other hand is meant to speak about how best to organise our society, yet continuously proffers an erroneous, detached and out-of-touch worldview that might sound 'real' to cloistered free market think-tanks and politicians. But only them.

Market malice

None of this would be a problem if economics was confined to the endowed chairs of the academy, esoteric journal articles and boring conferences. But the lexicon of neoclassical economics is the leading language game in (post-)neoliberal societies of control. And this economisation of life in general has only gathered strength following the global financial crisis, an event that mainly become notable because it affects rich people (the Global South has had its own global crisis for many years, it's called poverty). The marginal nothingness that marks theoretical economics is seductive if you get too close to it and can spirit the enthusiast away from reality very quickly. When it is accepted as the practical basis for organising large patterns of human behaviour, however, deep dissonances appear and reality starts to go crazy because it cannot cope with that kind of nihilistic self-referentiality. This is what 'utility maximisation' and 'enhanced revenue streams' mean for everyone *beyond* the corporate boardroom.

Here are a few disconcerting examples of what happens when social values drop out of the picture and profit is perused purely for its own sake, the dominion of lost means that actually end up defying the mandate of 'practically' in the wider sense of the term. Given the popularity of the horror porn genre in British youth culture, a company called Hunters Knives and Swords made a killing by selling thousands of 'Zombie Knives' over the last few years. These are machetes, swords and hand-blades inspired by horror films. When a teenager was murdered by an assailant wielding a 'Zombie Killer' machete, the police called for them to be banned. As far as they were concerned, the weapons had no value to society whatsoever. An official stated,

> 'Zombie knives' are monstrous weapons that serve no practical use whatsoever. They are being banned because they are dangerous and companies should act responsibly. They are not your average kitchen knife or garden tool: they are pointless, over the top weapons that glamorise violence with names such as Head Splitter and Death Dagger. After a year of campaigning by my office, I am glad they are finally being banned.[6]

But the firm was mesmerised by the economics of nothingness or what an undergraduate university student learning the correct lingo might call utility maximisation. Means – shifting more units – were all that mattered. Even the above reminder of value-based ends by the police couldn't shake the spell. When the impending ban was announced the firm merely intensified its advertising campaign on its website: 'Order now – after 16th August 2016 you will no longer be able to purchase zombie knives in the UK, so grab them while you can!'[7] It would be fascinating to have the opportunity to sit down with the CEO of Hunters Knives and Swords, so clearly besotted by marginal cost issues, and press him or her about what purpose the company fundamentally serves. Beyond the blatant profiteering (which is also a means without substantive ends), the answer would probably be found in the pointless knives themselves: certainly *nothing* … but perhaps even *less than nothing*.

The second example comes from the USA. Food politics is a huge sore point in the neoliberal capitalist global economy. The use of so-called markets and the predominance of only a handful of multinational firms has created artificial scarcity, a decline in biodiversity and eroded the self-sufficiency of growers. Not to mention an obesity epidemic. The ultimate point of any food supply system ought to be the efficient, safe production and allocation of foodstuffs to the consumer, even according to the official narrative of capitalism.

However, once again the means for achieving this objective (particularly quantitative measures) have taken front seat and now the tail is undeniably wagging the dog. This is the case not only in terms of abstract profits (e.g., the completely unsustainable meat supply chain) but also the actual, physical food itself. For example, a recent report found that the US food industry probably discards *half* of everything it produces because the apples, tomatoes or whatever don't have the right appearance. While we know that 'down-stream' waste (in households and restaurants, for example) is a serious problem, it is incredible that 'up-stream' foodstuff corporations intentionally rubbish perfectly fine fruit and vegetables because of the way they look. And all of this in the context of widespread hunger and poverty. According to a fruit and vegetable merchant in Florida, 'It's all about blemish-free produce ... What happens in our business today is that it is either perfect, or it gets rejected. It is perfect to them, or they turn it down. And then you are stuck.'[8] Similarly shocking figures can be found in relation to unsold supermarket food. In the UK, for example, 115,000 tonnes of surplus food is thrown out every year.[9] Each tonne is equivalent to 2380 meals. At the same time, 875,000 Londoners admit to having at some time experienced financial difficulty in paying for their next meal.[10]

In reality, the market economy has nothing to do with the competent distribution of scarce resources. It instead represents a tyranny of pure means unconnected to the logic of social needs. This is what markets have actually amounted to in the era of wreckage economics. It seems like they only gain traction by positing an expansive chasm of nothingness where values ought to stand (e.g., what is the final purpose of the food industry? That is not my concern). Utility without purpose and a spiralling value-of-nothing myopia drives mainstream business models and much of its consumer culture.

The last example takes us back into the workplace. Huntley Mount Engineering in Manchester took advantage of a government youth apprentice scheme that allowed the firm to hire teenagers and pay them £3 per hour. In July 2015, 16-year-old Cameron Minshull was employed under the programme. As he was working at a lathe his oversized overalls became caught in the rotating chuck and turned metal, tossing him onto the equipment in a split second.[11] The injury was fatal. An investigation revealed the worst aspect of the economics of nothingness – the treatment of people as no more than an instrumental means rather than an ends in themselves, a violation of the great Kantian ethical code.

The case almost epitomises wreckage economics for a number of reasons. First, the apprentice scheme was part of the overall campaign by the government to deepen the ideology of work in society. Whether the work serves any useful social function or provides a fulfilling way of life is secondary to the imperative of simply having a job. As we noted in an earlier chapter, jobs become a quantitative *output* (politicians only talk about them in terms of faceless numbers) rather than a qualitative or substantive *input* that might serve some wider social and existential role. In other words, a job is no longer a means to achieve other things but a (dead) end in itself.

Second, the owners of Huntley Mount Engineering were only interested in the apprenticeship scheme because it provided a source of extraordinarily cheap labour. Since they had little concern for Cameron Minshull's wellbeing more generally, they gave him dangerously ill-fitting work wear (which eventually led to the accident), no safety training and permitted youngsters to work unsupervised.

And third, Lime People Training Solutions, the recruitment agency that placed Cameron, fast-tracked his application in order to receive a £4500 fee from the government's Skills Funding Agency. At the court hearing the engineering firm was found guilty of corporate manslaughter, with one of the boss's receiving a prison sentence and a large fine. Cameron's mother was interviewed about the tragedy:

> Our child going to work on a pittance apprentice wage through a proper agency on a government approved apprenticeship. How could this happen? Where was the safety? Where was the training to help my boy? No day is ever going to be the same and it is all caused by people failing to pay that little bit of attention to make sure our boy was safe.[12]

For her, Cameron was everything. Without a price. For Huntley Mount Engineering he was nothing, only a price.

Subprime justice?

These examples – and we could reel out many more – typify the commercial standpoint that prevails today, spellbound by money and reducing everyone and everything to a negative exchange value. Of course, the means/ends inversion has probably always been an elemental component of capitalism given the way it relies so heavily on objectification and exploitation. And as Max Weber alerted us to many years ago, bureaucratic managerialism, which has engulfed everyday life on a scale even he wouldn't believe, has converted the instruments of life into a purpose(less) way of living as such. The price-fixation of everything, excessive auditing, aggressive performance targets and monetarisation of even the air we breathe all fit hand in glove with neoliberal capitalism because it yields to the myth of *commensurability*; namely, that it is possible to create systems of measurement that permit the diverse, variegated and disparate entity we call society to be approached from a singular cash-perspective, especially given now values no longer matter. It is no surprise, then, that the business mind, something that almost every institution has adopted today (e.g., we demand x many widgets, students, surgical operations, etc.), becomes so detached from the professed *raison d'être* of civilisation, mechanically pursuing 'units' (money, savings, etc.) for their own sake; increasingly to the point of madness and self-destruction.

Perhaps above all this fetishisation of means serves to depoliticise the popular imagination. Rationality is mistaken to reside in the financial exchanges that are now the only way the social body can function. It's like an addict hooked on 'ice', the worse type of meth-amphetamine ever concocted. Nothing seems more reasonable than to chase another hit. Similarly, rent, debt, marginal utility, market clearing price and all of the other arithmetical interactions that have been modelled to death have nothing to say about the broader normative question of whether any of this is right. Economic rationality might look like the most sobering act of demystifica-tion since it exposes the naked self-interestedness at the centre of reality and can be calculated with mathematical accuracy. But the opposite is probably the case. It runs on a crazy ideological fuel, pregnant with distortion, nonsense and misrepresentation.

Was this not the lesson of the September 2008 subprime debacle and the litany of injustices that have ensued ever since, often draped in the incontrovertible language of necessity? Economic rationality turned out to be nothing more than the deformed bastard child of reason. Not a glorious sun of coming prosperity but an *anti-sun*, eclipsing the face of the globe under a formidable dead eye that has darkened the world. Now we're only allowed to be obsessed with the microrelations between subsets (a, b and c) and never the master set itself. Seldom are we called upon to consider whether ours is a worthy world, whether it should exist. That represents a significant abnormality in our society. Major collective pathologies have been born from less.

To see the totality again we need to foreshadow ourselves, the 99%-ers, and move out of the pallid gloom that the economics-for-the-1% has cast across the face of society. Given the preceding discussion, reclaiming perception (or perspective) and challenging capitalism's ontological precedence is the most urgent task we face today. The wildly financialised 'pseudo-realities' that have infiltrated our imagined non-communities are falling apart and dying. Perhaps they were never alive in the first place. But make no mistake. The growing winter of a wasted world, a vapid monoculture of nothingness, is encircling us as we speak, and it's time to leave. That ticket isn't going to be served on a paper plate. For the future to begin again and history to be made, one has to be correctly poised. Be ready. And therein lies the most important question: will we ever be *worthy* of that history, still yet to come, but certainly demanding a response from us very soon.

Notes

Introduction

1. King, M. (2017). *The End of Alchemy: Banking, the Global Economy and the Future of Money.* New York: W.W. Norton & Company.
2. The Equality Trust (2016). 'UK taxation – unfair and unclear'. Available at www.equalitytrust.org.uk/uk-taxation-unfair-and-unclear
3. See Vaughn, L. and Finch, G. (2017). *The Fix: How Bankers Lied, Cheated and Colluded to Rig the World's Most Important Number.* Chichester: John Wiley & Sons; Kolhatka, S. (2017). *Black Edge: Inside Information, Dirty Money and the Quest to Bring Down the Most Wanted Man on Wall Street.* New York: Random House; Sekka, P. (2017). 'A British snub of the EU investigation into the Panama Papers is short-sighted'. *Guardian.* Available at www.theguardian.com/commentisfree/2017/feb/21/british-snub-eu-investigation-panama-papers-treasury-hmrc
4. Gilman, N., Goldhammer, J. and Weber, S. (2011). *Deviant Globalization: Black Market Economy in the 21st Century.* New York: Continuum.
5. For example, see O'Neill, S. (2015). 'Cash from crime lords drives up house prices'. *The Times.* Available at www.thetimes.co.uk/tto/news/uk/crime/article4508163.ece
6. See Worley, W. (2017). 'Rupert Murdoch's News Corp "enjoys astounding access" to government, research shows'. *Independent.* Available at www.independent.co.uk/news/media/rupert-murdoch-news-corp-access-government-downing-street-prime-minister-chancellor-a7566016.html; Stewart, J. (2017). 'Goldman Sachs completes return from wilderness to the White House'. *New York Times.* Available at www.nytimes.com/2017/01/12/business/goldman-sachs-completes-return-from-wilderness-to-the-white-house.html
7. YouGov (2017). '37% of British workers think their jobs are meaningless'. Available at https://yougov.co.uk/news/2015/08/12/british-jobs-meaningless/
8. *Work Front* (2017). *2016–2017 State of Enterprise Work Report: U.S. Edition.* Available at https://resources.workfront.com/ebooks-whitepapers/2016-state-of-enterprise-work-report-u-s-edition
9. National Oceanic and Atmospheric Administration (2017). 'The Great Pacific garbage patch'. Available at https://marinedebris.noaa.gov/info/patch.html

10. Earle, J., Moran, C. and Ward-Perkins, Z. (2016). *The Econocracy: The Perils of Leaving Economics to the Experts*. Manchester: University of Manchester Press.

11. Romer, P. (2016). 'The trouble with macroeconomics'. Available at https://paulromer.net/wp-content/uploads/2016/09/WP-Trouble.pdf

12. Resolution Foundation (2017). 'Living standards 2017: the past, present and possible future of UK incomes'. Available at www.resolution foundation.org/publications/living-standards-2017-the-past-present-and-possible-future-of-uk-incomes/

13. Quoted in Belluz, J. (2016). 'It may have seemed like the world fell apart in 2016. Steven Pinker is here to tell you it didn't'. *Vox*. Available at www.vox.com/science-and-health/2016/12/22/14042506/steven-pinker-optimistic-future-2016

14. Pinker, S. (2012). *The Better Angels of Our Nature: A History of Violence and Humanity*. New York: Penguin, p. xxv.

15. Laven-Morris, F. (2017). 'Oxfam's wealth statistics are persistently misleading – Ben Southwood comment'. Adam Smith Institute. Available at www.adamsmith.org/news/oxfams-wealth-statistics-are-persistently-misleading-ben-southwood-comment

16. Fisher, M. (2014). *Ghosts of My Life: Writings on Depression, Hauntology and Lost Futures*. London: Zero.

17. Milanovic, B. (2016). *Global Inequality: A New Approach for the Age of Globalization*. Cambridge, MA: Harvard University Press.

18. See Sayer, A. (2015). *Why We Can't Afford the Rich*. Bristol: Policy Press; Dorling, D (2014). *Inequality and the 1%*. London: Verso.

19. Mann, G. (2017). *In the Long Run We Are All Dead: Keynesianism, Political Economy and Revolution*. London: Verso.

Chapter 1

1. *Herald Scotland* (2009). 'Shock but little grief for Isabella in neighbourhood where pensioner lay dead in her flat for five years'. Available at www.heraldscotland.com/news/12765623.Shock_but_little_grief_for_Isabella_in_neighbourhood_where_pensioner_lay_dead_in_her_flat_for_five_years/

2. BBC (2009). 'Body may have lain for five years'. Available at http://news.bbc.co.uk/1/hi/scotland/edinburgh_and_east/8132642.stm

3. Laing, O. (2015). 'The future of loneliness'. *Guardian*. Available at www.theguardian.com/society/2015/apr/01/future-of-loneliness-internet-isolation

4. Rhodes, D. (2017). 'Social care system "beginning to collapse" as 900 carers quit every day'. BBC. Available at www.bbc.co.uk/news/uk-england-39507859

5. *Scotsman* (2009). 'Pensioner lies dead in flat for five years'. Available at www.scotsman.com/news/pensioner-lies-dead-in-flat-for-five-years-1-1211321

6. Ibid.

7. Mullen, S. (2010). 'Cousin of woman who lay dead in flat for five years gets fortune'. *Daily Record*. Available at www.dailyrecord.co.uk/news/scottish-news/cousin-of-woman-who-lay-dead-1072975

8. Cederstrom, C. and Fleming, P. (2013). *Dead Man Working*. London: Zero Books.

9. Crewe, T. (2016). 'The strange death of municipal England'. *London Review of Books*. Available at www.lrb.co.uk/v38/n24/tom-crewe/the-strange-death-of-municipal-england

10. Chiu, J. (2016). 'Bottled air started as a joke. Now China can't get enough'. *Mashable*. Available at http://mashable.com/2016/05/12/china-bottled-air-demand/#KeTTrCnTcGqI

11. King, M. (2017). *The End of Alchemy: Banking, the Global Economy and the Future of Money*. New York: W.W. Norton & Company.

12. Benjamin, W. (2009). *One-way Street and Other Writings*. London: Penguin, p. 39.

13. See Verhaeghe, P. (2014). *What About Me? The Struggle for Identity in a Market-based Society*. London: Scribe Books; Fisher, M. (2014). *Ghosts of My Life: Writings on Depression, Hauntology and Lost Futures*. London: Zero Books.

14. See Wilkinson, R. and Pickett, K. (2009). *The Spirit Level: Why More Equal Societies Almost Always Do Better*. London: Penguin.

15. BBC (2017). 'United Airlines: shares drop after passenger dragging video'. Available at www.bbc.co.uk/news/world-us-canada-39563570

16. *Telegraph* (2016). 'George Osbourne fires Rambo-style machinegun in Vietnam'. Available at www.telegraph.co.uk/news/2016/08/19/george-osborne-fires-rambo-style-machine-gun-in-vietnam/

17. *Southland Times* (2013). 'English denies "bullying" academic'. Available at www.stuff.co.nz/southland-times/news/8922539/English-denies-bullying-academic

18. Rancière, J. (2006). *Hatred of Democracy*. London: Verso.

19. Quoted in Konnikova, M. (2017). 'Trump's lies vs. your brain'. *Politico Magazine*. Available at www.politico.com/magazine/story/2017/01/donald-trump-lies-liar-effect-brain-214658

20. Bowden, G. (2017). 'Daily Mail banned as "reliable source" on Wikipedia in unprecedented move'. *Huffington Post*. Available at www.huffingtonpost.co.uk/entry/daily-mail-banned-from-wikipedia_uk_589c3e13e4b07685621810f8

21. Mason, P. (2015). *Postcapitalism: A Guide to Our Future*. London: Verso.

22. See Crouch, C. (2011). *The Strange Non-death of Neoliberalism*. Cambridge: Polity; Quiggin, J. (2010); *Zombie Economics: How Dead*

Ideas Still Walk Among Us. Princeton: Princeton University Press; Dupuy, P. (2014); *Economy and the Future: A Crisis of Faith.* Lansing: Michigan State University Press.

23. White, A. (2016). *Shadow State: Inside the Secret Companies that Run Britain.* London: One World Publications.

24. West, K. (2012). 'Rail fat cats send £700m to offshore tax havens'. *Sunday Times.* Available at http://www.thesundaytimes.co.uk/sto/business/Industry/article1042196.ece

25. Jenkins, P. (2016). '"Negligible" link found between executive pay and performance'. *Financial Times.* Available at www.ft.com/content/abc7085e-c857-11e6-9043-7e34c07b46ef

26. Equality Trust (2017). 'Pay tracker'. Available at www.equalitytrust.org.uk/sites/default/files/Pay%20Tracker%20%28March%202017%29_1.pdf

27. McDonald, D. (2017). 'Harvard Business School and the propagation of immoral profit strategies'. *News Week.* Available at www.newsweek.com/2017/04/14/harvard-business-school-financial-crisis-economics-578378.html

28. Ahmed, K. (2017). 'Farewell to pay growth'. BBC. Available at www.bbc.co.uk/news/business-39578270

29. Farnsworth, K. (2015). 'The British corporate welfare state: public provision for private businesses'. Available at http://speri.dept.shef.ac.uk/wp-content/uploads/2015/07/SPERI-Paper-24-The-British-Corporate-Welfare-State.pdf

30. Trade Union Centre (2017). 'Rise in insecure work is costing Exchequer £4bn a year, warns TUC'. Available at www.tuc.org.uk/industrial-issues/workplace-issues/rise-insecure-work-costing-exchequer-%C2%A34bn-year-warns-tuc

31. *Independent* (2014). 'Northumbria NHS trust saves £67m by freeing itself from PFI deal'. Available at www.independent.co.uk/life-style/health-and-families/health-news/northumbria-nhs-trust-saves-67m-by-freeing-itself-from-pfi-deal-9517844.html

32. Ibid.

33. Young, A. (2013). 'Cheney's Halliburton made $39.5 billion on Iraq War'. *Reader Supported News.* Available at http://readersupportednews.org/news-section2/308-12/16561-focus-cheneys-halliburton-made-395-billion-on-iraq-war

34. *Independent* (2008). 'Funeral flights bring in best profits, says Ryanair boss'. Available at www.independent.ie/business/irish/funeral-flights-bring-in-best-profits-says-ryanair-boss-26452014.html

35. Luthra, S. (2017). 'Massive price hike for lifesaving opioid overdose antidote'. *Scientific American.* Available at www.scientificamerican.com/article/massive-price-hike-for-lifesaving-opioid-overdose-antidote1/

36. Step Change Debt Charity (2014). 'The social cost of problem debt in the UK'. Available at www.stepchange.org/policy-and-research/social-cost-of-debt.aspx

37. Warren, E. (2017). 'Senator Elizabeth Warren questions Betsy DeVos at Senate confirmation hearing'. YouTube. Available at www.youtube.com/watch?v=ld6k2b-AEfU&t=147s

38. Reddit (2014). 'What led to your becoming a NEET?' Available at www.reddit.com/r/NEET/comments/2cww5t/what_led_to_your_becoming_a_neet/

39. Paul, K. (2017). 'Millennials are more depressed at work than any other generation'. *New York Post*. Available at http://nypost.com/2017/02/14/millennials-are-more-depressed-at-work-than-any-generation/

40. Piketty, T. (2013). *Capital in the Twenty-first Century*. Cambridge, MA: Harvard University Press.

41. Savage, M. (2015). *Social Class in the 21st Century*. London: Pelican.

42. Mayer, J. (2016). *Dark Money: The Hidden History of the Billionaires Behind the Rise of the Radical Right*. New York: Doubleday.

43. Dorling, D. (2014). *All That is Solid: How the Great Housing Disaster Defines Our Times, and What We Can Do About It*. London: Penguin.

44. Desmond, M. (2017). *Evicted: Poverty and Profit in the American City*. New York: Penguin.

45. Temin, P. (2017). *The Vanishing Middle Class: Prejudice and Power in a Dual Economy*. Cambridge, MA: MIT Press.

46. Barr, C. and Malik, S. (2016). 'Revealed: the 30-year economic betrayal dragging down Generation Y's income'. *Guardian*. Available at www.theguardian.com/world/2016/mar/07/revealed-30-year-economic-betrayal-dragging-down-generation-y-income; Resolution Foundation (2017). 'As time goes by: shifting incomes and inequality between and within generations'. Available at www.resolutionfoundation.org/publications/as-time-goes-by-shifting-incomes-and-inequality-between-and-within-generations/

47. Peck, T (2016). 'Scrap the triple-lock on pensions to tackle generational inequality, MPs say'. *Independent*. Available at www.independent.co.uk/news/uk/politics/scrap-the-triple-lock-on-pensions-mps-say-a7399721.html

48. Oxfam (2014). 'Number of billionaires doubled since financial crisis as inequality spirals out of control'. Available at www.oxfam.org.uk/blogs/2014/10/number-of-billionaires-doubled-since-financial-crisis-as-inequality-spirals-out-of-control. Also see *Guardian* (2015). 'Recession rich: Britain's wealthiest double net worth since crisis'. Available at www.theguardian.com/business/2015/apr/26/recession-rich-britains-wealthiest-double-net-worth-since-crisis

49. Gallup (2013). 'Worldwide, 13% of employees are engaged at work'. Available at www.gallup.com/poll/165269/worldwide-employees-engaged-work.aspx
50. *The Economist* (2015). 'When what comes down doesn't go up'. Available at www.economist.com/news/briefing/21650086-salaries-rich-countries-are-stagnating-even-growth-returns-and-politicians-are-paying
51. Pew Research Centre (2014). 'For most workers, real wages haven't budged for decades'. Available at www.pewresearch.org/fact-tank/2014/10/09/for-most-workers-real-wages-have-barely-budged-for-decades/
52. International Labour Organization (2014). 'Working poverty reduction stalled'. Available at www.ilo.org/global/about-the-ilo/newsroom/news/WCMS_234030/lang--en/index.htm
53. *Guardian* (2016). 'Angela felt pressured into work. Now she's struggling to pay the bills'. Available at www.theguardian.com/commentisfree/2016/jun/16/jobcentre-advisers-pressure-work-carer
54. National Housing Federation (2016). 'Private landlords double takings from public purse to £9 billion'. Available at www.housing.org.uk/press/press-releases/private-landlords-double-takings-from-public-purse-to-9-billion/
55. Booth, R. (2016). 'More than 7m Britons now in precarious employment'. *Guardian*. Available at www.theguardian.com/uk-news/2016/nov/15/more-than-7m-britons-in-precarious-employment
56. Weckler, A. (2016). 'Google Ireland pays €47m in tax on sales of €22.6bn'. *Independent*. Available at www.independent.ie/business/technology/news/google-ireland-pays-47m-in-tax-on-sales-of-226bn-35189644.html
57. See Young, C., Varner, C., Lurie, I. and Prisinzano, R. (2016). 'Millionaire migration and taxation of the elite: evidence from administrative data'. *American Sociological Review*, 81(3): 421–46.
58. Mason, R. (2017). 'Data watchdog looks at whether No 10 covered up Uber correspondence'. *Guardian*. Available at www.theguardian.com/technology/2017/apr/13/data-watchdog-no-10-cameron-uber-correspondence-regulation
59. Tapscott, D. and Tapscott, A. (2016). *Blockchain Revolution: How the Technology Behind Bitcoin is Changing Money, Business and the World*. New York: Portfolio Penguin.
60. Indeed.co.uk (2015). 'Hermes'. Available at www.indeed.co.uk/cmp/Hermes/reviews
61. Livingston, J. (2016). 'Fuck work'. *Aeon*. Available at https://aeon.co/essays/what-if-jobs-are-not-the-solution-but-the-problem
62. Giuffo, J. (2012). 'MissTravel.com: dating site or Travel Ho dating site?' *Forbes*. Available at www.forbes.com/sites/johngiuffo/2012/04/27/misstravel-com-dating-site-or-travel-ho-dating-site/#5f07a4b34d1c

63. Hajibagheri, S. (2015). 'Sugar Babies: students selling sex'. Sky News. Available at http://news.sky.com/story/sugar-babies-students-selling-sex-10341851

64. Noor, P. (2017). 'Sex for rent? It's the logical extension of leaving housing to the market'. *Guardian*. Available at www.theguardian.com/comment isfree/2017/apr/19/sex-rent-logical-extension-leaving-housing-to-market

65. OECD (2016). 'Policy brief on the future of work: automation and independent work in a digital economy'. Available at www.oecd.org/employment/Policy%20brief%20-%20Automation%20and%20Independent%20Work%20in%20a%20Digital%20Economy.pdf

66. Sundararajan, A. (2016). *The Sharing Economy: The End of Employment and the Rise of Crowd-based Capitalism*. Cambridge, MA: MIT Press.

67. See Williams, C. (2014). 'Out of the shadows: a classification of economies by their size and character of their informal sector'. *Work, Employment and Society*, 28(5): 735–53; Neuwirth, R. (2012). *Stealth of Nations: The Global Rise of the Informal Economy*. New York: Anchor Books.

68. For example, see Milton Friedman's arguments against formal union organisations in medicine, namely, the American Medical Association. In Friedman, M. and Friedman, R. (1980). *Free to Choose: A Personal Statement*. San Diego: Harcourt.

69. Hilton, S. (2015). *More Human: Designing a World Where People Come First*. New York: W.H. Allen.

70. McGregor, J. (2015). 'At Zappos, 210 employees decide to leave rather than work with no bosses'. *Washington Post*. Available at www.washingtonpost.com/news/on-leadership/wp/2015/05/08/at-zappos-210-employees-decide-to-leave-rather-than-work-with-no-bosses/

71. National Careers Service (2016). 'What are the "soft skills" employers want?' Available at https://nationalcareersservice.direct.gov.uk/aboutus/newsarticles/Pages/Spotlight-SoftSkills.aspx

72. Deleuze, G. (1992). 'Postscript on the societies of control'. *October*, 59(Winter): 3–7, p. 6.

73. Scheiber, N. (2017). 'How Uber uses psychological tricks to push its drivers' buttons'. *New York Times*. Available at www.nytimes.com/interactive/2017/04/02/technology/uber-drivers-psychological-tricks.html?_r=1

74. Packard, V. (1957). *The Hidden Persuaders*. New York: David McKay Company.

75. Sunstein, C. and Thaler, R. (2009). *Nudge: Improving Decisions About Health, Wealth and Happiness*. New York: Penguin.

76. Scheiber, 'How Uber uses psychological tricks'.

77. Quoted in *The Irish News* (2017). 'Ella's kitchen founder puts family first at mealtimes'. Available at www.irishnews.com/lifestyle/2017/04/04/

news/ella-s-kitchen-founder-puts-family-first-at-mealtimes-984537/;
also see Lindley, P. (2017). *Little Wins: The Huge Power of Thinking Like a Toddler*. London: Penguin.

78. Davies, R. (2017). 'Sick Parcelforce couriers can be charged up to £250 if they can't find cover'. *Guardian*. Available at www.theguardian.com/business/2017/mar/06/sick-parcelforce-couriers-royal-mail-mands-john-lewis-hamleys-dpd

79. Booth, R. (2017). 'UK Mail driver who was unable to work after car accident charged £800'. *Guardian*. Available at www.theguardian.com/business/2017/mar/19/uk-mail-driver-unable-to-work-car-accident-charged-800-pounds

80. *Financial Times* (2017). 'India strike curb Uber's ambitions'. Available at www.ft.com/content/9653ace2-f1d9-11e6-8758-687615182a16

81. *Guardian* (2016). 'Collective action via social media brings hope to gig economy workers'. Available at www.theguardian.com/money/2016/aug/19/collective-action-via-social-media-brings-hope-to-gig-economy-workers

82. Adorno, T.W. (1968). 'Late Capitalism or Industrial Society? Opening Address to the 16th German Sociological Congress'. Available at www.marxists.org/reference/archive/adorno/1968/late-capitalism.htm

Chapter 2

1. Schwartz, J. (2013). 'Internet activist, a creator of RSS, is dead at 26, apparently a suicide'. *New York Times*. Available at www.washingtonpost.com/news/on-leadership/wp/2015/05/08/at-zappos-210-employees-decide-to-leave-rather-than-work-with-no-bosses/

2. Scheiber, N. (2013). 'The inside story of why Aaron Swartz broke into MIT and JSTOR'. *New Republic*. Available at https://newrepublic.com/article/112418/aaron-swartz-suicide-why-he-broke-jstor-and-mit

3. United States District Court (2011). 'United States of America v. Aaron Swartz (Defendant)'. Available at www.documentcloud.org/documents/217117-united-states-of-america-v-aaron-swartz

4. US Attorney's Office District of Massachusetts (2011). 'Alleged hacker charged with stealing over four million documents from MIT network'. Available at https://web.archive.org/web/20120526080523/www.justice.gov/usao/ma/news/2011/July/SwartzAaronPR.html

5. Cullen, K. and Ellement, J. (2014). 'MIT hacking case lawyer says Aaron Swartz was offered plea deal of six months behind bars'. *Boston Globe*. Available at http://archive.boston.com/metrodesk/2013/01/14/mit-hacking-case-lawyer-says-aaron-swartz-was-offered-plea-deal-six-months-behind-bars/hQt8sQI64tnV6FAd7CLcTJ/story.html

6. Franceschi-Bicchierai, F. (2014). 'Aaron Swartz's girlfriend explains "why Aaron died"'. *Mashable*. Available at http://mashable.com/2013/02/05/aaron-swartz-girlfriend-why-he-died/#vQSSsNySEkqR

7. Guy, S. (2013). 'Aaron Swartz was "killed by government," father says at funeral'. *Chicago Sun Times*. Available at https://web.archive.org/web/20140824225658/www.suntimes.com/business/17594002-420/aaron-swartz-memorialized-at-service.html#.WCBYyNWLTX5

8. Ibid.

9. Swartz, A. (2008). 'Guerilla open access manifesto'. Available at https://archive.org/stream/GuerillaOpenAccessManifesto/Goamjuly2008_djvu.txt

10. Ibid.

11. Day, E. (2013). 'Aaron Swartz: hacker, genius … martyr?' *Guardian*. Available at www.theguardian.com/technology/2013/jun/02/aaron-swartz-hacker-genius-martyr-girlfriend-interview

12. Reese, F. (2013). 'The death of Aaron Swartz: why we may never know the truth'. Mint News Press. Available at www.mintpressnews.com/the-federal-government-and-the-death-o-aaron-swartz-why-we-may-never-know-the-truth/47261/

13. Singel, R. (2009). 'FBI investigated coder for liberating paywalled court records'. *Wired*. Available at www.wired.com/2009/10/swartz-fbi/

14. Hollister, S. (2013). 'Aaron Swartz's legacy lives on: SecureDrop is a WikiLeaks for any journalist'. *The Verge*. Available at www.theverge.com/2013/10/16/4843484/securedrop-aaron-swartz-freedom-of-the-press-dead-drop-wikileaks

15. Ball, J. (2014). 'Guardian launches SecureDrop system for whistleblowers to share files'. *Guardian*. Available at www.theguardian.com/technology/2014/jun/05/guardian-launches-securedrop-whistleblowers-documents

16. US House Judiciary Committee (2013). 'H.R. 3261 stop online piracy bill'. Available at www.webcitation.org/630CICqjh

17. Aaron Swartz (2013). 'Freedom to connect: Aaron Swartz (1986–2013) on victory to save open internet, fight online censors'. *Democracy Now*. Available at www.democracynow.org/2013/1/14/freedom_to_connect_aaron_swartz_1986

18. Ibid.

19. Ibid.

20. Waugh, R. (2012). 'U.S Senators withdraw support for anti-piracy bills as 4.5 million people sign Google's anti-censorship petition'. *Daily Mail*. Available at www.dailymail.co.uk/sciencetech/article-2088860/SOPA-protest-4-5m-people-sign-Googles-anti-censorship-petition.html#ixzz4PK3i4TDy

21. Smith, L. (2012). 'Statement from Chairman Smith on Senate delay of vote on PROTECT IP Act'. Committee on the Judiciary. Available at

https://judiciary.house.gov/_files/news/01202012.html?scp=2&sq=
lamar%20smith&st=cse

22. Monbiot, G. (2011). 'Academic publishers make Murdoch look like a
    socialist'. *Guardian*. Available at www.theguardian.com/commentisfree/
    2011/aug/29/academic-publishers-murdoch-socialist; Gusterson, H.
    (2012). 'Want to change academic publishing? Just say no'. *Chronicle of
    Higher Education*. Available at www.chronicle.com/article/Want-to-
    Change-Academic/134546/

23. Sample, I. (2012). 'Harvard University says it can't afford journal
    publishers' prices'. *Guardian*. Available at www.theguardian.com/
    science/2012/apr/24/harvard-university-journal-publishers-prices?
    CMP=share_btn_fb

24. JSTOR (2013). 'JSTOR statement: misuse incident and criminal case'.
    Available at http://about.jstor.org/news/jstor-statement-misuse-incident-
    and-criminal-case

25. Quoted in Thomas, O. (2013). 'Family of Aaron Swartz blames MIT,
    prosecutors for his death'. *Business Insider*. Available at www.
    businessinsider.com/statement-family-aaron-swartz-2013-1?IR=T

26. Mazzucato, M. (2013). *The Entrepreneurial State: Debunking Public vs.
    Private Sector Myths*. London: Anthem Press; Patkar, M. (2015). 'Con
    jobs: 5 things everyone thinks Apple invented (wrongly)'. *Make Use Of*.
    Available at www.makeuseof.com/tag/con-jobs-5-things-apple-didnt-
    invent-internet-wont-shut/

27. Perelman, M. (2002). *Steal this Idea: Intellectual Property and the
    Corporate Confiscation of Creativity*. New York: Palgrave Macmillan,
    p. 76.

28. Mills, J. (2016). 'A crash is coming if we don't begin real investment'.
    Telegraph. Available at www.telegraph.co.uk/business/2016/06/16/a-
    crash-is-coming-if-we-dont-begin-real-investment/

29. Jobs, S. (2013). 'Steve Jobs – the lost interview (1995)'. Available at www.
    youtube.com/watch?v=TRZAJY23xio

30. Ibid.

31. Johnson, G. (1990). 'Once again, a man with a mission'. *New York Times*.
    Available at www.nytimes.com/1990/11/25/magazine/once-again-a-
    man-with-a-mission.html?pagewanted=all

32. *Forbes* (2012). 'How much money did Jonas Salk potentially forfeit by
    not patenting the polio vaccine?' Available at www.forbes.com/sites/
    quora/2012/08/09/how-much-money-did-jonas-salk-potentially-
    forfeit-by-not-patenting-the-polio-vaccine/#3bc3627e1c2d

33. Rutherford, H. (2013). 'Government to ignore asset sales referendum'.
    Stuff. Available at www.stuff.co.nz/national/politics/8412749/
    Government-to-ignore-asset-sales-referendum

34. Drutman, L. (2015). 'How corporate lobbyists conquered American
    democracy'. *The Atlantic*. Available at www.theatlantic.com/business/

archive/2015/04/how-corporate-lobbyists-conquered-american-democracy/390822/

35. Holden, D. (2014). 'TTIP: the biggest threat to democracy you've never heard of'. *New Statesman*. Available at www.newstatesman.com/politics/2014/09/ttip-biggest-threat-democracy-youve-never-heard

36. Oxfam (2016). 'An economy for the 1%: how privilege and power in the economy drive extreme inequality and how this can be stopped'. Available at http://policy-practice.oxfam.org.uk/publications/an-economy-for-the-1-how-privilege-and-power-in-the-economy-drive-extreme-inequ-592643

37. Credit Suisse (2014). *Global Wealth Report*. Available at http://economics.uwo.ca/people/davies_docs/credit-suisse-global-wealth-report-2014.pdf

38. Babrook, B. and Cameron, A. (1995). 'The Californian Ideology'. *Mute*. Available at www.metamute.org/editorial/articles/californian-ideology

39. Babrook, B. and Cameron, A. (2007). 'The Californian Ideology'. *Imaginary Futures*. Available at www.imaginaryfutures.net/2007/04/17/the-californian-ideology-2/

40. Jobs, 'Steve Jobs – the lost interview'.

41. Chafkin, M. (2016). 'The strange politics of Peter Thiel, Trump's most unlikely supporter'. *Bloomberg Business Week*. Available at www.bloomberg.com/news/articles/2016-07-21/the-strange-politics-of-peter-thiel-trump-s-most-unlikely-supporter

42. Mason, P. (2015). *Postcapitalism: A Guide to the Future*. London: Allen Lane.

43. Ibid., p. 143.

44. Coutts, K. and Gudgin, G. (2015). 'The macroeconomic impact of liberal economic policies in the UK'. Available at http://insight.jbs.cam.ac.uk/assets/2015_cbr-report_macroeconomic-impact-of-liberal-policies-in-the-uk.pdf, p. 11.

45. Weldon, D. (2015). 'Shareholder power "holding back economic growth"'. BBC. Available at www.bbc.co.uk/news/business-33660426

46. Ibid.

47. Reinhart, C.M. and Rogoff, K.S. (2010). 'Growth in the time of debt'. *American Economic Review*, 100(2): 573–8.

48. Jay, P. (2013). '28-year old PhD student debunks the most influential austerity study'. *The Real News*. Available at http://therealnews.com/t2/index.php?option=com_content&task=view&id=31&Itemid=74&jumival=10099#newsletter1

49. Glaser, E. (2015). 'Nation-states aren't households: debating their economies as if they are is stupid'. *New Statesman*. Available at www.newstatesman.com/politics/2015/03/nation-states-arent-households-debating-their-economies-if-they-are-stupid

50. Olen, H. (2013). 'Why the Federal budget can't be managed like a household budget'. *Guardian*. Available at www.theguardian.com/

money/us-money-blog/2013/mar/26/federal-budget-household-finances-fed

51. Blanchard, O. and Leigh, D. (2013). 'Growth forecast errors and fiscal multipliers'. IMF Working Paper. Available at www.imf.org/external/pubs/ft/wp/2013/wp1301.pdf

52. Ostry, J., Loungani, P. and Furceri, D. (2016). 'Neoliberalism: oversold?' Available at www.imf.org/external/pubs/ft/fandd/2016/06/ostry.htm

53. Ibid.

54. OECD (2016). 'Elusive global growth outlook requires urgent policy response'. Available at www.oecd.org/economy/elusive-global-growth-outlook-requires-urgent-policy-response.htm

55. McTague, T. (2015). 'George Osborne on course to privatise more public assets than any Chancellor since 1979'. Independent. Available at www.independent.co.uk/news/uk/politics/george-osborne-on-course-to-sell-off-more-public-assets-than-any-chancellor-for-more-than-30-years-a6786926.html

56. Beattie, J. (2015). 'Polls shows massive opposition to George Osborne's privatisation plan – and even Tory voters are against it'. Mirror. Available at www.mirror.co.uk/news/uk-news/polls-shows-massive-opposition-george-6990108

57. Ibid.

58. Meek, K. (2015). Private Island: Why England Now Belongs to Someone Else. London: Verso.

59. Ralfe, J. (2016). 'BT's mountainous pension liabilities hampers spin-off'. Financial Times. Available at www.ft.com/content/3fd971f6-e539-11e5-a09b-1f8b0d268c39

60. Palmer, K. (2016). 'BT pension black hole risks dividends'. Financial Times. Available at www.telegraph.co.uk/business/2016/05/28/bt-pension-black-hole-risks-dividends/

61. Cable, V. (2013). 'Business, Innovation and Skills Committee – Minutes of Evidence'. House of Commons. Available at www.publications.parliament.uk/pa/cm201415/cmselect/cmbis/539/131009.htm

62. Bennett, A. (2013). Royal Mail nears FTSE 100 as Vince Cable defends cheap sale'. Huffington Post. Available at www.huffingtonpost.co.uk/2013/12/11/royal-mail-ftse100_n_4423934.html

63. Business, Innovation and Skills Committee (2014). First Report: Royal Mail Privatization. Available at www.publications.parliament.uk/pa/cm201415/cmselect/cmbis/539/53902.htm

64. Farrell, S. (2014). 'Royal Mail sale underpriced by £1bn, says scathing select committee report'. Guardian. Available at www.theguardian.com/uk-news/2014/jul/11/royal-mail-sale-lost-1bn-says-select-committee

65. Business, Innovation and Skills Committee, First Report.

66. Neate, R. (2014). 'Lazard advised on Royal Mail shares then profited by £8m in flotation'. Guardian. Available at www.theguardian.com/

uk-news/2014/apr/30/lazard-bank-royal-mail-shares-profit-flotation-margaret-hodge

67. Ibid.
68. Ibid.
69. BBC (2014). 'Taxpayers "lost £1bn" on Royal Mail sale, MPs say'. Available at www.bbc.co.uk/news/business-28250963
70. Collinson, P. (2016). 'Big cuts in store for Royal Mail and Post Office workers' pensions'. *Guardian*. Available at www.theguardian.com/money/2016/aug/10/royal-mail-pension-post-office-hit-brexit-defined-benefit
71. This is Money (2015). 'Royal Mail boss who axed 5,500 staff sees pay rise 13% to £1.5million: revelation will anger staff after thousands are made redundant'. Available at www.thisismoney.co.uk/money/news/article-3102959/Royal-Mail-boss-Moya-Greene-receives-1-5m-pay-bonanza.html#ixzz4PQsJeyds
72. Jones, R. (2016). 'Royal Mail raises first class stamp price to 64p'. *Guardian*. www.theguardian.com/business/2016/mar/28/royal-mail-raises-first-class-stamp-price-to-64p
73. Armstrong, A. (2015). 'Government nets £750m from Eurostar stake sale'. *Telegraph*. Available at www.telegraph.co.uk/finance/newsbysector/transport/11448231/Government-nets-750m-from-Eurostar-stake-sale.html
74. National Audit Office (2015)'. The sale of Eurostar'. Available at www.nao.org.uk/report/the-sale-of-eurostar/
75. Ibid.
76. BBC (2013). 'NHS IT system one of "worst fiascos ever", say MPs'. Available at www.bbc.co.uk/news/uk-politics-24130684
77. El-Gingihy, Y. 2015). *How to Dismantle the NHS in 10 Easy Steps*. London: Zero Books.
78. Lawrence, F. (2013). 'Private health contractor's staff told to cut 999 calls to meet targets'. *Guardian*. Available at www.theguardian.com/society/2013/jan/23/private-health-contractor-999-calls?INTCMP=SRCH
79. Ibid.
80. Lawrence, F. (2012). 'Serco investigated over claims of "unsafe" out-of-hours GP service'. *Guardian*. Available at www.theguardian.com/society/2012/may/25/serco-investigated-claims-unsafe-hours-gp
81. *Telegraph* (2016). 'Five G4S police control room staff suspended amid 999 "test calls" investigation'. Available at www.telegraph.co.uk/news/2016/05/23/five-g4s-police-control-room-staff-suspended-amid-999-test-calls/
82. Quoted in Cowburn, A. (2016). 'G4S workers suspended amid allegations of bogus 999 calls'. *Independent*. Available at www.independent.co.uk/

news/uk/five-g4s-workers-suspended-amid-allegations-of-bogus-999-calls-a7044406.html

83. Crewe, T. (2016). 'The strange death of Municipal England'. *London Review of Books*. Available at www.lrb.co.uk/v38/n24/tom-crewe/the-strange-death-of-municipal-england

84. See Bowman, A (ed.) (2015). *What a Waste: Outsourcing and How It Goes Wrong*. Manchester: Manchester University Press.

85. Hood, C. and Dixon, R. (2015). *Government that Worked Better and Cost Less? Evaluating Three Decades of Reform and Change in UK Central Government*. Oxford: Oxford University Press.

86. Ibid., p. 1.

87. Meek, *Private Island*.

88. Ibid.

89. MacGregor, J. (1992). House of Commons. 'Points of Order'. www.publications.parliament.uk/pa/cm199293/cmhansrd/1992-05-18/Debate-1.html

90. Hadley, P. (2015). 'The four big myths of UK rail privatisaton'. Action for Rail. Available at http://actionforrail.org/the-four-big-myths-of-uk-rail-privatisation/

91. Murray, D. (2014). '245% train fares increase in 20 years since privatisation'. *Evening Standard*. Available at www.standard.co.uk/news/transport/245-train-fares-increase-in-20-years-since-privatisation-9225958.html

92. BBC (2016). 'Average age of British passenger trains is 21, study says'. Available at www.bbc.co.uk/news/uk-38450117

93. Boffey, D. (2013). 'East Coast Mainline: profitable and publicly owned – so why sell it?' *Guardian*. Available at www.theguardian.com/uk-news/2013/oct/26/east-coast-mainline-why-privatise

94. TCU (2015). 'The start of East Coast Mainline privatization marks a costly mistake'. Available at www.tuc.org.uk/economic-issues/public-spending/industrial-issues/transport-policy/start-east-coast-main-line

95. Moore-Bridger, B. (2016). 'City worker who pays £6,000 for train ticket forced to sit in tiny cleaning cupboard on packed trains'. *Evening Standard*. Available at www.standard.co.uk/news/transport/city-worker-who-pays-6k-for-train-ticket-forced-to-sit-in-tiny-cleaning-cupboard-on-packed-trains-a3163931.html

96. Ibid.

97. BBC (2016). 'Southern Rail co-owner Go-Ahead reports £100m profits'. Available at www.bbc.co.uk/news/uk-england-37253789

98. High Pay Centre (2014). 'FTSE 100 bosses now paid an average 130 times as much as their employees'. Available at http://highpaycentre.org/blog/ftse-100-bosses-now-paid-an-average-143-times-as-much-as-their-employees

99. Economic Policy Institute (2015). 'Top CEOs make 300 times more than typical workers'. Available at www.epi.org/publication/top-ceos-make-300-times-more-than-workers-pay-growth-surpasses-market-gains-and-the-rest-of-the-0-1-percent/

100. Adam Smith Institute (2016). 'Ben Southwood discusses CEO pay on BBC News'. Available at www.adamsmith.org/news/ben-southwood-discusses-ceo-pay-on-bbc-news

101. Fisman, R. and Sullivan, T. (2013). *The Org: The Underlying Logic of the Office*. New York: Hachette Book Group.

102. Davidson, L. (2015). 'Want a new job? You could probably earn more walking dogs'. *Telegraph*. Available at www.telegraph.co.uk/finance/jobs/11624564/Want-a-new-job-You-could-probably-earn-more-walking-dogs.html

103. Economic Policy Institute, 'Top CEOs make 300 times more than typical workers'.

104. Macalister, T. (2016). 'BP chief receives 20% pay hike despite record loss and 7,000 axed jobs'. *Guardian*. Available at www.theguardian.com/business/2016/mar/04/bp-chief-executive-20-per-cent-pay-package-hike-record-loss-axed-jobs

105. McDonald, D. (2017). *The Golden Passport: Harvard Business School, the Limits of Capitalism and the Moral Failure of the MBA Elite*. New York: HarperCollins.

106. Leftly, M. (2015). 'Pizza Express faces protests over fee on waiters' tips'. *Independent*. Available at www.independent.co.uk/news/business/news/pizza-express-faces-protests-over-fee-on-waiters-tips-10434050.html

107. Batchelor, L. (2015). 'Restaurants' tipping policy "forces waiters to pay to work"'. *Guardian*. Available at www.theguardian.com/lifeandstyle/2015/aug/23/restaurant-tipping-policy-forces-waiters-to-pay-to-work

108. McIntyre, N. (2017). 'Harrods restaurants keep up to 75% of waiters' tips, claims union'. *Independent*. Available at www.independent.co.uk/news/uk/home-news/harrods-restaurants-75-waiters-tips-service-charge-union-a7506471.html

109. Batchelor, 'Restaurants' tipping policy.

110. Blanchard, J (2016). 'David Cameron's Trade Union Bill may be illegal warns his own human rights watchdog'. *Mirror*. Available at www.mirror.co.uk/news/uk-news/david-camerons-trade-union-bill-7154118

111. Harvey, G., Rhodes, C., Vachhani, S.J. and Williams, K. (2017). 'Neo-villeiny and the service sector: the case of hyper flexible and precarious work in fitness centres'. *Work, Employment and Society*, 31(1): 19–35.

112. Taylor, C. (2014). 'Plantation neoliberalism'. *The New Inquiry*. Available at http://thenewinquiry.com/essays/plantation-neoliberalism/

113. Barr, C. and Malik, S. (2016). 'Revealed: the 30-year economic betrayal dragging down Generation Y's income'. *Guardian*. Available at www.

theguardian.com/world/2016/mar/07/revealed-30-year-economic-betrayal-dragging-down-generation-y-income

114. Liverpool Victoria (2016). 'Raising a child more expensive than buying a house'. Available at www.lv.com/about-us/press/article/cost-of-a-child-2016

115. Age UK (2016). 'Invisible but invaluable army of carers save state billions'. Available at www.ageuk.org.uk/richmonduponthames/news--campaigns/invisible-but-invaluable-army-of-carers-save-state-billions/

116. BBC (2016). '"Hidden army" of carers in their 80s, says Age UK'. Available at www.bbc.co.uk/news/health-36310617

117. BBC (2016). 'Third bankruptcy of BHS buyer revealed'. Available at www.bbc.co.uk/news/business-36241660

118. Ruddick, G. and Butler, S. (2016). 'BHS paid more than £25m to owner in 13 months before administration'. *Guardian*. Available at www.theguardian.com/business/2016/apr/25/bhs-owner-retail-acquisitions-25m-administration

119. Steiner, R. (2016). 'MPs demand Tina Green explains how money passes between companies registered to her overseas'. *Daily Mail*. Available at www.dailymail.co.uk/news/article-3653518/Lady-Shifty-told-details-tax-haven-firms-MPs-demand-Tina-Green-explains-money-passes-companies-registered-overseas.html#ixzz4Pbhv3I8D

120. Butler, S. (2016). 'How Philip Green's family made millions as value of BHS plummeted'. *Guardian*. Available at www.theguardian.com/business/2016/apr/25/bhs-philip-green-family-millions-administration-arcadia

121. Eagle, A. (2016). '2016 speech on BHS'. Available at www.ukpol.co.uk/2016/04/26/angela-eagle-2016-speech-on-bhs/

122. Atterbury, G. (2016). 'Diary of a BHS worker: "If there were a Dignitas for department stores, I would make the call"'. *Guardian*. Available at www.theguardian.com/business/2016/jul/25/bhs-worker-diary-department-store-jobs

123. Chakrabortty, A. (2016). 'How Boots went rogue'. *Guardian*. Available at www.theguardian.com/news/2016/apr/13/how-boots-went-rogue

124. Aston, H. (2010). 'Alliance Boots deals pension blow to 15,000 staff'. *This is Money*. Available at www.thisismoney.co.uk/money/article-1247176/Alliance-Boots-deals-pension-blow-15-000-staff.html#ixzz4ZnuqAhVo

125. Ibid.

126. Chakrabortty, 'How Boots went rogue'.

127. Ibid.

128. Ibid.

129. Ibid.

130. United Nations Conference on Trade and Development (2013). '80% of trade takes place in "value chains" linked to transnational corporations'.

Available at http://unctad.org/en/pages/PressRelease.aspx?Original VersionID=113

131. Bowers, S. (2016). 'Google pays €47m in tax in Ireland on €22bn sales revenue'. *Guardian*. Available at www.theguardian.com/business/2016/nov/04/google-pays-47m-euros-tax-ireland-22bn-euros-revenue

132. Tax Justice Network (2012). 'The price of offshore, revisited'. Available at www.taxjustice.net/2014/01/17/price-offshore-revisited/

133. Fioretti, J. (2016). 'Apple appeals against EU tax ruling, Brussels says no cause for low tax bill'. *Reuters*. Available at http://uk.reuters.com/article/us-eu-apple-taxavoidance-idUKKBN148007

134. Public Account Committee (2017). 'Collecting tax from high net worth individuals'. Available at www.publications.parliament.uk/pa/cm201617/cmselect/cmpubacc/774/77403.htm#_idTextAnchor004

135. National Audit Office (2016). 'The quality of service for personal taxpayers'. Available at www.nao.org.uk/report/the-quality-of-service-for-personal-taxpayers/

136. Royal Society for the Protection of Birds (2015). 'Using regulation as a last resort? Assessing the performance of voluntary approaches'. Available at www.rspb.org.uk/Images/usingregulation_tcm9-408677.pdf

137. Ibid.

138. Perrett, M. (2016). 'FSA budget cuts: what it means for food safety'. *Food Manufacture*. Available at www.foodmanufacture.co.uk/Food-Safety/Food-safety-implications-of-FSA-budget-cuts?utm_source=copyright&utm_medium=OnSite&utm_campaign=copyright

139. BBC (2015). 'Viewpoint: the rejected vegetables that aren't even wonky'. Available at www.bbc.co.uk/news/magazine-34647454

140. Ibid.

141. Friedman, M. (1979). 'Interview: Milton Friedman on capitalism and greed'. Available at www.slobodaiprosperitet.tv/en/node/847

142. Gaspar, V. and De Mooij, R. (2016). 'Imagine what fiscal policy could do for innovation'. Available at https://blog-imfdirect.imf.org/2016/03/31/imagine-what-fiscal-policy-could-do-for-innovation/

143. Ibid.

144. Gordon, R. (2012). 'Is U.S. economic growth over? Faltering innovation confronts the six headwinds'. National Bureau of Economic Research. Available at www.nber.org/papers/w18315

145. Ibid., p. 10.

146. Ibid., p. 2.

147. Ibid., p. 9.

148. Christensen, C.M. (1997). *The Innovator's Dilemma: When New Technologies Cause Great Firms to Fail*. Boston, MA: Harvard University Press.

149. Christensen, C.M. (2012). 'Disruptive innovation explained'. Available at www.youtube.com/watch?v=qDrMAzCHFUU

150. Gorz, A. (2012). *Capitalism, Socialism, Ecology.* London: Verso, p. 81.
151. Collini, S. (2017) *Speaking of Universities.* London: Verso.
152. Martin, R. (2011). *Under New Management: Universities, Administrative Labour and the Professional Turn.* Philadelphia: Temple University Press.
153. University and College Union (2016). 'Words used so far to describe Newcastle University's "Raising the Bar" target-based performance management scheme'. Available at http://newcastle.web.ucu.org.uk/words-used-so-far-to-describe-newcastle-universitys-raising-the-bar-target-based-performance-management-scheme/
154. University and College Union (2016). 'Report reveals university heads' pay rises and perks'. Available at www.ucu.org.uk/article/8096/Report-reveals-university-heads-pay-rises-and-perks
155. Demianyk, G. (2016). 'Oxford graduate sues university for £1m, claiming "appallingly bad" tuition cost him high-flying job'. *Huffington Post.* Available at www.huffingtonpost.co.uk/entry/oxford-graduate-sues-university-for-1m-claiming-appallingly-bad-tuition-cost-him-high-flying-job_uk_584463e1e4b00b318b1001c3
156. For example, see Reich, R. (2015). *Saving Capitalism: For the Many, Not the Few.* New York: Knopf; Standing, G. (2016). *The Corruption of Capitalism: Why Rentiers Thrive and Work Does Not Pay.* London: Biteback Publishing.
157. Holland, E.W. (2011). *Nomad Citizenship: Free-market Communism and the Slow-motion General Strike.* Minneapolis: University of Minnesota.
158. Kobek, J. (2016). *I Hate the Internet.* Los Angeles: We Heard You Like Books, p. 213.
159. Mason, *Postcapitalism.*
160. Klein, N. (2014). *This Changes Everything: Capitalism vs. The Climate.* New York: Simon and Schuster.

Chapter 3

1. Gani, A. (2016). 'DWP told woman she was not ill enough for benefit on day she died'. *Guardian.* Available at www.theguardian.com/society/2016/jan/07/dwp-told-dawn-amos-not-ill-enough-for-benefit-day-she-died
2. Smith, I.D. (2015). 'Rt Hon Iain Duncan Smith MP: speech on work, health and disability'. *Reform.* Available at www.reform.uk/publication/rt-hon-iain-duncan-smith-mp-speech-on-work-health-and-disability/
3. Johnson, C. (2016). 'Braintree mum Dawn Amos, 67, told she's too healthy for sick benefits on the day she dies'. *Clacton Gazette.* Available at www.clactonandfrintongazette.co.uk/news/north_essex_news/14185620.Mum_told_she_s_too_healthy_for_sick_benefits_on_the_day_she_dies/
4. Mann, T. (2016). 'Mother told she's not ill enough for benefits on the day she dies'. *Metro.* Available at http://metro.co.uk/2016/01/07/mother-told-

shes-not-ill-enough-for-benefits-on-the-day-she-dies-5608662/
#ixzz4OwVEwloJ

5. Ibid.

6. Ibid.

7. BBC (2015). 'More than 2,300 died after Fit for Work assessment – DWP figures'. Available at www.bbc.co.uk/news/uk-34074557

8. Armour, R. (2016). 'Police asked to investigate former DWP ministers'. *Third Force News*. Available at http://thirdforcenews.org.uk/tfn-news/ police-asked-to-investigate-former-dwp-ministers#5vZHW 51klPVrsEdf.99

9. Bloom, D. (2016). 'Private firms rake in half a BILLION pounds for cruel disability benefit assessments'. *Daily Mirror*. Available at www.mirror. co.uk/news/uk-news/private-firms-rake-half-billion-9515131

10. Hattenstone, S. (2013). 'Students and depression: the struggle to survive'. *Guardian*. Available at www.theguardian.com/education/2013/mar/23/ student-suicide-depression-debt-recession

11. Ibid.

12. Gore, A. (2012). 'Overdrawn student killed himself over just £8,000 of debt and left a suicide note written on the back of a letter from his bank'. *Daily Mail*. Available at www.dailymail.co.uk/news/article-2242259/ Student-Toby-Thorn-killed-just-8-000 debt-wrote-suicide-note-BANK-letter.html#ixzz4OwmJKyGa

13. Groves, N. (2012). 'Student suicides rise during recession years'. *Guardian*. Available at www.theguardian.com/higher-education-network/2012/nov/30/student-suicide-recession-mental-health

14. Ibid.

15. Johannsen, C.C. (2012). 'The ones we've lost: the student loan debt suicides'. *Huffington Post*. Available at www.huffingtonpost.com/c-cryn-johannsen/ student-loan-debt-suicides_b_1638972.html

16. US Department of Education (2016). 'Official cohort default rates for schools'. Available at www2.ed.gov/offices/OSFAP/defaultmanagement/ cdr.html

17. Student Loan Hero (2016). 'A look at the shocking student loan debt statistics for 2016'. Available at https://studentloanhero.com/student-loan-debt-statistics/

18. Warrell, H. and Hale, T. (2017). 'UK to sell record £4bn of student loans to investors'. *Financial Times*. Available at www.ft.com/content/2b66bfaa-ec7a-11e6-930f-061b01e23655

19. Perraudin, F. and Adams, R. (2016). 'UK student loans: "we will trace and prosecute borrowers who don't pay"'. *Guardian*. Available at www. theguardian.com/uk-news/2016/feb/12/student-loans-we-will-trace-prosecute-borrowers-dont-pay

20. Politically Corrected New Zealand (2016). 'John Key talks free tertiary education'. Available at https://politicallycorrectednz.wordpress. com/2016/02/02/john-key-talks-free-tertiary-education/
21. Jones, N. (2016). 'New Zealanders scared to come home due to student loan arrest threat'. *New Zealand Herald.* Available at www.nzherald.co. nz/business/news/article.cfm?c_id=3&objectid=11649957
22. Rhodes, S. (2015). 'Suspect accused of shooting, killing boss in NE Houston turns self in'. *Click2Houston.* Available at www.click2houston. com/news/suspect-accused-of-shooting-killing-boss-in-ne-houston-turns-self-in
23. Ibid.
24. Biddle, S. (2011). '1 in 10 dead bosses are murdered'. *Gizmodo.* Available at http://gizmodo.com/5835821/1-in-10-dead-bosses-are-murdered
25. Furlong, S. (2015). '7 disgruntled employees who killed their bosses'. *Career Addict.* Available at www.careeraddict.com/7-disgruntled-employees-who-killed-their-bosses
26. Anonymous (2016). 'Thread regarding Chevron layoffs'. *The Layoff.com.* Available at www.thelayoff.com/t/Fje2ifr
27. PRMG Security (2016). 'Many business opt for employee termination security'. Available at www.prmgsecurity.com.
28. Howker, E and Malik, S. (2013). *Jilted Generation: How Britain Has Bankrupted Its Youth.* London: Icon.
29. Ellen, B. (2016). 'It's boom time for bank of mum and dad – if you chose the right parents'. *Guardian.* Available at www.theguardian.com/global/commentisfree/2016/may/07/mortgage-home-loan-parents-bank-mum-dad-borrowing
30. BBC (2014). 'FCA: credit cards can encourage excessive debts'. BBC. Available at www.bbc.co.uk/news/business-26867309
31. Karabell, S. (2014). 'Fear as a management technique'. *Forbes.* Available at www.forbes.com/forbes/welcome/?toURL=www.forbes.com/sites/shelliekarabell/2014/09/25/fear-as-a-management-technique/&refURL=&referrer=#107a77e57bab
32. Chartered Institute of Personal Development (2016). 'Employee outlook survey'. Available at www.cipd.co.uk/Images/employee-outlook-spring-2016_tcm18-10903.pdf
33. Ibid.
34. Wessel, D. (2015). 'The typical male U.S. worker earned less in 2014 than in 1973'. Brookings. Available at www.brookings.edu/opinions/the-typical-male-u-s-worker-earned-less-in-2014-than-in-1973/
35. Berlant, L. (2011). *Cruel Optimism.* Durham: Duke University Press.
36. Davies, W. (2015). *The Happiness Industry: How the Government and Big Business Sold Us Well-being.* London: Verso; Enhrenreich, B. (2009). *Smile or Die: How Positive Thinking Fooled America and the World.*

London: Granta; Cederstrom, C. and Spicer, A. (2015). *The Wellness Syndrome*. Cambridge: Polity Press.

37. Centre for Crime and Justice Studies (2016). 'Social murder kills thousands each year'. Available at www.crimeandjustice.org.uk/news/social-murder-kills-thousands-each-year

38. Ibid.

39. Quiggin, J. (2010). *Zombie Economics: How Dead Ideas Still Walk Among Us*. Princeton: Princeton University Press; Crouch, C. (2011). *The Strange Non-death of Neoliberalism*. Cambridge: Polity Press; Cederstrom, C. and Fleming, P. (2012). *Dead Man Working*. London: Zero Books; McNally, D. (2011). *Monsters of the Market: Zombies, Vampires and Global Capitalism*. Chicago: Haymarket Books; Harman, C. (2009). *Zombie Capitalism: Global Crisis and the Relevance of Marx*. London: Bookmarks.

40. Derrida, J. (1994). *Specters of Marx: The State of the Debt, the Work of Mourning, & the New International*. New York: Routledge.

41. Andrews, E. (2008). 'Greenspan concedes error on regulation'. *New York Times*. Available at www.nytimes.com/2008/10/24/business/economy/24panel.html; Elliott, L. (2013). 'George Osborne told by IMF chief: rethink your austerity plan'. *Guardian*. Available at www.theguardian.com/politics/2013/apr/18/george-osborne-imf-austerity

42. Slee, T. (2015). *What's Yours is Mine: Against the Sharing Economy*. New York: Orr Books.

43. Thaler, R.H. and Sunstein, C.R. (2008). *Nudge: Improving Decisions about Health, Wealth, and Happiness*. New Haven: Yale University Press; Ariely, D. (2008). *Predictably Irrational: The Hidden Forces that Shape Our Decisions*. New York: Harper Collins; Thaler, R. (2015). *Misbehaving: How Economics Became Behavioural*. New York: W.W. Norton.

44. Kahneman, D. and Tversky, A. (1979). 'Prospect theory: an analysis of decision under risk'. *Econometrica*, 47(2): 263–93.

45. Frank, R.H. (2011). *The Darwin Economy: Liberty, Competition, and the Common Good*. Princeton: Princeton University Press.

46. Halpern, D. (2015). *Inside the Nudge Unit: How Small Changes Can Make a Big Difference*. London: W.H. Allen.

47. The Behavioural Insights Team (2016). 'Inside the Nudge Unit'. Available at www.behaviouralinsights.co.uk/inside-the-nudge-unit/

48. Kahneman, D. (2003). 'Maps of bounded rationality: psychology for behavioral economics'. *American Economic Review*, 93(5): 1449–75, p. 1469.

49. Akerlof, G. and Shiller, R.J. (2015). *Phishing for Phools: The Economics of Manipulation and Deception*. Princeton: Princeton University Press.

50. Thaler, R. (2015). 'Richard Thaler: Misbehaving: the making of behavioural economics – talks at Google'. Available at www.youtube.com/watch?v=42qbHeFxdzE

51. Halpern, *Inside the Nudge Unit*.

52. Shane, S. (2010). *Born Entrepreneurs, Born Leaders: How Your Genes Affect Your Work Life*. Oxford: Oxford University Press.
53. Fitza, M. (2014). 'The use of variance decomposition in the investigation of CEO effects: how large must the CEO effect be to rule out chance?' *Strategic Management Journal*, 35(12): 1839–52.
54. *Science Daily* (2015). 'CEO effect on firm performance mostly due to chance'. Available at www.sciencedaily.com/releases/2015/10/1510229 2337.htm
55. Chartered Financial Analyst Institute (2016). *CFA UK Executive Remuneration Report 2016*. Available at www.cfauk.org/media-centre/cfa-uk-executive-remuneration-report-2016
56. Quoted in Roberts, C. (2012). 'Billionaire Gina Rinehart sparks controversy with $2-a-day pay remark'. *New York Daily News*. Available at www.nydailynews.com/news/world/billionaire-gina-rinehart-sparks-controversy-2-a-day-pay-remark-article-1.1152735
57. Piketty, T. (2013). *Capital in the Twenty-first Century*. Cambridge, MA: Harvard University Press.
58. The Sutton Trust (2016). 'Leading people 2016: the educational backgrounds of the UK professional elite'. Available at www.suttontrust.com/wp-content/uploads/2016/02/Leading-People_Feb16.pdf
59. Weale, S. (2016). 'Privately educated elite continues to take top jobs, finds survey'. *Guardian*. Available at www.theguardian.com/education/2016/feb/24/privately-educated-elite-continues-to-take-top-jobs-finds-survey
60. Pertaining to the US corporate sector, see Rivera, L. (2012). 'Hiring as cultural matching: the case of elite professional service firms'. *American Sociological Review*, 77(6): 999–1022.
61. Clare, A., Motson, N. and Thomas, S. (2013). 'An evaluation of alternative equity indices Part 1: Heuristic and optimised weighting schemes'. Cass Working Paper. Available at www.cass.city.ac.uk/news-and-events/news/2013/april/monkeys-beat-market-cap-indices
62; Ibid., p. 23.
63. Meek, J. (2015). *Private Island: Why Britain Now Belongs to Someone Else*. London: Verso.
64. Ibid., pp. 105–6.
65. BBC (2016). 'Sadiq Khan accuses Thames Water after three London floods'. Available at www.bbc.co.uk/news/uk-england-london-38287467
66. See Srnicek, N. (2016). *Platform Capitalism*. Cambridge: Polity Press.
67. See Bolton, D. (2016). 'The Fine bros withdraw controversial trademark plans following community backlash'. *Independent*. Available at www.independent.co.uk/life-style/gadgets-and-tech/news/the-fine-bros-brothers-trademark-licensing-react-world-apology-controversy-a6848331.html
68. Mazzucato, M. (2013). *The Entrepreneurial State: Debunking Public vs. Private Sector Myths*. London: Anthem Press.

69. Hutton, W. (2012). 'Thames Water – a private equity plaything that takes us for fools'. *Guardian*. Available at www.theguardian.com/commentisfree/2012/nov/11/will-hutton-thames-water-private-equity-plaything

70. Behar, R. (2016). 'Inside Israeli's secret start-up machine'. *Forbes*. Available at www.forbes.com/sites/richardbehar/2016/05/11/inside-israels-secret-startup-machine/#3ea02f6157d3

71. Goodyear, S. (2014). 'The ugly economics of subprime auto loans'. *The Atlantic*. Available at www.citylab.com/commute/2014/09/the-ugly-economics-of-subprime-auto-loans/380946/

72. Quoted in Corkery, M. and Silver-Greenberg, J. (2014). 'Miss a payment? Good luck moving that car'. *New York Times*. Available at http://dealbook.nytimes.com/2014/09/24/miss-a-payment-good-luck-moving-that-car/?_php=true&_type=blogs&_r=1

73. Ibid.

74. Brandist, C. (2014). 'A very Stalinist management model'. *Times Higher Education*. Available at www.timeshighereducation.com/comment/opinion/a-very-stalinist-management-model/2013616.article

75. Grove, J. (2016). 'UCU report: "academics work two days a week unpaid"'. *Times Higher Education*. Available at www.timeshighereducation.com/news/ucu-report-academics-work-two-days-week-unpaid

76. Schuman, R. (2014). 'Student evaluations of professors aren't just biased and absurd – they don't even work'. *Slate*. Available at www.slate.com/articles/life/education/2014/04/student_evaluations_of_college_professors_are_biased_and_worthless.html

77. Schuman, R. (2014). 'Sexist teaching evals'. Available at https://storify.com/pankisseskafka/sexist-student-evals

78. Edwards, M. and Roy, S. (2017). 'Academic research in the 21st century: maintaining scientific integrity in a climate of perverse incentives and hypercompetition'. *Environmental Engineering Science*, 34(1): 51–61.

79. Graeber, D. (2015). *The Utopia of Rules: On Technology, Stupidity and the Secret Joys of Bureaucracy*. Brooklyn: Melville House.

80. Overheard: Like to Discover (2015). 'The greatest "Ryanair" complaint letter in the world … ever!' Available at http://overheard.liketodiscover.com/the-greatest-ryan-air-complaint-letter-in-the-world-ever/

81. O'Hara, M. (2015). 'As a jobcentre adviser, I got "brownie points" for cruelty'. *Guardian*. Available at www.theguardian.com/society/2015/feb/04/jobcentre-adviser-play-benefit-sanctions-angela-neville

82. Ibid.

83. Deleuze, G. 'The irony of sadism lies in the two fold operation whereby he projects his dissolved ego outward and as a result experiences what is outside him as his only ego', (2006). *Coldness and Cruelty*. New York: Zone Books, p. 125.

84. Sartre, J. P. (1984). *Being and Nothingness*. New York: Washington Square Press.

85. Wu, T. (2014). 'Why airlines want to make you suffer'. *The New Yorker*. Available at www.newyorker.com/business/currency/airlines-want-you-to-suffer

86. Martin, H. (2014). 'Would you book a smaller, "Economy Minus" seat to save money?' *Los Angeles Times*. Available at www.latimes.com/business/la-fi-economy-minus-seat-20141031-story.html

87. Swinford, S. and Hope, C. (2016). 'George Osborne defends claim £130 million Google tax deal is "major success"'. *Telegraph*. Available at www.telegraph.co.uk/news/politics/georgeosborne/12126786/George-Osborne-defends-claim-130-million-Google-tax-deal-is-major-success.html

88. Murphy, R. (2015). *The Joys of Tax: How a Fair Taxation System Can Create a Better Society*. London: Penguin.

89. Brand, R. (2014). 'Russell Brand The Trews (E168)'. Available at www.youtube.com/watch?v=EX6_BXKtcV8

90. University of Oxford (2016). 'New study shows nearly half of US jobs at risk of computerisation'. Available at www.eng.ox.ac.uk/about/news/new-study-shows-nearly-half-of-us-jobs-at-risk-of-computerisation

91. PwC (2017). 'Consumer spending prospects and the impact of automation on jobs'. Available at www.pwc.co.uk/services/economics-policy/insights/uk-economic-outlook.html

92. Kaplin, J. (2015). *Humans Need Not Apply: A Guide to Wealth and Work in the Age of Artificial Intelligence*. New Haven: Yale University Press; Brynjolfsson, E. and Mcfee, A. (2014). *The Second Machine Age: Work, Progress and Prosperity in a Time of Brilliant Technologies*. New York: W.W. Norton; Ford, M. (2016). *The Rise of the Robots: Technology and the Threat of a Jobless Future*. New York: Basic Books.

93. See Susskind, R. and Susskind, D. (2016). 'Technology will replace many doctors, lawyers and other professionals'. *Harvard Business Review*. Available at https://hbr.org/2016/10/robots-will-replace-doctors-lawyers-and-other-professionals?utm_campaign=hbr&utm_source=facebook&utm_medium=social

94. See Autor, D.H. (2015). 'Why are there still so many jobs? The history and future of workplace automation'. *Journal of Economic Perspectives*, 29(3): 3–30.

95. Booth, R. (2016). 'More than 7m Britons now in precarious employment'. *Guardian*. Available at www.theguardian.com/uk-news/2016/nov/15/more-than-7m-britons-in-precarious-employment

96. Woodcock, J. (2016). *Working the Phones: Control and Resistance in a Call-centre*. London: Pluto Press.

97. Jorens, Y., Gillis, D., Valcke, L. and De Coninck, J. (2015). *Atypical Employment in Aviation: Final Report*. Available at https://biblio.ugent.be/publication/6852830/file/6853379.pdf

98. Oxfam America (2016). 'Lives on the line: the high human cost of chicken'. Available at www.oxfamamerica.org/livesontheline/

99. Silver, B. (2003). *Forces of Labor: Workers' Movements and Globalization Since 1870*. New York: Cambridge University Press; Cowen, D. (2014). *The Deadly Life of Logistics: Mapping Violence in Global Trade*. Minneapolis: Minnesota Press.

100. Bowman, R. (2014). 'Third-party logistics providers are shrinking in number, growing in size'. *Forbes*. Available at www.forbes.com/sites/robertbowman/2014/06/03/third-party-logistics-providers-are-shrinking-in-number-growing-in-size/#567254e75cfa

101. Gordon, R. (2013). 'Ted talks: the death of innovation, the end of growth'. Available at www.youtube.com/watch?v=PYHd7rpOTe8

102. Gallagher, J. (2014). 'Recession led to 10,000 suicides'. Available at www.bbc.co.uk/news/health-27796628

Chapter 4

1. Barber, L. (2015). 'Email overload: you spend 36 days a year writing emails'. *City AM*. Available at www.cityam.com/213658/email-overload-you-spend-36-days-year-writing-emails

2. Perez, S. (2012). '80% of Americans work "after hours," equaling an extra day of work per week'. *Tech Crunch*. Available at https://techcrunch.com/2012/07/02/80-of-americans-work-after-hours-equaling-an-extra-day-of-work-per-week/

3. *Daily Mail* (2015). 'How we spend 18 months of our lives commuting: average worker spends 13,870 hours getting to work and back'. Available at www.dailymail.co.uk/news/article-3069581/How-spend-18-months-lives-commuting-Average-worker-spends-13-870-hours-getting-work-back.html#ixzz4ONwL5O81

4. Feintzeig, R. (2015). 'The 4-hour work week is a thing of the past'. *Wall Street Journal*. Available at http://blogs.wsj.com/atwork/2015/05/05/the-40-hour-work-week-is-a-thing-of-the-past/

5. Althusser, L. (1971). *Lenin and Philosophy*. New York: Monthly Review Press.

6. Monbiot, G. (2015). 'Aspirational parents condemn their children to a desperate, joyless life'. *Guardian*. Available at www.theguardian.com/commentisfree/2015/jun/09/aspirational-parents-children-elite

7. Gerstacker, D. (2014). 'Sitting is the new smoking: ways a sedentary lifestyle is killing you'. *Huffington Post*. Available at www.huffingtonpost.com/the-active-times/sitting-is-the-new-smokin_b_5890006.html

8. Oster, S. (2014). 'Is work killing you? In China, workers die at their desks'. *Bloomberg*. Available at www.bloomberg.com/news/articles/2014-06-29/ is-work-killing-you-in-china-workers-die-at-their-desks

9. Mosbergen, D. (2016). 'French legislation suggests employees deserve the right to disconnect'. *Huffington Post*. Available at www.huffingtonpost. com/entry/work-emails-france-labor-law_us_57455130e4b03 ede4413515a

10. *BBC Magazine* (2014). 'Should holiday email be deleted?' Available at www.bbc.co.uk/news/magazine-28786117

11. Lewis, L. (2016). 'Dentsu president resigns after recruit's suicide'. *Financial Times*. Available at www.ft.com/content/6e7e7862-cd0a-11e6- 864f-20dcb35cede2

12. Reid, E. (2015). 'Embracing, passing, revealing, and the ideal worker image: how people navigate expected and experienced professional identities'. *Organization Science*, 26(4): 997–1017.

13. Graeber, D. (2013). 'On the phenomenon of bullshit jobs'. *Strike Magazine*, August: 7–8.

14. Lane, C. (2011). *A Company of One: Insecurity, Independence and the New World of White-collar Unemployment*. Ithaca: Cornell University Press.

15. Ibid., p. 71.

16. As Southwood (2011: 46) points out in *Non-stop Inertia* (London: Zero Books) after being rebranded as a 'job seeker', 'the only labour now exchanged at the job centre is the performative sort: empty gestures, feigned enthusiasm, containment of hostility, suppression of resentment'.

17. See Gibson, D.W. (2012). *Not Working: People Talk About Losing a Job and Finding Their Way in Today's Changing Economy*. New York: Orr Books.

18. Lane, *A Company of One*, p. 5.

19. Bolchover, D. (2005). *The Living Dead: Switched Off, Zoned Out – the Shocking Truth About Office Life*. London: Wiley Books.

20. Paulssen, R. (2014). *Empty Labour*. Cambridge: Cambridge University Press.

21. Southwood, *Non-stop Inertia*, p. 57.

22. Bolchover. *The Living Dead*, p. 2.

23. *The Economist* (2014). 'A guide to skiving'. Available at www.economist. com/news/business/21627649-how-thrive-work-minimum-effort- guide-skiving

24. Bolchover, *The Living Dead*, p. 2.

25. Bolchover, D. (2015). 'Office life today: too many jobs, not enough work?' BBC. Available at www.bbc.co.uk/programmes/p02kowbg

26. Hegel, G.W.F. (2010). *The Science of Logic*. Cambridge: Cambridge University Press, p. 511.

27. Marx, K. (1973). *Political Writings: Surveys from Exile Volume 2*. London: Penguin.

28. Foucault, M. (2008). *The Birth of Biopolitics: Lectures at the Collège de France, 1978–79*. London: Palgrave.

29. Moore, J. (2013). 'Financial crisis "led to the loss of 7m jobs"'. *Independent*. Available at www.independent.co.uk/news/business/news/financial-crisis-led-to-the-loss-of-7m-jobs-8847911.html

30. Bellamy-Foster, J. and McChesney, R. (2012). *The Endless Crisis: How Monopoly-finance Capital Produces Stagnation and Upheaval from the USA to China*. New York: Monthly Review Press, p. 145.

31. Dahlgreen, W. (2015). '37% of British workers think their jobs are meaningless'. YouGov. Available at https://yougov.co.uk/news/2015/08/12/british-jobs-meaningless/

32. Weber, M. (2002). *Protestant Ethic and the Spirit of Capitalism*. London: Penguin.

33. Friedrich, O. (1994). *The Kingdom of Auschwitz*. New York: Harper, pp. 2–3.

34. Haffner, S. (2002). *Defying Hitler: A Memoir*. London: Phoenix, p. 128.

35. Cadelli, M. (2016). 'The President of Belgian Magistrates: neoliberalism is a form of fascism'. Defend Democracy Press. Available at www.defenddemocracy.press/president-belgian-magistrates-neoliberalism-form-fascism/

36. See Agamben, G. (2000). *Means Without End: Notes on Politics*. Minneapolis: University of Minnesota Press.

37. Wallace, H. (1944). 'The danger of American Fascism'. *New York Times*, 9 April 1944. Available at http://newdeal.feri.org/wallace/haw23.htm

38. Ibid.

39. For example, see Bernanke, B. (2015). *The Courage to Act: A Memoir of a Crisis and Its Aftermath*. New York: W.W. Norton & Company.

40. Huang, D. (2015). 'The Ten Commandments for Wall Street interns'. *Wall Street Journal*. Available at http://blogs.wsj.com/moneybeat/2015/06/03/the-ten-commandments-for-wall-street-interns/

41. Huizinga, J. (1996). *The Autumn of the Middle Ages*. Chicago: University of Chicago Press.

42. BBC (2016). 'British Airways cabin crew to strike over Christmas'. Available at www.bbc.co.uk/news/business-38347181

43. Goodley, S. and Ashby, J. (2015). 'A day at "the gulag": what it's like to work at Sports Direct's warehouse'. *Guardian*. Available at www.theguardian.com/business/2015/dec/09/sports-direct-warehouse-work-conditions

44. Lawrence, F. (2015). 'This is a brutal and inhumane way to treat staff – and Sports Direct is not alone'. *Guardian*. Available at www.theguardian.com/commentisfree/2016/jun/08/inhumane-sports-direct-mike-ashley-workforce

45. Goodley and Ashby, 'A day at "the gulag"'.

46. Ibid.

47. BBC (2016). 'Sports Direct founder Mike Ashley admits pay errors'. Available at www.bbc.co.uk/news/business-36465404

48. Mills, K.A (2016). 'Mike Ashley turns up to Sports Direct meeting about zero-hour contracts – with MASSIVE wad of £50 notes'. *Mirror*. Available at www.mirror.co.uk/news/uk-news/mike-ashley-turns-up-sports-8786377

49. Chakrabortty, A. and Weale, S. (2016). 'Universities accused of "importing Sports Direct model" for lecturers' pay'. *Guardian*. Available at www.theguardian.com/uk-news/2016/nov/16/universities-accused-of-importing-sports-direct-model-for-lecturers-pay

50. Goodley, S. and Ashby, J. (2015). 'Revealed: how Sports Direct effectively pays below minimum wage'. *Guardian*. Available at www.theguardian.com/business/2015/dec/09/how-sports-direct-effectively-pays-below-minimum-wage-pay

51. Sheffield, H. (2016). 'Sir Philip Green snaps at MP to stop staring at him during BHS hearing'. *Independent*. Available at www.independent.co.uk/news/business/news/sir-philip-green-snaps-at-mp-to-stop-staring-at-him-during-bhs-hearing-a7083536.html

52. Brynjolfsson, E. and Mcfee, A. (2014). *The Second Machine Age: Work, Progress and Prosperity in a Time of Brilliant Technologies*. New York: W.W. Norton.

53. Avent, R. (2016). *The Wealth of Humans: Work, Power, and Status in the Twenty-first Century*. New York: St Martin's Press; Hanson, R. (2016). *The Age of Em Work, Love and Life When Robots Rule the Earth*. Oxford: Oxford University Press.

54. See Deloitte (2015). 'From brawn to brains: the impact of technology on UK jobs'. Available at www2.deloitte.com/content/dam/Deloitte/uk/Documents/Growth/deloitte-uk-insights-from-brawns-to-brain.pdf; Deloitte (2016). 'State of the state 2016–2017'. Available at file:///C:/Users/sbbj759/Downloads/deloitte-uk-state-of-the-state-2016-report.pdf

55. Marx, K. (1981). *Capital: Volume 3*. London: Penguin.

56. See Kliman, A. (2011). *The Failure of Capitalist Production: Underlying Causes of the Great Recession*. London: Pluto Press; Lapavitsas, C. (2013). *Profits Without Producing*. London: Verso; Shaikh, A. (2016). *Capitalism: Competition, Conflict, Crises*. Oxford: Oxford University Press.

57. See Barnett, A., Batten, S., Chiu, A., Franklin, J. and Sebastiá-Barriel, M. (2014). *Bank of England Quarterly Bulletin: The UK Productivity Puzzle*. Available at www.bankofengland.co.uk/publications/Documents/quarterlybulletin/2014/qb14q201.pdf

58. Ibid., p. 119.

59. Sheffield, H. (2016). 'UK wages drop 10% – worse than anywhere else in Europe apart from Greece'. *Independent*. Available at www.independent.

co.uk/news/business/news/uk-wages-drop-10-tuc-greece-recession-financial-crisis-brexit-a7157681.html
60. Kirby, D. (2015). 'Malnutrition and "Victorian" diseases soaring in England "due to food poverty and cuts"'. *Independent*. Available at www.independent.co.uk/life-style/health-and-families/health-news/malnutrition-and-other-victorian-diseases-soaring-in-england-due-to-food-poverty-and-cuts-a6711236.html
61. Deleuze, G. (1992). 'Postscript on the Societies of Control'. *October*, 59(Winter): 3–7.
62. Ross, K. (1988). *The Emergence of Social Space*. London: Verso, p. 70.
63. Badiou, A. (2008). 'The communist hypothesis'. *New Left Review*, 49: 29–42.
64. Keynes, J.M. (2009). 'Economic Possibilities For Our Grandchildren'. In *Essays in Persuasion*. Classic House Books: New York, pp. 191–202.
65. Saval, N. (2014). *Cubed: A Secret History of the Workplace*. New York: Doubleday.
66. Douglas, C.H. (1936). *The Tragedy of Human Effort*. Liverpool: K.R.P. Publications; Rifkin, J. (1995). *The End of Work: The Decline of the Global Labor Force and the Dawn of the Post-market Era*. New York: G.P. Putnam's Sons; Pistono, F. (2012). *Robots Will Steal Your Job But That's OK: How to Survive the Economic Collapse and Be Happy*. Creative Space; Ford, M. (2015). *The Rise of the Robots – Technology and the Threat of Mass Unemployment*. London: Oneworld Publications.
67. Black, B. (1985). *The Abolition of Work and Other Essays*. Port Townsend, WA: Loompanics Unlimited.

Chapter 5

1. Office for National Statistics (2014). 'The self-employment boom: key issues for the 2015 Parliament'. Available at http://webarchive.nationalarchives.gov.uk/20160105160709/http://www.ons.gov.uk/ons/dcp171776_374941.pdf; Bureau of Labor Statistics (2014). 'Self-employment: what to know to be your own boss'. Available at www.bls.gov/careeroutlook/2014/article/self-employment-what-to-know-to-be-your-own-boss.htm
2. Pink, D. (2002). *Free Agent Nation: The Future of Working for Yourself*. New York: Warner Books; Florida, R. (2012). *The Rise of the Creative Class Revisited*. New York: Basic Books.
3. Johns, T, and Gratton, L. (2013). 'The third wave of virtual work'. *Harvard Business Review*. Available at https://hbr.org/2013/01/the-third-wave-of-virtual-work/ar/1
4. See Miller, J.G and Miller, M. (2012). 'The rise of the super-temp'. *Harvard Business Review*. Available at https://hbr.org/2012/05/the-rise-

of-the-supertemp/; Stewart, H. (2013). *The Happiness Manifesto: Make Your Organization a Great Place Workplace*. London: Koogan Page.

5. Eccles, L. (2013). 'Ryanair pilots "bullied into silence over safety": two-thirds say they are not comfortable raising fears with their bosses'. *Daily Mail*, 12 August.

6. Hill, S. (2015). *Raw Deal: How the 'Uber Economy' and Runaway Capitalism are Screwing American Workers*. New York: St Martin's Press.

8. See Booth, R. (2016). 'More than 7m Britons now in precarious employment'. *Guardian*. Available at www.theguardian.com/uk-news/ 2016/nov/15/more-than-7m-britons-in-precarious-employment; Resolution Foundation (2016). 'Britain is on track for a million agency workers by 2020'. Available at www.resolutionfoundation.org/media/ press-releases/britain-is-on-track-for-a-million-agency-workers-by-2020/

8. Thompson, E.P. (1963). *The Making of the English Working Class*. London: Penguin; Thompson, E.P. (1967). 'Time, work-discipline and industrial capitalism'. *Past and Present*, 38: 56–103.

9. Montgomery, D. (1988). *The Fall of the House of Labor*. New York: Cambridge University Press; Edwards, R. (1979). *Contested Terrain: The Transformation of the Workplace in the Twentieth Century*. New York: Basic Books.

10. Taylor, F.W. (1911). *The Principles of Scientific Management*. Reprinted in 1967. New York: W.W. Norton and Company.

11. Ibid., p. 33.

12. Ibid., p. 70.

13. McGregor, D. (1960). *The Human Side of Enterprise*. New York: McGraw-Hill.

14. Friedman, A. (1977). *Industry and Labour: Class Struggle at Work and Monopoly Capitalism*. London: Macmillan.

15. Ouchi, W.G. (1980). 'Markets, bureaucracies and clans'. *Administrative Science Quarterly*, 25(1): 129–41; Deal, T. and Kennedy, A. (1982). *Corporate Cultures: The Rites and Rituals of Corporate Life*. New York: Perseus Books.

16. Peters, T. and Waterman, R.H. (1982). *In Search of Excellence*. New York: Harper and Row.

17. O'Reilly, C. and Chatman, J. (1996). 'Culture as social control: corporations, cults and commitment'. In B. Staw and L. Cummings (eds), *Research in Organization Behaviour*. Greenwich: JAI Press, pp. 157–200.

18. Collinson, D. (1992). *Managing the Shopfloor: Subjectivity, Masculinity, and Workplace Culture*. Berlin: Walter de Gruyter.

19. Berger, J. (1993). 'The pain of layoffs for ex-senior I.B.M. workers; in Dutchess County, a disorienting time for employees less hardened to job loss'. *New York Times*. Available at www.nytimes.com/1993/12/22/

nyregion/pain-layoffs-for-ex-senior-ibm-workers-dutchess-county-disorienting-time-for.html?pagewanted=all

20. Bains, G (2007) *Meaning Inc.* London: Profile Books.

21. Casey, C. (1995). *Work, Self and Society: After Industrialism.* London: Sage.

22. Ross, A. (2004). *No-collar: The Humane Workplace and its Hidden Costs.* Philadelphia: Temple University Press.

23. Richards, L. (2010). *Union-free America: Workers and Antiunion Culture.* Chicago: University of Illinois Press; Sundararajan, A. (2015). 'The "gig economy" is coming. What will it mean for work?' *Guardian.* Available at www.theguardian.com/commentisfree/2015/jul/26/will-we-get-by-gig-economy; Rashid, B. (2016). 'The rise of the freelancer economy'. *Forbes Magazine.* Available at www.forbes.com/sites/brianrashid/2016/01/26/the-rise-of-the-freelancer-economy/#77e63fc379a8

24. Boudreau, J. and Ramstad, P. (2007). *Beyond HR: The New Science of Human Capital.* Cambridge, MA: Harvard Business Review Press.

25. Becker, G.S. (2008). 'Human capital'. In *The Concise Encyclopaedia of Economics.* Available at www.econlib.org/library/Enc/HumanCapital.html

26. Schultz, T. (1961). 'Investment in human capital'. *American Economic Review,* 51(1): 1–17, p. 2.

27. Becker. G.S. (1962). 'Investment in human capital: a theoretical analysis'. *Journal of Political Economy,* 70(5): 9–49.

28. Ibid., p. 13.

29. Schultz, 'Investment in human capital', p. 15.

30. Ibid.

31. Ibid., p. 3.

32. Ehrenberg, R.G. and Smith, R.S. (1994). *Modern Labor Economics: Theory and Public Policy.* New York: HarperCollins; Davenport, T. (1999) *Human Capital: What Is It and Why People Invest in It.* San Francisco: Jossey-Bass.

33. Kunda, G. and Ailon-Souday, G. (2005). 'Managers, markets and ideologies – design and devotion revisited'. In S. Ackroyd, R. Batt, R. Thompson and P. Tolbert (eds), *Oxford Handbook of Work and Organization.* Oxford: Oxford University Press, pp. 200–19.

34. Drucker, P. (1993). *Post-capitalist Society.* New York: HarperCollins; Peters, P. (1999). *The Brand You 50: Or: Fifty Ways to Transform Yourself from an 'Employee' into a Brand that Shouts Distinction, Commitment, and Passion.* New York: Alfred A. Knopf Books.

35. Peters, *The Brand You 50.*

36. Ressler, C. and Thompson, J. (2008). *Why Work Sucks and How to Fix it: The Results Only Revolution.* New York: Portfolio.

37. Ibid., p. 61.

38. Pew Research Centre (2015). 'Three-in-ten U.S. jobs are held by the self-employed and the workers they hire'. Available at www.pewsocialtrends.org/2015/10/22/three-in-ten-u-s-jobs-are-held-by-the-self-employed-and-the-workers-they-hire/

39. Resolution Foundation (2016). 'The RF earnings outlook: quarterly briefing'. Available at www.resolutionfoundation.org/wp-content/uploads/2016/08/RF-Earnings-Outlook-Briefing-Q2-2016.pdf

40. Office for National Statistics, 'The self-employment boom'.

41. Reich, R. (2015). 'The sharing economy will be our undoing'. *Salon Magazine*. Available at www.salon.com/2015/08/25/robert_reich_the_sharing_economy_will_be_our_undoing_partner/

42. Semler, R. (2007). *The Seven-day Weekend*. New York: Penguin, p. 13.

43. Lane, C. (2011). *A Company of One: Insecurity, Independence, and the New World of White-collar Unemployment*. New York: ILR Press.

44. Trade Unions Congress (2014). 'The decent jobs deficit – the human cost of zero-hours working in the UK'. Available at www.tuc.org.uk/workplace-issues/employment-rights/decent-jobs-week/decent-jobs-deficit-human-cost-zero-hours

45. Gov UK (2016). 'Employment status'. Available at www.gov.uk/employment-status/employee

46. Monaghan, A. (2014). 'Self-employment at highest level for 40 years'. *Guardian*, 21 August, p. 25.

47. Resolution Foundation, 'The RF earnings outlook'.

48. Heywood, M. (2016). 'Life as a Hermes driver'. *Guardian*. Available at www.theguardian.com/money/2016/jul/18/life-asa-hermes-driver-they-offload-all-the-risk-on-to-the-courier

49. Ibid.

50. Gregg, M. (2011). *Work's Intimacies*. Cambridge: Polity.

51. Foucault, M. (2008). *The Birth of Biopolitics: Lectures at the Collège de France, 1978–79*. London: Palgrave.

52. Lambert, C. (2015). *Shadow Work: The Unpaid, Unseen Jobs that Fill Your Day*. Berkley: Counterpoint; Bobo, K. (2009). *Wage Theft in America: Why Millions of Working Americans are Not Getting Paid – and What We Can Do About It*. New York: New Press.

53. Chartered Management Institute (2016). 'Quality of working life'. Available at www.managers.org.uk/~/media/Files/Quality%20of%20working%20life/Quality%20of%20Working%20Life%20-%20full%20report%20-%20January%202016.pdf

54. Chakrabortty, A. (2015). 'The £93bn handshake: businesses pocket huge subsidies and tax breaks'. *Guardian*. Available at www.theguardian.com/politics/2015/jul/07/corporate-welfare-a-93bn-handshake

55. Becker, 'Investment in human capital'.

56. Friedman, M. (1962). *Capitalism and Freedom*. Chicago: University of Chicago Press.

57. *The Dearing Report* (1997). Available at www.educationengland.org.uk/ documents/dearing1997/dearing1997.html, p. 11.

58. Ross, A. (2014). *Creditocracy and the Case for Debt Refusal*. New York: Or Books.

59. Institute for Fiscal Studies (2014). 'Payback time? Student debt and loan repayments: what will the 2012 reforms mean for graduates?' Available at www.ifs.org.uk/comms/r93.pdf

60. The Intergeneration Foundation (2016). 'The graduate premium: manna, myth or plain miss-selling?' Available at www.if.org.uk/wp-content/ uploads/2016/07/Graduate_Premium_final.compressed.pdf

61. Burns, J. (2016). 'Student debts wipe out most graduate pay premiums – report'. BBC. Available at www.bbc.co.uk/news/education-36916009

62. Howker, E. and Malik, S. (2013). *Jilted Generation: How Britain has Bankrupted its Youth*. London: Icon.

63. For example, see *Huffington Post* (2013). 'Toby Thorn, 23-year-old student, wrote suicide note on back of £3,000 overdraft statement'. Available at www.huffingtonpost.co.uk/2012/12/04/toby-thorn-suicide-overdraft_n_2236386.html

64. Callender, C. and Jackson, J. (2005) 'Does the fear of debt deter students from higher education?' *Journal of Social Policy*, 34(4): 509–40.

65. Autor, D. and Dorn, D. (2013). 'The growth of low-skill service jobs and the polarization of the US labor market'. *American Economic Review*, 103(5): 1553–97; O'Connor, S. (2015). 'UK economy shows shift to low-skilled jobs'. *Financial Times*. Available at www.ft.com/cms/ s/0/6a8544ae-9d9e-11e4-8ea3-00144feabdc0.html#axzz41wva1aTT

66. See Gordon, R. (2016). *The Rise and Fall of American Growth: The U.S. Standard of Living Since the Civil War*. Princeton: Princeton University Press; Broadbent, B. (2015). 'Compositional shifts in the labour market'. Speech to the Bank of England Conference. Available at www. bankofengland.co.uk/publications/Pages/speeches/2015/842.aspx

67. Gordon, R. (2012). 'Is U.S. economic growth over? Faltering innovation confronts the six headwinds'. National Bureau of Economic Research. Available at www.nber.org/papers/w18315; *The Economist* (2015). 'A lack of skilled workers and managers drags the country down'. Available at www.economist.com/news/britain/21648003-lack-skilled-workers-and-managers-drags-country-down-mind-gap

68. Bell, D. (1974). *The Coming Post-industrial Society*. New York: Basic Books.

69. Quoted in Kroft, S. (2014). 'Falling apart: America's neglected infrastructure'. CBS News. Available at www.cbsnews.com/news/falling-apart-america-neglected-infrastructure/

70. Davidson, L. (2016). 'Its official: British offices are the coldest and ugliest in the world'. *Telegraph*. Available at www.telegraph.co.uk/

business/2016/06/07/its-official-british-offices-are-the-coldest-and-ugliest-in-the/

71. Bargh, J. and Shalev, I. (2012). 'The substitutability of physical and social warmth in daily life'. *Emotion*, 12(1): 154–62.
72. Woo, J.M. and Postolache, T. (2008). 'The impact of work environment on mood disorders and suicide: evidence and implications'. *International Journal on Disability and Human Development*, 7(2): 185–200.
73. Morrison, A., Therrien, A. and Ailes, E. (2016). 'Is there such a thing as bore out?' BBC. Available at www.bbc.co.uk/news/magazine-36195442
74. Ibid.
75. Bitton, A. and Shipley, A. (2010). 'Bored to death'. *International Journal of Epidemiology*, 39(2): 370–1.
76. Gorz, A. (2010). *Immaterial*. London: Seagull Books.
77. Kleinknecht, A., Kwee, Z. and Budyanto, L. (2016). 'Rigidities through flexibility: flexible labour and the rise of management bureaucracies'. *Cambridge Journal of Economics*, 40(4): 1137–47, p. 1137 (emphasis in the original).
78. Gordon, D. (1996). *Fat and Mean: The Corporate Squeeze of Working Americans and the Myth of Managerial Downsizing*. New York: Simon and Schuster.
79. Waterson, J. (2016). 'Daily Telegraph installs workplace monitors on journalists' desks'. *BuzzFeed*. Available at www.buzzfeed.com/jimwaterson/telegraph-workplace-sensors#.wd05Qj4lP
80. Kantor, J. and Streitfeld, D. (2015). 'Inside Amazon: wrestling big ideas in a bruising workplace'. *New York Times*. Available at www.nytimes.com/2015/08/16/technology/inside-amazon-wrestling-big-ideas-in-a-bruising-workplace.html?_r=0
81. Anonymous (2016). 'No phones, low pay, sent home for purple hair – life on a zero-hours contract'. *Guardian*. Available at www.theguardian.com/commentisfree/2016/jul/19/no-phones-low-pay-sent-home-purple-hair-life-zero-hours-contract
82. Ibid.
83. Anonymous (2016). 'I worked on Facebook's Trending team – the most toxic work experience of my life'. *Guardian*. Available at www.theguardian.com/technology/2016/may/17/facebook-trending-news-team-curators-toxic-work-environment
84. Hilton, S. (2015). *More Human: Designing a World Where People Come First*. New York: W.H. Allen.
85. See Mortensen, D. (2010). 'Markets with search friction and the DMP model'. Nobel Prize Lecture. Available at www.nobelprize.org/nobel_prizes/economic-sciences/laureates/2010/mortensen-lecture.pdf
86. Roose, K. (2014). 'Sharing economy isn't about trust it's about desperation'. *New York Magazine*. Available at http://nymag.com/daily/intelligencer/2014/04/sharing-economy-is-about-desperation.html

87. Quoted in Khaleeli, H. (2016) 'The truth about working for Deliveroo, Uber and the on-demand economy'. *Guardian*. Available at www.theguardian.com/money/2016/jun/15/he-truth-about-working-for-deliveroo-uber-and-the-on-demand-economy

88. Hill, S. (2015). 'Welcome to the "1099 economy": the only things being shared are the scraps our corporations leave behind'. *Salon Magazine*. Available at www.salon.com/2015/12/29/the_sharing_economy_partner/

89. Ibid.

90. Society of Motor Manufacturers and Traders (2016). 'Largest ever number of vans recorded on British roads as Commercial Vehicle Show 2016 opens'. Available at www.smmt.co.uk/2016/04/largest-ever-number-of-vans-recorded-on-british-roads-as-commercial-vehicle-show-2016-opens/

91. Gates, B. (1995). *The Road Ahead*. New York: Viking Press.

92. Vaughn, A. (2015). 'Nearly 9,500 people die each year in London because of air pollution – study'. *Guardian*. Available at www.theguardian.com/environment/2015/jul/15/nearly-9500-people-die-each-year-in-london-because-of-air-pollution-study

93. Crouch, D. (2015). 'Ryanair closes Denmark operation to head off union row'. *Guardian*. Available at www.theguardian.com/business/2015/jul/17/ryanair-closes-denmark-operation-temporarily-to-sidestep-union-dispute

94. Ibid.

95. Ibid.

96. Evans, R. (2016). 'Construction firms apologise in court over blacklist'. *Guardian*. Available at www.theguardian.com/business/2016/may/11/construction-firms-apologise-in-court-over-blacklist

97. Osbourne, H. (2016). 'Uber loses right to classify UK drivers as self-employed'. *Guardian*. Available at www.theguardian.com/technology/2016/oct/28/uber-uk-tribunal-self-employed-status

98. Eidelson, J. (2013). 'Alt-labour'. *The American Prospect*. Available at http://prospect.org/article/alt-labor; *Weber Shandwick* (2015). 'Employees rising: seizing the opportunity in employee activism'. Available at www.webershandwick.com/uploads/news/files/employees-rising-seizing-the-opportunity-in-employee-activism.pdf

99. Woodcock, J. (2016). 'Learning lessons from Deliveroo and UberEATS'. Pluto Press blog. Available at https://plutopress.wordpress.com/2016/08/31/learning-lessons-from-deliveroo-and-ubereats/; BBC (2016). 'Deliveroo offers concessions in pay row'. Available at www.bbc.co.uk/news/business-37076706; Wong, J.C. (2016). 'Uber reaches $100m settlement in fight with drivers, who will stay contractors'. *Guardian*. Available at www.theguardian.com/technology/2016/apr/21/uber-driver-settlement-labor-dispute-california-massachusetts

100. Roy, E.A. (2016). 'Zero-hours contracts banned in New Zealand'. *Guardian.* Available at www.theguardian.com/world/2016/mar/11/zero-hour-contracts-banned-in-new-zealand

101. Bregman, R. (2016). *Utopia for Realists: The Case for a Universal Basic Income, Open Borders, and a 15-Hour Workweek.* Amsterdam: The Correspondent.

102. Stern, A. (2016). *Raising the Floor: How a Universal Basic Income Can Renew Our Economy and Rebuild the American Dream.* New York: PublicAffairs.

103. Stout, L. (2012). *The Shareholder Value Myth: How Putting Shareholders First Harms Investors, Corporations, and the Public.* San Francisco: Berrett-Koehler.

104. Battostoni, A. (2017). 'The false promise of universal basic income'. *Dissent.* Available at www.dissentmagazine.org/article/false-promise-universal-basic-income-andy-stern-ruger-bregman

105. Slee, T. (2015). *What's Yours is Mine: Against the Sharing Economy.* New York: Or Books.

106. For example, see Mason, P. (2015). *Postcapitalism: A Guide to Our Future.* London: Verso.

107. Lucas, R.E. (1988). 'On the mechanics of economic development'. *Journal of Monetary Economics,* 22: 3–42, p. 36.

108. Quoted in Osbourne, H. (2016). 'Graduate whose loan grew by £1,800 in one year says students were misled'. *Guardian.* Available at www.theguardian.com/education/2016/may/25/simon-crowther-loan-grew-by-1800-a-year-says-government-misled-students

109. Ibid.

110. Warrell, H. and Hale, T. (2017). 'UK to sell record £4bn of student loans to investors'. *Financial Times.* Available at www.ft.com/content/2b66bfaa-ec7a-11e6-930f-061b01e23655

111. See Ross, *Creditocracy.*

Chapter 6

1. Shaw, D. (2010). 'Air steward's amazing tantrum over rude flier'. *Mirror.* Available at www.mirror.co.uk/news/uk-news/air-stewards-amazing-tantrum-over-240878

2. *Free Republic* (2010). 'Investigators question flight attendant's tale'. Available at www.freerepublic.com/focus/f-news/2569789/posts

3. Waxon, T. (2010). 'Update on the biggest, most important aviation story ever'. *Dallas News.* Available at www.dallasnews.com/business/airlines/2010/08/12/update-on-biggest-aviation-sto

4. NBC New York (2010). 'Fed-up flight attendant out of jail, says he's appreciative'. Available at www.nbcnewyork.com/news/local/Airline-Steward-at-JFK-Pulls-Emergency-Chute-Flies-Coop-100286494.html

5. Gross, D. (2010). 'Cursing, beer-grabbing flight attendant grabs spotlight'. Available at http://edition.cnn.com/2010/TRAVEL/08/10/new.york. escape.chute.opened/index.html

6. Quoted in Jones, C. and Moore, M. (2010). 'JetBlue flight attendant strikes a nerve with stressed workers'. *USA Today.* Available at http://usatoday30.usatoday.com/money/industries/travel/2010-08-11-1Aattendants11_CV_N.htm

7. *Social Times* (2010). 'Flight attendant Steven Slater becomes Facebook star'. Available at www.adweek.com/socialtimes/steven-slater-fans/320155

8. Ibid.

9. Noonan, P. (2010). 'We pay them to be rude to us: in the service economy, all of us want to take the chute'. *Wall Street Journal.* Available at www.wsj.com/articles/SB10001424052748704407804575425983109795768

10. Spreier, S. (2010). 'How to head off the Steven Slater in your organization'. *Forbes.* Available at www.forbes.com/2010/08/19/steven-slater-jetblue-workplace-outburst-leadership-managing-advice.html?boxes=leadershipchannellatest

11. Ibid.

12. Johnson, A. (2013). 'Nobody ever just snaps'. *Health and safety Magazine.* Available at www.safetyandhealthmagazine.com/articles/-no-one-ever-just-snaps-2

13. Ibid.

14. Larkin, P. (1955). 'Toads'. In *The Less Deceived.* Hull: Marvell Press.

15. Foucault, M. (2008). *The Birth of Biopolitics: Lectures at the Collège de France, 1978–79.* London: Palgrave, p. 67.

16. Deleuze, G. (1978). 'On Spinoza's Concept of Affect'. Lecture at Cours Vincennes. Available at www.gold.ac.uk/media/images-by-section/departments/research-centres-and-units/research-centres/centre-for-the-study-of-invention/deleuze_spinoza_affect.pdf

17. Agamben, G. (2011). *Nudies.* Stanford: Stanford University Press.

18. Ibid., p. 43.

19. Ibid., p. 44.

20. Chamayou, G. (2012). *Manhunts: A Philosophical History.* Princeton: Princeton University Press.

21. Price, S. (2008). *How to Disappear in America.* New York: Leopard Press.

22. Chamayou, *Manhunts*, p. 152.

23. Ibid., p. 153.

24. Ibid., p. 154.

25. Conway, F. and Siegelman, J. (2005). *Snapping: America's Epidemic of Sudden Personality Change.* New York: Stillpoint Press.

26. Ibid., p. 280.

27. Scranton, R. (2015). *Learning to Die in the Anthropocene: Reflections on the End of a Civilization.* San Francisco: City Lights Books.

28. Quoted in Goldenberg, S. (2016). 'Arctic sea ice extent breaks record low for winter'. *Guardian*. Available at www.theguardian.com/environment/2016/mar/28/arctic-sea-ice-record-low-winter

29. Gillis, J. (2017). 'Earth sets a temperature record for the third straight year'. *New York Times*. Available at www.nytimes.com/2017/01/18/science/earth-highest-temperature-record.html?_r=0

30. Vaughn, A. (2015). 'Nearly 9,500 people die each year in London because of air pollution – study'. *Guardian*. Available at www.theguardian.com/environment/2015/jul/15/nearly-9500-people-die-each-year-in-london-because-of-air-pollution-study

31. Quoted in Carrington, D. (2016). 'One in five of world's plant species at risk of extinction'. *Guardian*. Available at www.theguardian.com/environment/2016/may/10/one-in-five-of-worlds-plant-species-at-risk-of-extinction

32. Grantham Centre for Sustainable Futures (2015). 'Soil loss: an unfolding global disaster'. University of Sheffield. Available at http://grantham.sheffield.ac.uk/soil-loss-an-unfolding-global-disaster/

33. World Wildlife Fund (2016). 'Half of global wildlife lost'. Available at www.worldwildlife.org/press-releases/half-of-global-wildlife-lost-says-new-wwf-report

34. Pauly, D. (2006). 'Fisheries on the brink'. YouTube Video. Available at www.youtube.com/watch?v=Tf1EgeHDxpA

35. BBC (2015). 'Stop saying rhinos have gone extinct – the last subspecies died off in 2011'. Available at www.bbc.co.uk/newsbeat/article/32323058/stop-saying-rhinos-have-gone-extinct---the-last-subspecies-died-off-in-2011

36. Slezak. M. (2015). 'Revealed: first mammal species wiped out by human-induced climate change'. *Guardian*. Available at www.theguardian.com/environment/2016/jun/14/first-case-emerges-of-mammal-species-wiped-out-by-human-induced-climate-change

37. Kolbert, E. (2014). *The Sixth Extinction: An Unnatural History*. New York: Henry Holt & Company.

38. Davies, J. (2016). *The Birth of the Anthopocene*. Los Angeles: University of California Press.

39. Moore, J. (2015). *Capitalism in the Web of Life: Ecology and the Accumulation of Capital*. London: Verso.

40. Shaviro, S. (2015). *No Speed Limit: Three Essays on Accelerationism*. Minneapolis: University of Minnesota Press, p. 2.

41. Camatte, J. (1976/1995). *This World We Must Leave and Other Essays*. Brooklyn: Autonomedia.

42. Ibid., p. 151.

43. Jensen, D. (2006). *Endgame*. New York: Seven Stories Press; Greer, J.M. (2008). *The Long Dissent: A Guide to the End of the Industrial Age*.

Gabriola Island: New Society Publishers; Weisman, A. (2007). *The World Without Us*. London: Virgin Books.

44. Weisman, A. (2007). 'On the world without us'. Big Think Video. Available at http://bigthink.com/videos/alan-weisman-on-the-world-without-us

45. *Australian Mining Magazine* (2011). 'Gina Rinehart urges Australians to fight against carbon and mining taxes'. Available at www.australianmining.com.au/news/gina-rinehart-urges-australians-to-fight-against-carbon-and-mining-taxes/

46. Jensen, D. (2012). 'End Game lecture'. Available at www.youtube.com/watch?v=hOOuGb_E86Q

47. Berardi, F. (2015). *Heroes: Mass Murder and Suicide*. London: Verso, p. 3.

48. Madsen, M. (2010). *Into Eternity: A Film For the Future*. Available at www.youtube.com/watch?v=wke01Porz2Q

49. Ibid.

50. Ibid.

51. Hardt, M. and Negri, A. (2000). *Empire*. Cambridge, MA: Harvard University Press; Hardt, M. and Negri, A. (2009). *Commonwealth*. Cambridge, MA: Harvard University Press.

52. Institute for Experimental Freedom. (2009). *Politics is Not a Banana*. Available at www.infoshop.org/pdfs/politics-banana3.pdf, p. 156.

53. Gottschall, J. (2016). *The Professor in the Cage: Why Men Fight and Why We Like to Watch*. New York: Penguin.

54. Ibid., p. 3.

55. Bogost, I. (2015). 'No one cares that you quit your job'. *The Atlantic*. Available at www.theatlantic.com/notes/2015/09/no-one-cares-that-you-quit-your-job/404467/

56. *Communists in situ* (2015). 'Mario Tronti: I am defeated'. Available at https://cominsitu.wordpress.com/2015/03/08/mario-tronti-i-am-defeated/

57. Murphey, G. (Director) (1985). *The Quiet Earth*. Mirage Films.

58. Kelsey, J. (1995). *The New Zealand Experiment: A World Model for Structural Adjustment?* Auckland: University of Auckland Press.

59. Baudrillard, J. (1996). *The Perfect Crime*. London: Verso, p. 125.

Conclusion

1. See Derrida, J. (1994). *Spectres of Marx: The State of Debt, the Work of Mourning and the New International*. New York: Routledge, p. 52.

2. Collier, P. (2017). 'How to save capitalism from itself'. *Times Literary Supplement*. Available at www.the-tls.co.uk/articles/public/how-to-save-capitalism/

3. Lucas, R.E. (2003). 'Macroeconomic priorities'. *American Economic Review*, 93(1): 1–14, p. 1.

4. Ionesco, E. (1959). *Rhinoceros*. New York: Grover Press.
5. Mance, H. (2016). 'Britain has had enough of experts, says Gove'. *Financial Times*. Available at www.ft.com/content/3be49734-29cb-11e6-83e4-abc22d5d108c
6. Halliday, J. (2016). '"Zombie knife" seller urges shoppers to buy before ban takes effect'. *Guardian*. Available at www.theguardian.com/uk-news/2016/aug/16/zombie-knife-seller-urges-shoppers-buy-before-ban-hunters-knives-swords
7. Ibid.
8. Goldenberg, S. (2016). 'Half of all US food produce is thrown away, new research suggests'. *Guardian*. Available at www.theguardian.com/environment/2016/jul/13/us-food-waste-ugly-fruit-vegetables-perfect
9. Cohen, D. (2016). 'What a waste: we launch a major investigation into the scandal of wasted food'. *Evening Standard*. Available at www.standard.co.uk/news/foodforlondon/what-a-waste-we-launch-a-major-investigation-into-the-scandal-of-wasted-food-a3348306.html
10. Ibid.
11. Keogh, G. (2015). 'Factory boss jailed over teen who died in horrific accident while on £3-an-hour government apprenticeship scheme'. *Mirror*. Available at www.mirror.co.uk/news/uk-news/factory-boss-jailed-over-teen-6065802
12. Ibid.

Index